THEORY OF TEACHING THINKING

Across the world education for 'thinking' is seen as the key to thriving in an increasingly complex, globalised, technological world. The OECD suggests that teaching thinking is key to growing a more successful economy; others claim it is needed for increased democratic engagement and well-being.

Theory of Teaching Thinking discusses what is meant by 'thinking' in the context of teaching and takes a global perspective incorporating contributions from neurocognitive, technological, Confucian, philosophical, and dialogical viewpoints.

Questions explored throughout this edited volume include:

- what is thinking?
- how can thinking be taught?
- what does 'better thinking' mean, and how can we know it if we see it?
- what is the impact on wider society when thinking is taught in the classroom?

Extensively researched and at the cutting edge of this field, this book provides the context for teaching thinking that researchers, teachers, and policy-makers need. As the first book in a brand new series, *Research on Teaching Thinking and Creativity*, it is a much-needed introduction and guide to this critical subject.

Laura Kerslake is a philosophy lecturer currently conducting research into Philosophy with Children at the University of Cambridge. She is the creator of the Philosophize project, and has wide experience of teaching thinking in education from Early Years to Higher Education.

Rupert Wegerif is a professor of education at the University of Cambridge. He has written several books and many research articles on teaching thinking and educational theory. He is co-director of the Cambridge Educational Dialogue Research Group (CEDiR) and founder and co-convenor of the Educational Theory Special Interest Group of the European Association for Research on Learning and Instruction.

Research on Teaching Thinking and Creativity

Research on Teaching Thinking and Creativity is a new international series edited by Li Li, James Kaufmann, and Rupert Wegerif. The idea of teaching thinking skills is now widely shared across the world and initiatives have been set up in the US, China, Brazil, Malaysia, and Russia. These initiatives lead to questions about what is meant by terms like 'creativity' and 'teaching thinking', questions raised, discussed, and answered in this new book series. The aims of the series are to:

- enhance reader understanding and knowledge about theories of the growth of thinking and creativity, both individual and collective;
- provide readers with insights and key principles that emerge from research into teaching thinking and creativity in a range of specific areas;
- inform readers of the main approaches being used globally to develop and assess thinking and creativity, including changes in technology and pedagogical strategies;
- give readers tangible, practical suggestions for improving their own or other people's thinking and creativity based on theory and research.

This series consists of books researching different social, cultural, and educational contexts in America, Europe, and Asia. Researchers, postgraduate students, and policy makers will be able to refer to this series.

Theory of Teaching Thinking
International Perspectives
Edited by Laura Kerslake and Rupert Wegerif

THEORY OF TEACHING THINKING

THINKING

International Perspectives

Edited by Laura Kerslake and Rupert Wegerif

Routledge
Taylor & Francis Group

LONDON AND NEW YORK

First published 2018
by Routledge
2 Park Square, Milton Park, Abingdon, Oxon OX14 4RN

and by Routledge
711 Third Avenue, New York, NY 10017

Routledge is an imprint of the Taylor & Francis Group, an informa business

British Library Cataloguing in Publication Data
A catalogue record for this book is available from the British Library

Library of Congress Cataloging in Publication Data
A catalog record for this book has been requested

ISBN: 978-1-138-29789-0 (hbk)
ISBN: 978-1-138-29790-6 (pbk)
ISBN: 978-1-315-09894-4 (ebk)

Typeset in Bembo
by Sunrise Setting Ltd, Brixham, UK

For Holly, Clara, and Beth, who enrich my thinking.

CONTENTS

CONTRIBUTORS

Carl Bereiter is a professor emeritus at the University of Toronto and co-founder, with Marlene Scardamalia, of the Institute for Knowledge Innovation and Technology (IKIT). Over a long career, his research and publications have dealt with many different areas of educational thought and practice. His contributions are profiled in the Routledge Key Guide, *Fifty Modern Thinkers on Education*.

Valerie A. Brown is the Director of the Local Sustainability Project, a collaborative research programme working with whole-of-community change in Australia and overseas. She is now Emeritus Professor of the University of Western Sydney after being its Foundation Chair of Environmental Health 1996–2002. Awarded an Officer of the Order of Australia for national and international advocacy for sustainable development, she is the author of thirteen books and over 100 papers on socio-environmental issues, social transformation and collective thinking. Valerie was a member of the National Health and Medical Research Council 1984–1992, and CSIRO Council 1986–2004. In 1999 she was appointed an Officer of the Order of Australia for national and international research, policy development, and advocacy for sustainable development. Valerie is currently working on collective learning as a tool for transformational change.

Robert Burden, 1940–2014, conducted research in educational psychology which covered a wide range of topics but shared a concern with improving the quality of children's experience of school. His influential 'Myself as a Learner Scale' revealed the importance of how children think about and respond to education. In 2005, when he became a Professor Emeritus, he established the Cognitive Education Centre at Exeter, which later became the Cognitive Education Development Unit. This promoted his whole school approach to teaching thinking and has had an impact not only in the UK, where there are now many 'Thinking Schools' accredited by Bob and his team, but also in countries around the world.

Steve Higgins is Professor of Education at Durham University. His research interests include the effective use of digital technologies in schools, understanding how children's thinking and reasoning develops, and how teachers can be supported in developing the quality of teaching and learning in their classrooms. He has a particular interest in the educational philosophy of Pragmatism, the application and warrant of meta-analysis and the implications of both of these for teaching and learning.

Laura Kerslake is conducting research into Philosophy with Children at the University of Cambridge. Her work looks at how philosophy with young children is augmented by the introduction of a pictorial-based talking framework to help to create a dialogic space in the classroom. She is the creator of the Philosophize project and also lectures on a philosophy course at the University of Exeter. She has held positions as a classroom teacher and as a research assistant at the University of Exeter. She is completing her PhD under the supervision of Rupert Wegerif.

Li Li is Senior Lecturer at the University of Exeter. Her main research interests include language teacher cognition, classroom discourse, developing thinking skills and the use of new technologies. She has published in these areas in both Chinese and English. She is author of Social Interaction and Teacher Cognition (EUP, 2017), and New Technologies in Language Learning (Palgrave, 2017). She also co-edited (with Rupert Wegerif and James C Kaufman) *The Routledge International Handbook of Research on Teaching Thinking* (Routledge, 2015).

Douglas P. Newton PhD DSc is based in the School of Education, Durham University, UK, where he currently teaches trainee teachers and higher degree students about purposeful thought and how to foster it. A recent book on the subject is *Teaching for Understanding* (Routledge, 2012). He is particularly interested in the interaction of emotions and purposeful thought, and wrote the well-received book, *Thinking with Feeling* (Routledge, 2014). On a similar subject is his monograph *In Two Minds* (ICIE, 2016).

Marlene Scardamalia holds the Presidents' Chair in Education and Knowledge Technologies at the University of Toronto and is the Director of the Institute for Knowledge Innovation and Technology (http://ikit.org). She is the inventor of CSILE (Computer Supported Intentional Learning Environments), recognized as the first networked collaborative learning environment. 'Knowledge building', a term now widely used in education and knowledge management, originated with the CSILE/Knowledge Building project.

Baruch B. Schwarz is the Isadore and Bertha Gudalsky Chair of Early Education at the School of Education, Hebrew University of Jerusalem. His research focuses on argumentation, dialogue and learning, with a special interest in computer-supported collaborative learning. He has published a number of books and journal articles on these subjects, including the recent *Argumentation, Education and Dialogue*.

Benzion Slakmon is a post-doctoral research fellow at the Laboratory for the Study of Pedagogy at the Department of Education, Ben Gurion University of the Negev. His research deals with the relationship between pedagogical design and students' modes of talk and thinking in the humanities and the social sciences. He has a strong interest in questions of equity, ethics and political education, dialogic and collaborative learning.

Rupert Wegerif is Professor of Education (2000) at the University of Cambridge. His research focuses on education for dialogue, thinking and creativity in the context of the Internet Age. This interest can be seen in his work developing theory in the field of the psychology of education, and his research on ways of teaching dialogue in classrooms and thinking and 'learning to learn together' with technology. He has gained over £2 million in research funding as principal investigator and published nine books, as well as over fifty peer-reviewed papers. He is a member of the steering committee of the Cambridge Educational Dialogue Research Network (CEDiR) and founding lead editor of the Elsevier SSCI journal *Thinking Skills and Creativity* as well as founder and co-convenor (with Gert Biesta) of the Educational Theory SIG of EARLI.

Emma Williams is Assistant Professor in the Centre for Education Studies at the University of Warwick, where she researches and teaches the philosophy of education. She writes particularly on the theme of thinking in education, and especially on the relation between thinking and language. Her work has been published in leading journals such as the *Journal of Philosophy of Education*, and in edited collections. Her monograph, *The Ways We Think*, is published by Wiley-Blackwell.

INTRODUCTION

Laura Kerslake and Rupert Wegerif

Introduction

There is a great deal of interest in teaching thinking. Governments are particularly concerned about how education can respond to the way in which automation is transforming the world of work. A recent report on the Future of Work estimates that perhaps '65% of children entering primary school today will ultimately end up working in completely new job types that don't yet exist' (WEF, 2016, p. 3). One of the recommendations of this report is to re-think education systems and 'to imagine what a true 21st century curriculum might look like'. Many experts, in the face of this challenge, recommend teaching for more general and transferable skills including creativity and critical thinking (e.g. Neelen & Kirschner, 2017). Implementing these sort of exhortations to re-think education for the 21st century by teaching more thinking is held up by the difficult challenge of conceptualising exactly what thinking is, and how it can be taught and learnt. A lack of an adequate theoretical understanding of the issues is probably the main reason why thinking is not more central to every state curriculum.

Another driver behind the growing interest in teaching thinking is a concern for the quality of civic life and democratic debate. In an increasingly globalised world there is a concern that schools are not providing students with the skills that they need to take part adequately in debates about the challenges that will face them. The apparently growing appeal of simplistic extremist solutions to problems and the election of a reality television star as president of the United States are taken by some commentators as signs that we need to teach more thinking of the kind that will enable future voters and citizens to make good decisions. But what kind of teaching is required to prepare students more adequately to participate in the kind of complex decisions that we will all face as voters in the future?

Why we need this book

The interest in teaching for thinking and creativity around the world has led to a great many publications of practical 'recipes' for teaching thinking pedagogy. Each package claims to be based on research but these claims are almost always based on cherry-picking the research findings that seem to fit the approach adopted, rather than on building an approach that comes out of a serious conceptual analysis of the issues or a serious review of the research findings. Without really understanding how difficult and complex it is to teach thinking, governments and businesses are at risk of buying packages that claim to make everything easy but that end up giving the whole enterprise of teaching thinking a bad name. At world conferences on teaching thinking, the voices of gurus with commercial solutions drown out the more modest voices of serious educational researchers with theoretical concerns about the nature of thinking and the best ways to teach it. This is why we need this volume. All the contributors to this volume are university researchers interested in making an impact through teaching thinking but only through teaching thinking in a way that is soundly grounded on good theory. The chapters are not promoting packages or any commercial product but are instead exploring the principles that underlie the success or failure of different approaches to teaching thinking.

Why more theory is essential: the limitations of psychology

Some might imagine that, rather than engage in a range of varied theoretical approaches to teaching thinking, it would be better to start with the hard science of what thinking is: the kind of rigorous science engaged in by cognitive psychologists. This is naïve because thinking is not so easy to define. Although some cognitive psychologists like to write as if they know what it is and simply need to do a little more research on how best to teach it, this is not true. It is almost amusing to see the perhaps inevitable circularity of definitions of thinking make by those who make it their business to directly study thinking. Here is a recent example from a pair of highly respected cognitive psychologists, Holyoak and Morrison, defining 'thinking' in the introduction to the *Cambridge Handbook of Thinking and Reasoning* (2005): 'Thinking is the systematic transformation of mental representations of knowledge to characterize actual or possible states of the world, often in service of goals'.

The word 'mental' plays an important role in this definition but 'mental' is essentially another way of saying thinking. So the definition is ultimately the tautologous claim that 'thinking is a kind of thinking'. They themselves modestly refer to their definition as pointing out a direction of research rather than substantively defining the field. They further claim that their definition is useful partly because of what it excludes. The implication of this claim is that their definition helps us to focus in on what is of most importance, and indeed this definition excludes a lot that others might connect with thinking: consciousness, for example, and creative imagination or perceptions such as insights. And, of course, dialogue and relationships are not mentioned at all. Thinking, according to this definition, seems to be something done within the head of an isolated individual willed and directed by that individual. There is a reference to goals which might imply a social context, but no suggestion that these goals must have arrived from somewhere other than the head of the individual thinker.

The older psychological tradition of behaviourism, a tradition largely replaced by cognitivism in the most powerful schools and journals in the 1960s, offered a completely different definition: 'thinking is talking to yourself' wrote Watson (1928, p. 480). Initially this sounds quite promising. It sounds close to a definition often attributed to Plato, who puts the following claim into the mouth of an Eleatic stranger in his dialogue 'Sophist': 'Thinking and discourse are the same thing, except that what we call thinking is, precisely, the inward dialogue carried on by the mind itself without a spoken sound' (Plato, 2015, 263e). The word translated as 'discourse' here is 'λόγος' (logos), which has played a major role in Western philosophy as a key term for reason or rationality. Through the multiple meanings of the term logos linking spoken word, discourse and reason we can see that the ancient Greeks did not distinguish as closely as recent cognitive psychologists do between silent inner thought of 'mental representations' and external audible thought in the form of speech, especially speech in the form of dialogues. In the Phaedrus, Plato (2011) quoted Socrates making it very clear that the highest form of thinking is to be found in face-to-face dialogue. He does not mean individual thinking here but real visible and audible thinking as an exchange of words carried by warm breath. In fact Socrates is quite dismissive of individual thinking, suggesting it might be an amusing occupation for an old man to recall and write down some of the better dialogues he participated in when in his prime. But of course this might be a bit of gentle self-mockery on the part of Plato who sat alone writing down the dialogues of Socrates which he had participated in as a younger man. Vygotsky could be seen as at least partly following in this Greek tradition, albeit in a form mediated by Hegel and by Marx, when he argued that the inner thought of individuals – what he called 'the higher mental functions' – develops as an internalised form of dialogue (Vygotsky, 1987). So all of these considerations makes Watson's claim that thinking is talking to yourself sound quite interesting from a theory of thinking and teaching thinking point of view. Unfortunately closer examination of Watson's (1928) text shows that he is simply trying to reduce thinking to a form of measurable behaviour. He explains his claim that 'thinking is talking to yourself' as a behaviour that takes the form of sub-vocalisation and so can be seen and measured in the micro-movements of throat muscles. He was expressly trying to distance thinking from modes of experience such as emotion, and to explain thought as biological reaction.

If we put the behaviourist definition together with the cognitivist definition one can see that what they both have in common is putting a concern with research methods (epistemology) over a concern with the real nature of thinking (ontology). In the first case, cognitivism, we have researching thinking through building models that can be tested using maths and computers and in the second the older idea of science as systematic observation. Basically these definitions are just two variations on the old joke about the drunken man found on his hands and knees late at night, searching for his keys near a lamp post. When asked where he had lost the keys he waved towards an area of darkness where there were no street lamps. When asked why he was searching for them here if he had lost them over there he replied: 'It's obvious: there is no point searching over there – I can't see anything – it is too dark!'

Transdisciplinary theory as the way forward

Historically, psychologists have used many different metaphors for thinking: Babbage's 19th century claim that thinking could be modelled by clockwork morphed, after the first computers were built, into the very similar claim that thinking could be modelled by electronic computers. The alternative claim that thinking is just behaviour is now returning in the new form of 'thinking is just neural activity' with a focus on the new method of brain scanning. One complication here is that we are always already within thinking whenever we set out to think about thinking and so whatever metaphor or model we choose is just going to be one aspect of thinking unable to exhaustively grasp all of its possibilities. It is as if we had hold of a powerful torch and were using it to explore a cave while asking the question 'What is this light?' Whatever the light reflects from, be it a plaster bust of a god, an old engine, or a computer or even an image of the open brain, we say 'that must be the source of this light' but of course the torch cannot shine back upon itself to see itself and know itself directly.

One response to the problem that psychologists refuse to search for truth in the dark where it is hard to understand might be to give up on empirical science and leave the field to the data-free conceptual research of philosophy. Philosophers famously are not afraid of the dark, and many love to write as if they had answers in the face of deep mysteries. Unfortunately philosophy also does not have a good track record of delivering useful truths out of their encounters with the void. An alternative way forward for a genuine science of thinking and teaching requires that we revise the underlying understanding of what it means to do science. The reason so many cognitive psychologists seem to run scared of facing the real issues in research on thinking is because of their misguided 'scientistic' understanding of scientific method. They want to be engaged in finding the truth where they have a good grasp of one single model of how things are and each individual experiment that disproves a hypothesis adds in some small, incremental way to the body of truth. In fact, despite their naive ontological assumptions, experiments conducted under the behaviourist research programme and those conducted under the cognitivist research programme have both enriched our understanding of thinking. The answer to this seeming paradox requires a shift in our understanding of science from an ever-more-accurate single representation of the truth to being an ongoing dialogue with multiple voices trying to find more-or-less useful answers to questions of shared concern. Understanding science as essentially a dialogue between a variety of different voices allows us to see the many different metaphors of thinking offered by psychology as neither true nor false but as offering different insights. This is the new transdisciplinary approach to scientific advancement advocated by Helga Nowotny, recently retired leader of the European Research Council (Nowotny, Scott, & Gibbons, 2001). This is the approach that is taken by this book. It is not so much the philosophy of teaching thinking as the transdisciplinary theory of teaching thinking offering a range of lenses and metaphors to illuminate the central focus: what it means to teach thinking.

Developments in the field

When David Perkins surveyed developments in the field of teaching thinking in his valedictory address at Harvard (2011), he stressed a particular shift from a focus on teaching skills to teaching for the development of enduring dispositions. Research suggests that cognitive skills often do not transfer from the context in which they are taught and so a focus on teaching for positive thinking dispositions is an answer to this challenge. Dispositions are tendencies to act in certain ways that people carry with them across different situations. This shift from understanding teaching thinking as teaching skills or abilities to understanding teaching thinking also in terms of teaching for positive thinking dispositions is implicit behind several chapters in this book: Emma Williams's re-thinking of teaching thinking as situated questioning; Wegerif's focus on developing dialogic dispositions; Newton's exploration of the significance of emotional responses; and Higgins and Burden's chapter on assessment.

The increasing roles given to creativity in the literature on teaching thinking and to developing dispositions are perhaps part of a broader movement away from a focus on discrete cognitive skills of the kind that can be measured in a laboratory and towards an understanding of thinking as always embedded in complex real-world contexts and so needing to be taught in a way that takes context into account.

Traditionally, teaching thinking has focused on individuals, and yet there are a significant number of papers in this volume that consider extended cognition. The Community of Inquiry (CoPI) is a pedagogy in which children think together, providing an example of thinking that is demonstrated by a plurality of minds (see Kerslake, Chapter 4, this volume). Wegerif's account of the dialogic theory of teaching thinking similarly considers the relationships between individuals as they think together. It is only quite recently that there has been clear research demonstrating that collective thinking is a real, separate phenomenon with its own unique features that can be measured and can be taught (Woolley, Chabris, Pentland, Hashmi, & Malone, 2010).

Collective thinking depends upon communication and research on collective thinking is often linked to research on tools that support collective thinking (e.g. Stahl, 2006). This very new approach to teaching thinking is brought out in

Brown's chapter, which explores how we can teach thinking together to solve global problems. Her chapter presents an account of how theories of collective thinking have an application in helping to remedy problems in society today. She details the collective thinking approach employed in the Landcare project in Australia, which aimed to allow the views of those with a stake in the land, such as farmers, environmentalists and landowners, to be heard. Such an issue is known as a 'wicked' problem: this is not in a moral sense, but in the sense that it was brought about by a particular way of thinking and cannot be resolved by recourse to the same way of thinking. New ways of thinking must be found in order to move forward from a wicked problem. Her account of the Landcare project highlights the importance of teaching thinking not only in formal classroom learning environments, but in the community arena as well. It is an example of the ways in which thinking skills have a lifelong application, and are not a time-limited package only for classroom learning, and is a new development that follows the logic of the general shift towards more situated approaches to thinking and teaching thinking.

Traditional views of cognition have been derived from the Cartesian mind-body duality, locating thinking as a process or states that are based in the mind. Emma Williams's chapter in this volume highlights that in addition to the mind-body duality, Descartes also gives us the concept of representational thinking – that the aim of the thinking processes that take place in the mind is to accurately represent what is 'out there'. This has the effect of separating the human thinker from the world, and also of valuing the kind of thinking that most accurately represents what is 'out there'. Human thinkers become dispassionate, third party observers. It might seem, then, that teaching thinking means teaching humans to become the sort of being that exemplifies this sort of thinking – or as Williams writes, the 'valorisation of the cerebral and cognitive endowments of the human being' (p. 47). The implication is that the value placed on cognitive endowment is at the expense of other ways of exemplifying human thinking. This critique has also been made by a number of proponents of Philosophy with Children (PwC) programmes (see Kerslake, Chapter 4, this volume), who see some PwC approaches as critical thinking programmes. Martens (2013, p. 161) sees such an approach to teaching thinking pedagogies as the 'dark side' of pedagogy arising since the Enlightenment that 'enforces a discipline of alleged clarity of reasoning in children'.

From the examples given above, it is clear that theory, even when it is not at the forefront, informs the practice of teaching thinking that takes place in classrooms (Williams refers to this as the 'anchor' of Cartesian thought). Placing theory in the spotlight allows us to more clearly understand the teaching thinking practices that occur in classrooms. It also allows us to engage in dialogue about the relationship between theory and practice, which can be quite complex. Higgins (Chapter 1, this volume) uses the examples of such teaching thinking programmes as brain gym, which have been dismissed by theorists because they don't 'work', and yet remain popular with education practitioners, indicating that on some level they do 'work'. He cautions against dismissing such programmes, and instead encourages a commitment to engaging with practice and further understanding what we really mean when we say that a teaching thinking approach 'works': an approach that, again, goes beyond a narrow scientific understanding and encompasses the transdisciplinary approach.

The structure of the book

The contributions to this book offer the reader in-depth consideration of a number of theoretical perspectives in the teaching of thinking. They highlight issues relevant to the practice of teaching thinking in today's classrooms and communities, providing the theoretical background to the pedagogy. There are a number of important questions that are explored in this book: What is thinking? How can thinking be taught? What does 'better thinking' mean? How can we know it if we see it? What is the impact on wider society when thinking is taught in the classroom?

Highlighting the transdisciplinary approach, the chapters in the volume are concerned with understanding teaching thinking in what Rowlands (2010) describes as (1) *embodied*, (2) *embedded*, (3) *enacted*, and (4) *extended* thinking. This view considers thinking as embodied in bodily (not only neural) structures and processes, embedded in an extra-neural environment, enacted within that environment, and extended beyond the head of an individual. These different strands of thinking encompass a number of theories which are exemplified in the chapters in this book, and show the breadth of a transdisciplinary approach.

Newton's chapter emphasises the role of emotions in thinking, and the teaching of thinking. Some of his points – like the detrimental effect of a teacher who provokes negative emotions such as fear or shame – seem clearly problematic to effective thinking. He also points out that even positive emotions such as feeling cheerful or joyful are not conducive to detailed reasoning, as research has shown that those in a joyful state of mind are more likely to make generalisations rather than pay attention to detail. This is interesting as it asks what state of mind we want the children in our classrooms to be in; it also resonates with recent trends (and their criticisms) in primary school teaching, where teachers are encouraged to use a 'hook' to get children interested in a new topic. This is typically a high-impact event, such as getting children to believe that aliens have landed in the school, or dinosaur bones have been dug up on the school field. While this generates a great deal of excitement, questions have been raised about exactly what it is the child remembers from that event. The theories of mood and emotion and their impact on teaching thinking that Newton raises are of great importance to teachers – for example, it is common practice in UK classrooms (particularly at primary level) to change 'learning partners' quite frequently, to encourage children to work with those they haven't before. However, Newton cautions that bringing strangers together might not result in creative output because the feeling of caution will be unlikely to result in a creative frame of mind.

Philosophy for Children is a pedagogy that has gained significant momentum as a teaching thinking practice. Its growth as a practice and a research base is indicated by the three chapters in this volume that consider it as a teaching thinking pedagogy. Laura Kerslake's chapter considers the theoretical basis of philosophy with children (PwC) and the Community of Philosophical Inquiry (CoPI). Starting with Lipman (1998), who is also cited by Steve Higgins in this volume, she presents the pragmatist origins of PwC. The intervening decades since Lipman's original 1970s work have seen PwC expand globally, employing a plethora of techniques and pedagogies. Despite this, the CoPI has remained at the forefront of PwC pedagogy. In addition to this, new conceptions of the child and childhood, the role of the education system and the aims and objectives of PwC practice have emerged, leading to a theoretical shift.

Kerslake's chapter explores PwC and the CoPI from their pragmatist beginnings to an emergent posthuman position advocated by Karin Murris. She sets CoPI practice against this theoretical background, asking if the tenets of the CoPI are compatible with those of posthumanism. In her chapter, 'Thinking beyond rationalism', Emma Williams points out that some commentators, such as Winstanley, locate PwC practice firmly within the practice of critical thinking. For posthumanists, and some Continental philosophy commentators on PwC (e.g. Weber, see Kerslake, Chapter 4), the critical thinking focus of PwC is detrimental to children's development as children, and they seek PwC practice that takes a whole-child approach.

Bereiter and Scardamalia also theorise an area which is highly prominent in today's education world: the relationship between skills and knowledge. In the UK today, concern about the inferior status given to knowledge is shared by a number of education reformers. In particular, E.D. Hirsch's book *Cultural Literacy* (1988) has been highly influential in US and UK education policy, credited with the turnaround of the Massachusetts' school system, and known as the 'Massachusetts Miracle'. In the UK, the 2014 National Curriculum reforms set out by Michael Gove were influenced by Hirsch's work, particularly his claims that each child needs a substantial knowledge base from which to operate thinking skills. While highlighting the importance of thinking skills, they argue that a focus on thinking skills can be to the detriment of content. Knowledge can end up as fragmented and used in the service of skills, which are seen as superior.

Bereiter and Scardamalia further claim that the foundations of teaching thinking lie in the way in which children are positioned in their earliest years. To treat children in the way which is conducive to the development of thinking skills, adults must start by 'treating them seriously…giving them responsibilities, talking to them candidly' (p. 74). This is reminiscent of Murris's view presented in Kerslake's chapter that children, thought of by adults only as 'childish and immature' are the subject of ontological prejudice. All of these chapters consider the need for a reconceptualisation of what thinking is and who is capable of it. As Williams remarks, while reasoning and rationality may be vital to thinking, 'there are different ways of reasoning and of exemplifying rationality' (p. 44).

William's chapter goes on to state that while rationality, reasoning and argument are central to theories of thinking, they are not necessarily problematic in themselves. However, the foundations of thinking since Descartes have set the thinking human apart from the world, disengaging the human from the world and excluding that which does not exemplify or embody formal thinking. As such we have come to prioritise this above all else. Posthumanists make this point too, remarking that children are positioned as deficient until they are capable of formalised, critical thinking in the way that adults are.

All of these chapters consider the need for a reconceptualization of what thinking is and who is considered to be capable of it. Li Li's chapter on the Confucian perspective on teaching thinking reminds us that some of these issues, such as Cartesian heritage, have a Western focus. Other cultures, such as those with a Confucian heritage, or the African tradition of Ubuntu, already have in place a paradigm of collective rather than individualistic thinking. This makes a globalised approach of great importance as we consider how to teach thinking not only for educational outcomes but also for greater understanding and resolution of social issues.

The emphasis on educational outcomes has been of considerable focus in schools, with drives to 'raise standards', 'add value' and 'narrow the gap'. This is not only a Western focus – the advent of global organisations such as PISA, which test and compare students' abilities from a range of countries, have made this a global issue. Such a focus on attainment and measurement has also made this an issue for the teaching of thinking: can it be measured, and how can this be done? This is a complex issue that is explored in two chapters in this book. Burden and Higgins consider the range of issues that come into play when assessing and researching thinking skills; Slakmon and Schwarz comment on the current emphasis on collaborative work in teaching thinking and what this means for assessment.

In providing the theoretical background to teaching thinking, this book provides a substantial grounding in the traditions that have underpinned current practice. It provides a coherent and considered way forward for the teaching of thinking in globalised societies. It also offers suggestions for the future of teaching thinking by using the theoretical basis to ask and answer questions about how methods, technology, evaluation and research might look in years to come.

References

Hirsch, E. D. (1988). *Cultural literacy: What every American needs to know*. New York, NY: Random House.

Holyoak, K., & Morrison, R. (Eds.). (2005). *The Cambridge handbook of thinking and reasoning*. Cambridge: Cambridge University Press.

Lipman, M. (1998). *Philosophy goes to school*. Philadelphia, PA: Temple University Press.

Martens, E. (2013). *Philosophieren mit Kindern. Eine Einführung in die Philosophie* (S. Rimmington, Trans., 2017). *Philosophising with children: An introduction to philosophy*. Stuttgart: Reclam. Full translation available: sarahrimmington66@gmail.com

Neelen, M., & Kirschner, P. (2017). A three stage plan to prepare our youth for jobs that don't exist (yet). Retrieved October 4, 2017, from https://3starlearningexperiences.wordpress.com/2017/08/18/a-three-stage-plan-to-prepare-our-youth-for-jobs-that-dont-exist-yet/

Nowotny, H., Scott, P., & Gibbons, M. (2001). *Re-thinking science: Knowledge and the public in an age of uncertainty*. Cambridge: Polity Press.

Perkins, D. (2011). *40 years of teaching thinking: Revolution, evolution, and what next?* Retrieved October 4, 2017, from www.youtube.com/watch?v=-nmt1atA6ag

Plato. (2011). *Phaedrus* (H. Yunis, Ed.). Cambridge: Cambridge University Press.

Plato. (2015). *Theaetetus and sophist* (C. Rowe, Ed.). Cambridge: Cambridge University Press.

Rowlands, M. (2010). *The new science of the mind: From extended mind to embodied phenomenology.* Cambridge, MA: MIT Press.

Stahl, G. (2006). *Group cognition: Computer support for building collaborative knowledge.* Cambridge, MA: MIT Press.

Vygotsky, L. S. (1987). Thinking and speech. In R. W. Rieber & A. S. Carton (Eds.), *The collected works of L. S. Vygotsky, Volume 1: Problems of general psychology* (pp. 39–285). New York, NY: Plenum Press. (Original work published 1934).

Watson, J. B. (1928). *Psychological care of infant and child.* New York, NY: W. W. Norton.

Woolley, A. W., Chabris, C. F., Pentland, A., Hashmi, N., & Malone, T. W. (2010). Evidence for a collective intelligence factor in the performance of human groups. *Science, 330*(6004), 686–688. doi:10.1126/science.1193147

World Economic Forum. (2016). The future of jobs: Employment skills and workforce strategy for the fourth industrial revolution. Retrieved October 2, 2017, from www3.weforum.org/docs/WEF_Future_of_Jobs.pdf

1

A RECENT HISTORY OF TEACHING THINKING

Steve Higgins

Introduction

There have always been arguments about what the terms 'teaching thinking' (Sternberg & Berg, 1992) and 'thinking skills' mean since they first came into vogue in the late 1970s (McGregor, 2007). Indeed some argue that the concept of teaching general thinking or thinking skills is misguided, while others focus on its utility in the classroom to provoke more complex thinking and to help teachers develop appropriate pedagogies to support learners' development (Higgins & Baumfield, 1998). A host of different programmes and approaches have advocated teaching thinking skills. See Nickerson, Perkins, & Smith (1985) for an account of developments, particularly in North America through the 1970s and the early 1980s and Hamers, van Luit, & Csapó (1999) for a European perspective up to the turn of the century, or McGregor (2007) for more recent developments. One way to understand the development of teaching thinking is to start with the influence of three key individuals who exemplify the different strands of teaching thinking in schools. Each has pioneered a different approach, and their ideas have influenced and inspired other programmes and approaches over the last 60 years. Subsequently, as teachers have adopted these ideas, and as researchers have explored their effects, there has been a cross-fertilisation of ideas, with increasing emphasis on the impact of different approaches so their inclusion can be justified in an increasingly scrutinised curriculum. At the same time there have been criticisms about the focus in teaching thinking and about the development of skills and capabilities and how this relates to curriculum content and knowledge in particular.

Reuven Feuerstein and Instrumental Enrichment

After World War II, young people flooded into Israel. Many of them suffered traumatic experiences and alienation from anything which could be described as a coherent cultural inheritance. On intelligence and standardised tests many of these youngsters scored so badly as to appear ineducable. Rather than simply accept this conclusion and deny any chance of recovery, Reuven Feuerstein devised ways of finding out:

- exactly what cognitive functions they were deficient in,
- how they could be helped to develop these functions,
- what was each individual's potential for learning.

Feuerstein developed a set of techniques that helped these learners succeed on subsequent tests. These methods were termed 'dynamic', in that they were studying changes in the *process* of learning, as opposed to 'static' traditional assessments. He argued that this process was much more likely to predict how someone might learn in the future (Feuerstein, Rand, Hoffman, & Miller, 1980; see also Feuerstein, Jensen, Hoffman, & Rand, 2014). The complex diagnostic instrument which he and his colleagues developed was called the Learning Potential Assessment Device (LPAD). It measures an individual's intellectual change, known as 'cognitive modifiability' (Sharron & Coulter, 1994). Twenty different tasks or 'instruments' were devised, to tackle different underlying difficulties involving 200–300 hours of interaction. As the whole process is an enriching one, the programme was labelled *Instrumental Enrichment*. Feuerstein's ideas have influenced work on teaching thinking: his innovative theory of mediated learning in particular which led to the development of dynamic assessment (Haywood, & Lidz, 2007; Tzuriel, 2001) and more broadly, his cognitive, task-based approach supported by teacher mediation: for evidence impact see Romney and Samuels (2001). The instruments do not contain specific content or knowledge so are both additional to and separate from the traditional school curriculum, though Feuerstein & Falik (2010) argue that structural cognitive teaching should be seen as a separate and distinct curricular intervention.

Matthew Lipman and Philosophy for Children (P4C)

Another important pioneer, in what in the United States is termed the Critical Thinking movement, is the American philosopher, Matthew Lipman. Originally a university philosophy professor, Lipman was unhappy at what he saw as the poverty of thinking in his students (Lipman, 2003). He became convinced that something was wrong with the way they had been taught in school when they were younger. They seemed to have been encouraged to learn facts and to accept authoritative opinions, but not to think for themselves. He therefore founded the Institute for the Advancement of Philosophy for Children (IAPC) at Montclair State College, New Jersey, in 1972. Since then and until his death in 2010, he and his colleagues developed material for use in schools, to help young people to think. One of Lipman's basic convictions is that children are natural philosophers, and view the world with curiosity and wonder. That is all that is needed as a starting-point for enquiry, which can legitimately be termed 'philosophical'. The Philosophy for Children (P4C) programme (Lipman, Sharp, & Oscanyan, 1980) rests on certain assumptions, such as that discussion skills precede and form the basis for better thinking. Through engaging in group dialogue and a 'community of enquiry', children can become more effective thinkers.

The IAPC has produced a number of novels, into which strange and anomalous points have been woven. As a class reads a page together, the text encourages them to raise questions. These queries form the basis of guided discussions. The teacher does not try to control what questions are asked, since it is the children's curiosity which needs to be tapped to promote active participation and learning. The text steers the children's questions into certain areas, suitable for exploration, and the novels provide a model of philosophical enquiry, describing fictional children engaging in argument, debate and discussion.

The adoption and impact of P4C has been worldwide, in countries from Australia (Splitter & Sharp, 1995) to Iceland (Sigurborsdottir, 1998) and in other subjects such as science (Sprod, 1998). It has been developed for younger children, through *Teaching Philosophy with Picture Books* and *Storywise* (Haynes & Murris, 2011; Murris, 1992; Murris & Haynes, 2001). Other school-age programmes draw on the 'community of enquiry' approach (Fisher, 1996, 1998; see also the work of the Society for the Advancement of Philosophical Enquiry and Reflection in Education (SAPERE) and Naji & Hashim, 2017). An interest in philosophical ideas, as opposed to psychological ones, predominates and the approach sees its lineage through Lipman to the work of John Dewey. This 'community of inquiry' approach has also expanded and influenced the development of online learning in universities (Garrison, Anderson, & Archer, 2010). For an overall synthesis of impact see Trickey & Topping's review (2004). P4C is usually taught as a separate set of lessons, additional to the school curriculum or replacing other lessons. In some adaptations of P4C teachers select a text with specific subject content (such as understanding in science), or to develop speaking and listening skills (Jones, 2008).

Edward de Bono's thinking tools

Edward de Bono's key contribution has been in developing a range of widely and easily applicable thinking tools which have captured popular imagination, accompanied by considerable commercial success. One of the first of these was *Lateral thinking* in 1967: solving problems with an indirect and creative approach, involving ideas that may not be obtainable by using only traditional step-by-step logic (de Bono, 1970). He has developed a range of other popular approaches, such as 'Six Thinking Hats', which is perhaps the most widely known. This is a tool for group discussion and individual thinking involving six coloured hats, with each hat representing a different kind of thinking. Six Thinking Hats and the associated idea of 'parallel thinking' aim to provide a way for people to plan their thinking in a more detailed and explicit way. Throughout his writings (e.g. 1970, 1992, 2010), de Bono stresses the importance of consciously practising certain strategies in order to become a more effective thinker. His CoRT (Cognitive Research Trust) materials refer to 'thinking tools', which are made easy for children to remember, with acronym titles such as PMI (Plus Minus Interesting) or CAF (Consider All Factors). He claims his tools are based on his understanding of the brain as a self-organizing system and that he has updated and developed his thinking tools as knowledge of the brain has developed (Dudgeon, 2001). However, his work has also been criticised from an academic perspective as lacking theoretical coherence (Sternberg & Lubart, 1999) and empirical validation (Moseley et al., 2005). Despite these criticisms his work remains internationally influential and widely used.

De Bono differs from the other approaches, on at least the following two counts. First, his theory of how the human mind works has tried to remain consistent with developing knowledge of how the brain functions and his tools and ideas are based on these inspirations. Second, he is more concerned with innovation and creativity than developing or proving psychological or educational theory.

Approaches such as Tony Buzan's *Mind Mapping* (2006) or Alistair Smith's *Accelerated Learning* (e.g. Smith, Call, & Baton, 1999) follow de Bono's inspiration and use information about the brain to inspire teachers and learners to adopt specific techniques. Other brain-based approaches have found the gap between neurological research and practice hard to bridge with tenable or testable theories, such as Neuro-Linguistic Programming (NLP), developed by Richard Bandler and John Grinder in the United States in the 1970s, or Paul and Gail Dennison's 'brain-gym' and 'educational kinesiology'. What is interesting with a number of these approaches, which can only be described as pseudo-scientific, is that they remain popular with practitioners, suggesting that although the theoretical explanations offered by the developers may not be coherent and certainly lack robust evidence, the practices undertaken in schools may have some educational value for other reasons. This has been ignored by academics and scientists who appear to believe the approaches cannot 'work', because the underlying theorisation is flawed. This displays a certain lack of critical (or scientific) thinking, as brain-gym or NLP may be reliably effective at achieving certain outcomes, just not for the reasons the proponents expound. Only rigorous experimental research can identify which causal outcomes (if any) are reliably associated with which particular practices and whether this is consistent with the underpinning theorisation. As our understanding of the brain develops, the promise of neuro-scientific explanations is seductive (Weisberg, Keil, Goodstein, Rawson, & Gray, 2008), but the gap between physiological understanding and educational practice remains challenging (Howard-Jones, 2010) and ultimately limited to questions of efficacy, rather than those of educational value (Davis, 2004). Just because an approach is 'brain-friendly' does not mean it is educationally desirable. Approaches such as de Bono's *Thinking Hats* or Buzan's *Mind Mapping* are taught discretely as skills or techniques, additional to the curriculum, but then are applied within subjects to specific curriculum content, according to the teachers' judgement.

The expansion of teaching thinking: cognitive perspectives

Each of these leading figures held similar beliefs about children and young people's abilities. They all consider that through specific and explicit thinking activities learners can improve their thinking and exceed the predicted competence that psychometric or school-based tests may have suggested is their limit. New thinking capabilities can be developed and extended with practice. Each of the pioneers has, in turn, fostered a series of developments growing from their three different initial perspectives of improving cognitive capabilities, applying thinking tools based on brain-based understanding, and promoting philosophical reasoning through discussion.

In the 1970s and 1980s work on teaching thinking burgeoned and inspired development in schools, often supported by academic theorising and research. One of the most ambitious of these collaborations was 'Project Intelligence', a partnership between the Venezuelan Government, Harvard University and BBN Technologies (originally Bolt, Beranek and Newman, all from Massachusetts Institute of Technology, who were the pioneers of computer networking, e-mail and the LOGO programming language). The project was the inspiration of Dr Luis Alberto Machado, the Minister of State for the Development of Human Intelligence, who was committed to the idea that every child should be able to develop to their full potential (Machado, 1978). The project developed and evaluated methods for teaching cognitive skills in seventh grade classrooms in Venezuela with materials to improve specific capabilities such as observation, classification, reasoning, problem solving, inventive thinking and decision-making. A fuller account of the programme and its impacts can be found in a range of publications (e.g. Hernstein, Nickerson, de Sanchez, & Swets, 1986; Nickerson, 1985; Nickerson et al., 1985).

This illustrates how the development of teaching thinking is often clustered around people, projects and places. Project Zero is the name associated with a number of independently sponsored research projects at the Harvard Graduate School of Education, many of which relate to teaching thinking. Since 1967, Project Zero has examined the development of learning processes in children, adults and organizations and includes the work of Howard Gardner and David Perkins on themes such as multiple intelligences, teaching for understanding and thinking dispositions (Gardner, 1983; Gardner & Perkins, 1988).

Many of the academic classifications of thinking and cognition have fostered their own specific tools and programmes (see Moseley and colleagues' (2005) analysis of over forty thinking frameworks). This includes examples such as the *Structure of Intellect* programme (Meeker, 1969) based on Guilford's (1967) model or *Science: a process approach* drawing on Gagné's ideas about structuring and sequencing (Klausmeier & Sipple, 1980), or Klauer's (1990) inductive reasoning with recent implementation in Australia (Barkl, Porter, & Ginns, 2012) and Hungary (Molnár, 2011). As early as 1985, Nickerson et al. (1985) could identify thirty different programmes based to varying degrees on cognitive approaches. Feuerstein's ideas are widely acknowledged to be seminal in this area and have also inspired other programmes, such as, in the

UK, the *Somerset Thinking Skills Course* (Blagg, Ballinger, & Gardner, 1988), aimed at secondary age pupils, and *Top Ten Thinking Tactics* (Baumfield & Higgins, 1997; Lake & Needham, 1993) for primary or elementary age children. Programmes following a cognitive approach tend to structure a series of tasks and activities according to their underlying cognitive theorisation. When these programmes are evaluated the emphasis is not purely on the efficacy of the approach in terms of improving learning in schools, but is often testing aspects of the underpinning theory.

An example of this is Piaget's stage theory of development and moving learners from concrete to formal operational thinking. This has inspired a number of approaches including 'Operational Enrichment' (Csapó, 1992) and 'Cognitive Acceleration through Science Education' (CASE). Cognitive acceleration was developed by Michael Shayer and Philip Adey in the early 1980s at King's College, London (Adey, Shayer, & Yates, 1995; Adey & Shayer, 2002). The approach builds on both Piaget's and Vygotsky's ideas and takes a broadly constructivist approach. CASE has been developed in other curriculum areas such as mathematics and technology education as well as for use with younger pupils (Let's Think) which has been successfully trialled in Finland (Aunio, Hautamäki, & Van Luit, 2005) and China (Hu, Adey, Jia, Liu, Zhang, Li, & Dong, 2011), though with varying results.

Socio-cultural approaches have similarly influenced thinking skills programmes and approaches. Drawing on the work of the Russian psychologist, Lev Vygotsky, the emphasis is on talking and discussion and 'scaffolded' experiences where children develop understanding through communicating their ideas and being exposed to others' ideas. The *Thinking Together* programme, developed by a team at the Open University (Dawes, Mercer, & Wegerif, 2000), draws explicitly on Vygotsky, while also incorporating wider theoretical ideas about talk, dialogue and interaction (Mercer, 2004; Wegerif, 2008; Wegerif, Mercer, & Dawes, 1999), in both the UK and Mexico (Wegerif, Perez Linares, Rojas-Drummond, Mercer, & Velez, 2005).

Pragmatic solutions

A number of further approaches to teaching thinking have looked at the extensive range of programmes and their underpinning theories and classroom techniques and have distilled key elements to produce an approach which can be more easily adopted by practitioners. Examples of these are Swartz and Parks' (1994) thinking diagrams and, in the UK, approaches such as *TASC: Thinking Actively in a Social Context* (Wallace & Adams, 1993) or *ACTS: Activating Children's Thinking Skills* (Dewey & Bento, 2009; McGuinness, 1999) or the *Thinking Through…* strategies developed by a team at Newcastle University (Baumfield & Leat, 2002; Higgins, 2001; Leat, 1998: see also van der Schee, Leat & Vankan, 2006). These techniques and approaches are infused into specific subjects through the use of 'powerful pedagogical strategies' (Leat & Higgins, 2002). Such 'thinking routines' (Ritchhart, Church, & Morrison 2011) help to provide a manageable unit of change for teachers and a practical way to try out such approaches in the classroom. As 'catalytic tools' (Baumfield, Hall, Higgins, & Wall, 2009) they also provide the opportunity for teachers to investigate the value of such approaches and sustain their use in their professional practice. These resulting hybrid approaches are then hard to classify though elements from the other approaches can be seen. Most programmes and approaches acknowledge the importance of language, articulation and discussion as a key element. From this perspective teaching thinking approaches chime with many practitioners' views and values about what is important in education and therefore often provide a productive arena for professional enquiry and development (Baumfield, 2006). Most of these approaches either embedded these cognitive (and meta-cognitive) approaches in curriculum areas (such as CASE in Science or Leat's (1998) *Thinking Through Geography*) or exemplified how they could be used to support curriculum teaching, indicating the challenge of balancing skills and content for teachers (Jones, 2008).

Challenges and controversies in teaching thinking

A key controversy which triggered the development of teaching thinking and which clearly influenced Feuerstein, de Bono and Lipman, was the notion of fixed ability or intelligence. This has now been reasonably conclusively answered by cognitive science, in favour of the views of the teaching thinking pioneers. Brain plasticity and patterns of neuronal development indicate that intelligence, at least when crudely conceptualised, is not fixed. Though we may not yet fully understand how to benefit from this understanding in designing educational programmes and activities to maximise any individual's potential, it has reinvigorated the challenge (Howard-Jones, 2010).

In the 1980s and 1990s much time was spent in arguments about how explicit or implicit approaches to teaching thinking should be. Each of the programmes and approaches can be categorised as to whether they adopt an 'enrichment' approach where they are taught through extra or separate lessons or 'infusion' where skills and practices are embedded in the curriculum (McGuinness, 2005). Evidence from meta-analysis (Abrami et al., 2008) indicates that the answer is an emphatic 'both'. Combined approaches where skills are taught explicitly as critical thinking lessons and combined with curriculum teaching which is infused with these skills, is the most effective approach (an effect size of 0.94). If you teach critical thinking separately, then learners do improve (an effect size of 0.38), but perhaps don't know how or when to employ these skills. If you teach skills embedded or infused into a curriculum, this is slightly more effective than teaching them separately (with an effect size of 0.54) but learners may not be so aware of them or of how they might need to be adapted for a different context or subject (see also Higgins, Hall, Baumfield, & Moseley, 2005).

Not all of the controversies have been answered so clearly. For Garnham and Oakhill (1994), the thorniest problem facing all teaching thinking programmes and approaches was that of transfer. This is one reason for developing both general and subject-specific programmes. There is insufficient space here to get involved in the complex transfer debate (e.g. Higgins & Baumfield, 1998), but one way through the controversy is through self-regulation. McGuinness & Nisbet (1991), in reviewing the European scene, pointed to two themes: a 'thinking curriculum' and 'a growing recognition of the importance of affective factors in thinking – attitudes, motivation and disposition – and of social factors in helping to establish appropriate habits of thought'. Motivation, renewal of belief in oneself as a learner and a disposition to want to learn may all be as important as an outcome of teaching thinking, as any improvement of a distinct aspect of thinking, such as inference or creativity.

The evolution of teaching thinking through cognitive tools, meta-cognitive approaches and self-regulation is reflected in the development of programmes adopted in Europe and North America (Hamers, van Luit, & Csapó, 1999). It can also be seen from an academic perspective with the recent focus on self-regulation in Europe (Dignath, Buettner, & Langfeldt, 2008). In North America the development of 'habits of mind' (Costa & Kallick, 2000) and 'thinking dispositions' (Perkins & Salomon, 2012) both aim to combine these cognitive and conative aspects of thinking.

Overall no single perspective has evidence of superior results in terms of either theoretical coherence or impact on learning outcomes (see also Burden & Higgins, Chapter 10, this volume). Researchers and developers of a wide range of teaching thinking programmes and approaches using different theoretical standpoints have all had some success.

However some implications are clear. Thinking skills approaches can enhance learning across the school age range (see Table 1.1), can benefit learning in specific

TABLE 1.1 Findings from meta-analyses of thinking skills approaches

Meta-analysis	Focus	Effect size
Abrami et al. (2008)	Critical thinking	0.34 (overall) 0.52 (primary pupils) 0.69 (secondary pupils)
Chiu (1998)	Meta-cognitive interventions for reading	0.67 (reading comprehension)
Dignath, Buettner, & Langfeldt (2008)	Self-regulated learning interventions	0.68 (primary pupils) 0.71 (secondary pupils)
Donker, De Boer, Kostons, Dignath van Ewijk, & Van der Werf (2014)	Learning strategy instruction	0.66 (overall) 0.80 (meta-cognitive strategies)
Higgins, Hall, Baumfield, & Moseley (2005)	Thinking skills approaches	0.62 (cognitive measures) 0.62 (curriculum measures)
Klauer & Phye (2008)	Inductive reasoning	0.69 (reasoning tests)
Trickey & Topping (2004)	Philosophy for Children	0.43 (all outcomes)
Shiell (2002)	Feuerstein's Instrumental Enrichment	0.58 (ability) 0.26 (general achievement)
Overall weighted mean effect size		0.62

subjects as well as improve more general skills (such as reasoning or reading comprehension). They should be taught both discretely and through subjects (Abrami et al., 2008) so that skills and knowledge both receive emphasis. It also suggests that although research and theorisation are working in productive areas for improvement, the concepts and ideas may benefit from further exploration, development and evaluation.

Teaching thinking and classroom talk

One of the areas where our understanding of the pedagogical rationale for teaching thinking has strengthened is in the nature of classroom talk. There is considerable evidence that most lessons in schools follow a similar interaction or 'discourse' pattern (Edwards & Westgate, 1994). This is described as 'Initiate Respond Evaluate' (I-R-E) or 'Initiate Respond Feedback' (I-R-F) (Sinclair & Coulthard, 1992). One of the advantages of this type of discourse structure is that the teacher is clearly in control of both the content and turn-taking in any classroom discussion. In addition, it may promote effective transmission of information, as pupils are encouraged mainly to recall information (Edwards, 1980; Edwards & Westgate, 1994, p. 156). The level of demand on students' thinking was an issue which Benjamin Bloom had observed in the 1950s and classified as 'lower order' (Bloom, 1974). Over the intervening decades an understanding of teachers' questioning, evaluation and feedback and how this sets the level of demand for learners' thinking has been described (Crooks, 1988). The value of collaborative work in enabling different kinds of talk is also now well established (Kutnick & Blatchford, 2014).

Teaching thinking approaches advocate a less directive role for the teacher which encourages mediation or scaffolding of pupils' thinking. Because of the difficulties of managing the turn-taking of a large numbers of pupils, some (Barnes & Todd, 1995) advocate the use of collaborative group work as a way of 'decentralising' classroom communication so as to encourage more pupils to participate in and practice forms of academic discourse normally dominated by the teacher. Proponents of teaching thinking approaches argue that such 'decentralising' can happen in both small groups and whole class situations such as the structuring of talk and turn-taking in P4C. The *Thinking Together* approach has also shown over a number of projects that children's individual reasoning (as measured by Raven's matrices, a standardised test of abstract reasoning) improves when they are taught how to discuss and exchange ideas in groups and by explicitly developing 'talk rules' to define social norms and make the meta-discursive rules explicit (Mercer, Wegerif, & Dawes, 1999). One perspective on teaching thinking approaches therefore is that they provide structures, tools or contexts for teachers to alter the default pattern of interaction in classrooms. Learners engage in and articulate more complex forms of thinking and develop their thinking through reasoning and discussion. This is often interpreted as more dialogic, more inclusive or more learner-centred teaching (Padget, 2012). Collaboration is often associated with greater improvement (e.g. Abrami et al., 2008; Chiu, 1998).

21st century skills and teaching thinking

Renewed interest in teaching thinking has been ignited by the development of digital and networked technologies (Wegerif, 2006; see also Wegerif, Chapter 6, this volume) and the emergence of '21st century skills' (Voogt, Erstad, Dede, & Mishra, 2013). The argument is that new technological tools and digital data have changed the nature of knowledge for the next generation of learners. While it has certainly changed the nature of information in terms of its representation, translation, and access, the nature of knowing is more problematic (Higgins, 2014). Overall the arguments that the digital world requires a different emphasis in the school curriculum is a persuasive one, particularly in terms of developing a critical understanding of the nature of information and its value to help answer particular questions or solve particular problems. Access to information is clearly a part of that process, and young people are certainly more adept at looking for information online to help them find out how to do something new. This has its limits however. While it may be possible to Google how to undertake brain surgery, the expertise required is more complex than simply having access to the information and watching a YouTube video. What is less commonly talked about in discussions of 21st century education is the potential of teaching thinking approaches, and the philosophical perspective in particular, being of value in communicating understanding. This includes the importance of being able to argue for a position or course of action, but also to be able to concede to stronger arguments and evidence. The role of knowledge and developing expertise may be under-emphasised in developing more complex thinking capabilities. As the history of teaching thinking has shown, this relationship is an intricate one, which can easily be misunderstood.

Conclusion

The teaching thinking movement has been and will continue to be of interest within education. It will continue to have a history. Its various strands stem from a reaction against the assumption implicit in much educational practice and theory that intelligence and ability are fixed. While there is a scientific basis for this belief it is also driven by values, reflecting a desire to help each individual student reach their full potential.

Teaching thinking will also continue to resonate because of the interaction between educational and psychological (or cognitive science) theories about thinking and learning. The challenge of operationalising such theories and enabling educational practice to benefit will always provide stimulus for educational development. There will always be programmes and approaches developed to test contemporary aspects of learning theory so programmes and approaches which promote more complex and more demanding thinking will continue to emerge. New understandings from neuro-science will no doubt also influence this interaction, both positively and negatively as they have in the past. Such physiological understandings will never withstand moral or ethical imperatives about educational values as these judgements about the aims and purposes of education, or desirable approaches from a value-based position, will always precede questions of efficiency and effectiveness, which an understanding of the brain may advance. Just because something is efficient or effective does not necessarily make it desirable. Technological developments will also challenge the nature of information and knowledge and their relevance to the school curriculum, again spurring on further debate about the teaching *of* and teaching *for* thinking. The philosophical perspective will also endure as this connects with educators' concerns about the role of developing reasoning and being able to reason with others. The balance between knowledge and skills will always be difficult for teachers to achieve, balancing the development of capability and expertise. These issues are at the core of a culture which seeks to maintain a democratic and pluralist society where its citizens (and teachers) are engaged in a process of inquiry into its maintenance, development and renewal (Dewey, 1916).

References

Abrami, P. C., Bernard, R. M., Borokhovski, E., Wade, A., Surkes, M. A., Tamim, R., & Zhang, D. (2008). Instructional interventions affecting critical thinking skills and dispositions: A stage 1 meta-analysis. *Review of Educational Research, 78*(4), 1102–1134.

Adey, P., & Shayer, M. (2002). *Really raising standards: Cognitive intervention and academic achievement.* London: Routledge.

Adey, P., Shayer, M., & Yates, C. (1995). *Thinking science: The curriculum materials of the CASE project.* London: Thomas Nelson and Sons.

Aunio, P., Hautamäki, J., & Van Luit, J. E. (2005). Mathematical thinking intervention programmes for preschool children with normal and low number sense. *European Journal of Special Needs Education, 20*(2), 131–146.

Barkl, S., Porter, A., & Ginns, P. (2012). Cognitive training for children: Effects on inductive reasoning, deductive reasoning, and mathematics achievement in an Australian school setting. *Psychology in the Schools, 49*(9), 828–842.

Barnes, D., & Todd, F. (1995). *Communication and learning revisited: Making meaning through talk.* Portsmouth, NH: Heinemann.

Baumfield, V. (2006). Tools for pedagogical inquiry: The impact of teaching thinking skills on teachers. *Oxford Review of Education, 32*(2), 185–196.

Baumfield, V., & Higgins, S. (1997). 'But no one has maths at a party': Pupils' reasoning strategies in a thinking skills programme. *Curriculum, 18*(3), 140–148.

Baumfield, V., & Leat, D. (2002). *Thinking through religious education.* Cambridge: Chris Kington Publishing.

Baumfield, V. M., Hall, E., Higgins, S., & Wall, K. (2009). Catalytic tools: Understanding the interaction of enquiry and feedback in teachers' learning. *European Journal of Teacher Education, 32*(4), 423–435.

Blagg, N., Ballinger, M., & Gardner, R. (1988). *Somerset thinking skills course handbook.* Oxford: Basil Blackwell.

Bloom, B. S. (1974). Implications of the IEA studies for curriculum and instruction. *The School Review, 82*(3), 413–435.

Buzan, T. (2006). *Mind mapping: Kick-start your creativity and transform your life.* London: Pearson Education.

Chiu, C. W. T. (1998). *Synthesizing metacognitive interventions: What training characteristics can improve reading performance?* Paper presented at the Annual Meeting of the American

Educational Research Association San Diego, CA, April 13–17, 1998. Retrieved from http://files.eric.ed.gov/fulltext/ED420844.pdf

Costa, A. L., & Kallick, B. (2000). *Discovering & exploring habits of mind. A developmental series, book 1.* Alexandria, VA: Association for Supervision and Curriculum Development.

Crooks, T. J. (1988). The impact of classroom evaluation practices on students. *Review of Educational Research, 58*(4), 438–481.

Csapó, B. (1992). Improving operational abilities in children. In A. Demetriou, M. Shayer, & A. Efklides (Eds.), *Neo-Piagetian theories of cognitive development: Implications and applications for education* (pp. 144–159). London: Routledge.

Davis, A. (2004). The credentials of brain-based learning. *Journal of Philosophy of Education, 38*(1), 21–36.

Dawes, L., Mercer, N., & Wegerif, R. (2000). *Thinking together: A programme of activities for developing thinking skills at KS2.* Birmingham: Questions Publishing.

De Bono, E. (1970). *Lateral thinking.* London: Penguin.

De Bono, E. (1992). *Teach your child to think.* London: Penguin.

De Bono, E. (2010). *Lateral thinking: Creativity step by step.* New York, NY: HarperCollins.

Dewey, J. (1916). *Democracy and education.* New York, NY: MacMillan.

Dewey, J., & Bento, J. (2009). Activating children's thinking skills (ACTS): The effects of an infusion approach to teaching thinking in primary schools. *British Journal of Educational Psychology, 79*(2), 329–351.

Dignath, C., Buettner, G., & Langfeldt, H. P. (2008). How can primary school students learn self-regulated learning strategies most effectively? A meta-analysis on self-regulation training programmes. *Educational Research Review, 3*(2), 101–129.

Donker, A. S., De Boer, H., Kostons, D., Dignath van Ewijk, C. C., & Van der Werf, M. P. C. (2014). Effectiveness of learning strategy instruction on academic performance: A meta-analysis. *Educational Research Review, 11*, 1–26.

Dudgeon, P. (2001). *Breaking out of the box: The biography of Edward de Bono.* London: Headline.

Edwards, A. D. (1980). Patterns of power and authority in classroom talk. In P. Woods (Ed.), *Teacher strategies* (pp. 237–253). London: Crook Helm.

Edwards, A. D., & Westgate, D. P. G. (1994). *Investigating classroom talk* (2nd ed.). London: The Falmer Press.

Feuerstein, R., & Falik, L. H. (2010). Learning to think, thinking to learn: A comparative analysis of three approaches to instruction. *Journal of Cognitive Education and Psychology, 9*(1), 4–20.

Feuerstein, R., Hoffman M. B., Jensen, M. R., & Rand, Y. (2014). Instrumental enrichment, an intervention program for structural cognitive modifiability: Theory and practice. In J. W. Segal, S. F. Chipman, & R. Glaser (Eds.), *Thinking and learning skills: Volume 1: Relating instruction to research* (pp. 43–82). London: Routledge.

Feuerstein, R., Rand, Y., Hoffman, M. B., & Miller, R. (1980). *Instrumental enrichment: An intervention programme for cognitive modifiability.* Baltimore, MD: University Park Press.

Fisher, R. (1996). *Stories for thinking.* Oxford: Nash Pollock.

Fisher, R. (1998). *Teaching thinking: Philosophical enquiry in the classroom.* London: Cassell.

Gardner, H. (1983). *Frames of mind: The theory of multiple intelligences.* New York, NY: Basic Books.

Gardner, H., & Perkins, D. N. (1988). *Art, mind, and education: Research from Project Zero.* Champaign, IL: University of Illinois Press.

Garnham, A., & Oakhill, J. (1994). *Thinking and reasoning.* Oxford: Blackwell.

Garrison, D. R., Anderson, T., & Archer, W. (2010). The first decade of the community of inquiry framework: A retrospective. *The Internet and Higher Education, 13*(1), 5–9.

Guilford, J. P. (1967). *The nature of human intelligence.* New York, NY: McGraw-Hill.

Hamers, J. H. M.; van Luit, J. E. H., & Csapó, B. (Eds.). (1999). *Teaching and learning thinking skills.* Abingdon: Swets and Zeitlinger.

Haynes, J., & Murris, K. (2011). *Picturebooks, pedagogy, and philosophy.* London: Routledge.

Haywood, H. C., & Lidz, C. S. (2007). *Dynamic assessment in practice: Clinical and educational applications.* Cambridge: Cambridge University Press.

Hernstein, R. J., Nickerson, R. S., de Sanchez, M., & Swets, J. A. (1986). Teaching thinking skills. *American Psychologist, 41*(11), 1279.

Higgins, S. (2001). *Thinking through primary teaching.* Cambridge: Chris Kington Publishing.

Higgins, S. (2014). Critical thinking for 21st-century education: A cyber-tooth curriculum? *Prospects, 44*(4), 559–574.

Higgins, S., & Baumfield, V. (1998). A defence of teaching general thinking skills. *Journal of Philosophy of Education, 32*(3), 391–398.

Higgins, S., Hall, E., Baumfield, V., & Moseley, D. (2005). A meta-analysis of the impact of the implementation of thinking skills approaches on pupils. In *Research evidence in education library.* London: EPPI-Centre, Social Science Research Unit, Institute of Education. Retrieved from http://eppi.ioe.ac.uk/cms/Default.aspx?tabid=338

Howard-Jones, P. (2010). *Introducing neuroeducational research: Neuroscience, education and the brain from contexts to practice.* Oxford: Taylor & Francis.

Hu, W., Adey, P., Jia, X., Liu, J., Zhang, L., Li, J., & Dong, X. (2011). Effects of a 'learn to think' intervention programme on primary school students. *British Journal of Educational Psychology, 81*(4), 531–557.

Jones, H. (2008). Thoughts on teaching thinking: Perceptions of practitioners with a shared culture of thinking skills education. *Curriculum Journal, 19*(4), 309–324.

Klauer, K. J. (1990). A process theory of inductive reasoning tested by the teaching of domain-specific thinking strategies. *European Journal of Psychology of Education, 5*(2), 191–206.

Klauer, K. J., & Phye, G. D. (2008). Inductive reasoning: A training approach. *Review of Educational Research, 78*(1), 85–123.

Klausmeier, H. J., & Sipple, T. S. (1980). *Learning and teaching concepts – A strategy for testing applications of theory.* New York, NY: Academic Press.

Kutnick, P., & Blatchford, P. (2014). Groups and classrooms. In P. Kutnick, & P. Blatchford (Eds.), *Effective group work in primary school classrooms* (pp. 23–49). Dordrecht: Springer Netherlands.

Lake M., & Needham, M. (1993). *Top ten thinking tactics.* Birmingham: Questions Publishing Company.

Leat, D. (1998). *Thinking through geography.* Cambridge: Chris Kington Publishing.

Leat, D., & Higgins S. (2002). The role of powerful pedagogical strategies in curriculum development. *The Curriculum Journal, 13*(1), 71–85.

Lipman, M. (2003). *Thinking in education.* Cambridge: Cambridge University Press.

Lipman, M., Sharp, A., & Oscanyan, F. (1980). *Philosophy in the classroom.* Princeton, NJ: Temple University Press.

McGregor, D. (Ed.). (2007). *Developing thinking; developing learning.* New York: McGraw-Hill International.

McGuinness, C. (1999). *From thinking skills to thinking classrooms: A review and evaluation of approaches for developing pupils' thinking.* London: DFEE Research Report RR115.

McGuinness, C. (2005). Teaching thinking: Theory and practice. *BJEP Monograph Series II, Number 3-Pedagogy-Teaching for Learning, 1*(1), 107–126.

McGuinness, C., & Nisbet, J. (1991). Teaching thinking in Europe. *British Journal of Educational Psychology, 61*, 174–186.

Machado, L. A. (1978). *El derecho a ser inteligente.* Barcelona: Seix Barral.

Meeker, M. N. (1969). *The structure of intellect, its interpretations and uses.* Columbus, OH: Charles Merrill.

Mercer, N. (2004). Development through dialogue. In T. Grainger (Ed.), *The Routledge Falmer Reader in Language and Literacy,* (pp. 121–137). London & New York: Routledge Falmer.

Mercer, N., Wegerif, R., & Dawes, L. (1999). Children's talk and the development of reasoning in the classroom. *British Educational Research Journal, 25*(1), 95–113.

Molnár, G. (2011). Playful fostering of 6-to-8-year-old students' inductive reasoning. *Thinking Skills and Creativity, 6*(2), 91–99.

Moseley, D., Baumfield, V., Elliott, J., Higgins, S., Miller, J., Newton, D. P., & Gregson, M. (2005). *Frameworks for thinking: A handbook for teaching and learning.* Cambridge: Cambridge University Press.

Murris, K. (1992). *Teaching philosophy with picture books*. London: Infoent.

Murris, K., & Haynes, J. (2001). *Storywise: Thinking through stories*. Newport: Dialogue Works.

Naji, S., & Hashim, R. (Eds.). (2017). *History, theory and practice of philosophy for children: international perspectives*. London: Routledge.

Nickerson, R. S. (1985). Project intelligence: An account and some reflections. *Special Services in the Schools, 3*(1–2), 83–102.

Nickerson, R. S., Perkins, D., & Smith, E. (1985). *The teaching of thinking*. London: Lawrence Erlbaum.

Padget, S. (Ed.). (2012). *Creativity and critical thinking*. London: Routledge.

Perkins, D. N., & Salomon, G. (2012). Knowledge to go: A motivational and dispositional view of transfer. *Educational Psychologist, 47*(3), 248–258.

Ritchhart, R., Church, M., & Morrison, K. (2011). *Making thinking visible: How to promote engagement, understanding, and independence for all learners*. San Francisco, CA: John Wiley.

Romney, D. M., & Samuels, M. T. (2001). A meta-analytic evaluation of Feuerstein's Instrumental Enrichment program. *Education and Child Psychology, 18*(4), 19–34.

Sharron, H., & Coulter, M (1994). *Changing children's minds: Feuerstein's revolution in the teaching of intelligence*. Birmingham: Questions Publishing Company.

Shiell, J. L. (2002). *A meta-analysis of Feuerstein's instrumental enrichment* (PhD Thesis). The University of British Columbia UBC, Vancouver. http://dx.doi.org/10.14288/1.0055041

Sigurborsdottir, I. (1998). Philosophy with children. *Foldaborg International Journal of Early Childhood, 30*(1), 14–16.

Sinclair, J., & Coulthard, M. (1992). Towards an analysis of discourse. In M. Coulthard (Ed.), *Advances in spoken discourse analysis* (pp. 1–34). London: Routledge.

Smith, A., Call, C., & Batton, J. (1999). *The ALPS approach: Accelerated Learning in Primary Schools* (revised edition). Stafford: Network Educational Press.

Splitter, L. J., & Sharp, A. M. (1995). *Teaching for better thinking: The classroom community of inquiry*. Melbourne: Australian Council for Educational Research.

Sprod, T. (1998). 'I can change your opinion on that': Social constructivist whole class discussions and their effect on scientific reasoning. *Research in Science Education, 28*(4), 463–480.

Sternberg, R. J., & Berg, C. A. (1992). *Intellectual development*. Cambridge: Cambridge University Press.

Sternberg, R. J., & Lubart, T. L. (1999). The concept of creativity. In R. J. Sternberg (Ed.), *Handbook of creativity* (pp. 3–15). Cambridge: Cambridge University Press.

Swartz, R. J., & Parks, S. (1994). *Infusing critical and creative thinking into content instruction: A lesson design handbook for the elementary grades*. Pacific Grove, CA: Critical Thinking Press & Software.

Trickey, S., & Topping, K. J. (2004). 'Philosophy for children': A systematic review. *Research Papers in Education, 19*(3), 365–380.

Tzuriel, D. (2001). *Dynamic assessment of young children*. Boston, MA: Springer US.

van der Schee, J., Leat, D., & Vankan, L. (2006). Effects of the use of thinking through geography strategies. *International Research in Geographical & Environmental Education, 15*(2), 124–133.

Voogt, J., Erstad, O., Dede, C., & Mishra, P. (2013). Challenges to learning and schooling in the digital networked world of the 21st century. *Journal of Computer Assisted Learning, 29*(5), 403–413.

Wallace, B., & Adams, H. B. (1993). *TASC: Thinking actively in a social context*. Oxford: AB Academic Publishers.

Wegerif, R. (2006). A dialogic understanding of the relationship between CSCL and teaching thinking skills. *International Journal of Computer-Supported Collaborative Learning, 1*(1), 143–157.

Wegerif, R. (2008). Dialogic or dialectic? The significance of ontological assumptions in research on educational dialogue. *British Educational Research Journal, 34*(3), 347–361.

Wegerif, R., Mercer, N., & Dawes, L. (1999). From social interaction to individual reasoning: An empirical investigation of a possible socio-cultural model of cognitive development. *Learning and Instruction, 9*(6), 493–516.

Wegerif, R., Perez Linares, J., Rojas-Drummond, S., Mercer, N., & Velez, M. (2005). Thinking together in the UK and Mexico: Transfer of an educational innovation. *Journal of Classroom Interaction, 40*(1), 40–48.

Weisberg, D. S., Keil, F. C., Goodstein, J., Rawson, E., & Gray, J. R. (2008). The seductive allure of neuroscience explanations. *Journal of Cognitive Neuroscience, 20*(3), 470–477.

2

EMOTIONS

Can't think with them, can't think without them

Douglas P. Newton

Introduction

There is a certain irony in the time, effort and money that goes into trying to make machines think like people while, in classrooms, we pretend that people think like machines. We are not dispassionate, infinitely patient devices, careless about what others think. The world bears upon us and shapes our thoughts, sometimes for the better and sometimes for the worse. We respond to the world, we are driven by goals and desires, and we care about how the world responds. Brain-computer analogies are seductive, but they have limits (Carbonell, Sánchez-Esguevillas, & Carro, 2016; Dielenberg, 2013). Exercising the intellect is important – very important – but inventing exercises for it may be the easy part. We might achieve more if we acknowledged, and enlisted, those things which bear upon that exercise, both in teaching and in research.

Many things influence students' facility with intellectual thought. Lack of sleep reduces the ability to learn (Stickgold, 2013), poor health can affect mental reactions (Schmidt, 2015), loud noise can impair reading comprehension (Clark, Head, & Stansfeld, 2013), and sources of stress compete for attention (Sliwinski, Smyth, Hofer, & Stawski, 2006). Exercise, on the other hand, can enhance cognitive function (Cooper, Dring, & Nevill, 2016; Hillman, Kamijo, & Pontifex, 2012), as can good weather and the arrival of spring (Brennan, Martinussen, Hansen, & Hjemdal, 1999; Keller et al., 2005). Even horoscopes affect creativity, at least for believers (Clobert, van Cappellen, Bourdon, & Cohen, 2016). And then there are moods and emotions: without them, there would be no thought (Damasio, 1994). Given the sway of moods and emotions over cognition, it may seem odd that only recently has there been a concerted effort to understand it. For over two millennia, moods and emotions were generally seen as primitive, fickle responses that are bad for thought, a threat to *Homo sapiens'* supremacy in the animal world, and something to be suppressed (Labouvie-Vief, 2015; Plamper, 2015). In education, proficiency in dispassionate thought is the goal, and, given its evident success in our mastery of the world, this is understandable. But, dispassionate thought is largely an illusion. Instead of being 'fickle and primitive', moods and emotions have a part in focusing and steering the intellect, and in promoting (and, yes, at times hindering) purposeful thought (Labouvie-Vief, 2015). In cultivating such thought, affect and cognition need to pull together if the intellect is to give of its best.

Thinking and feeling

Dijksterhuis & Nordgren (2006) offer a useful and parsimonious theoretical framework for thinking about thinking. They refer to two modes of thought, the conscious and the unconscious. Conscious thought is attention-dependent, low-capacity, relatively slow and rule-based; unconscious thought is automatic, high-capacity, fast and associative. Different kinds of purposeful thought may draw on these two modes to different degrees. Careful, step-by-step deduction in mathematics, for instance, generally requires focused attention and rule observance. Constructing an understanding of an historical event, on the other hand, is likely to benefit from imagination which brings together disparate ideas. As Dijksterhuis & Nordgren (2006, p. 102) write, 'conscious thought stays firmly under the searchlight, [whereas] unconscious thought ventures out into the dark and dusty and crannies of the mind'. Moods and emotions can be intimately involved in these processes.

Emotions are relatively brief affective responses to specific situations. Moods tend to last longer and reflect someone's subjective state of well-being (Newton, 2016). The emotional system automatically appraises situations for benefits and threats to well-being, and can generate fast responses to support self-interest. Resulting bodily changes are experienced as feelings (Lazarus (1991) constructed an early, influential appraisal theory, but there are variants; see e.g. Brosch & Sander (2013) and Keltner & Horberg (2015)). Emotions like fear at the sight of a predator and pleasure at the sight of a friend can, through the actions they prompt, enhance physical survival, but moods and emotions are also frequently generated in situations which threaten or benefit non-biological concerns, like personal goals, values and beliefs. Some of these, like interest, anticipation, enjoyment, joy, satisfaction, anxiety, disappointment, embarrassment and dread, are common in the classroom (Pekrun, Goetz, Titz, & Perry, 2002). They often arise from semi-conscious appraisals of classroom events. Dirkx (2001) described how he felt when he attended a short course. As the others expressed their views, he noted that,

> I felt myself grow tense. My face flushed and it seemed as if a tight knot was forming in the pit of my stomach. I was obviously upset and feeling even a little irritated and angry. I was at a loss as to why I was feeling so strongly about this discussion.
>
> *(Dirkx, 2001, p. 63)*

Dirxx had unconsciously perceived what was said as threatening his values and beliefs. His automatic response was to generate emotions prompting him to defend his beliefs, or leave the room. Of course, not all moods and emotions are generated in the classroom. Some are brought to it from elsewhere, but these, too, can have an effect.

Moods and emotions are often grouped by valence (+/-), strength, activation/deactivation, approach/avoidance, or some combination of these. This provides an economical and functional way of describing their effects. Some see this as over-simple and, instead, prefer to discuss the effects of individual moods and emotions within groups (see Narrow effects and Particular effects in Leblanc, McConnell & Monteiro, 2014). I begin with some broad effects, then describe more subtle effects on particular families of thought, and then point to other effects and some finer detail.

Broad effects

It hardly needs to be said that, at times, moods and emotions can impede, even overwhelm, purposeful, goal-directed thought (Newton, 2015). Strong moods and emotions can generate thoughts and actions which compete for mental resources with the task in hand. Rage, for instance, fills the mind with the offence that caused it; even moderate resentment at some unintended affront can distract attention for up to half-an-hour (Cram & Germinario, 2000; Greenleaf, 2005), while depression can lead to endless rumination about adversity, and excitement makes it difficult to stay on-task. What may seem less intense are what I call public performance emotions, such as those generated when answering questions, contributing to class discussions, group work or debates, and reporting orally on personal projects. Some students find such events very threatening, putting them at risk of looking foolish, or inadequate, or of revealing matters they prefer to be private. They respond with shyness, embarrassment, anxiety and stage fright, emotions strong enough to impede recall and reason, and often triggered by the need for a quick reply, or by a teacher lacking in empathy (Zarrinabadi, 2014). It also explains why students are inclined to be reticent when brought together for the first time (Todd, Forstmann, Burgmer, Wood Brooks, & Galinsky, 2015), and is well-known in language learning where students must respond orally, causing some to drop out at the first opportunity (He, 2013; Swain, 2013). High stakes examinations can generate anxiety which may be so intense that it impedes preparation and performance (Pekrun, Goetz, Titz, & Perry, 2002). Trying to motivate students by pointing out that their life's ambition depends on examination success is unhelpful (Newton, 2016). Even providing formative feedback, a highly favoured strategy, backfires if it prompts students to drop out when it threatens their self-esteem (Race, 2001; Young, 2000).

On the other hand, some emotions attract students to learning, and motivate them to persist with it. This is especially the case when their evaluation of the event suggests that it may offer satisfaction of a need for, for example, meaningfulness, novelty, competence, affiliation or, more instrumentally, access to a desired career, or avoidance of boredom or punishment (Fletcher, 2005; Newton, 1988). Such motivational properties did not escape Piaget (1954/1981) who saw affect as 'energizing' and 'regulating' the intellect, using the analogy that affect is like gasoline which activates an engine — without gasoline, the engine stops; without emotion, purposeful thought ceases. Even anxiety is not always bad for thought, if it is mild (Sieber, O'Neil, & Tobias, 2013; but note Corbett, 2015). And we must not forget memory; emotive matters generally attract attention, tend to be given more significance, produce more durable memories, and are easier to recall (Lindström & Bohlin, 2011). There is also a modest tendency for mood congruence in recall: it is a little better when the current mood matches that of the stored memory (Barry, Baus, & Rehm, 2004).

Such across-the-board, approach-avoidance effects apply more or less to all kinds of thinking and classroom work although their strength may vary with each student's temperament (Rothbart, 2012). Some interactions, however, are more selective, and have different, even complementary, effects in different families of thought.

Narrow effects

Methodical thought

Methodical thinking is characterised by the systematic and detailed processing of information, often involving analysis, formal logic and step-by-step reasoning (Newton, 2015). Deductive reasoning, typically associated with subjects like mathematics and the sciences, is an example, but is not, of course, confined to these subjects. The evaluation of mental products similarly requires careful, systematic thought, and those attempting to solve technological problems have to evaluate potential solutions likewise (Newton, 2016). Human thought is, of course, fallible; some methodical thinkers are less systematic than others, they make unwarranted assumptions and take short-cuts (Johnson-Laird, 2010). But, even without these imperfections, methodical thought is subject to the actions of moods and emotions.

As might be expected, strong emotions compete for those mental resources which could be useful in methodical thought, particularly when the task is demanding. Moreover, weaker reasoners tend to be affected more by moods and emotions they bring with them than those with some facility with methodical thought (Blanchette & Nougarou, 2017). But, less obviously, positive moods, like feeling cheerful or glad, widen attention, and give thought a broad brush stroke, so that details are disregarded in favour of generalities and broad perspectives (Blanchette & Richards, 2010). This is inimical to non-trivial methodical thought where close attention to detail is needed; it is better served by neutral, even low moods. As Andrews and Thomson (2009, p. 620) have put it, 'feeling blue' can be useful for 'analytical rumination'. Consequently, those feeling sad tend to take fewer moves to solve logical puzzles than those who are happy (Badcock & Allen, 2003). Sadness is generally not a preferred state of mind, at least in the West, but, while some dysphoria is a part of life, we would probably not want to recommend it to students simply to make them more effective computational devices. Nevertheless, we do need to recognise that there can be drawbacks to feeling forever joyful, and that a calm composure can have its rewards.

Constructive thought

Constructive thought is a second family of purposeful thought characterised by connection-making, relationship-finding and the imaginative synthesis of information into coherent wholes (Newton, 2016). In line with the constructivist paradigm, it involves the making of mental models of the world (Johnson-Laird, 2010; Richardson, 2003). Often, the models are those accepted by the academic community, and a teacher tries to support their construction as understandings. Students may also be expected to construct novel understandings (at least, novel to them) through creative thinking. Constructive thought cannot guarantee the veracity of such constructions, but it takes the risk of making them. (A partial exception is a fairly methodical kind of 'creative' problem solving, TRIZ, which offers a taxonomy of practical problems and solutions to facilitate the problem solving (Mann, 2002).)

Feeling moderately happy tends to support the noticing of patterns, connections and relationships. It seems that the state persuades the thinker that the situation is safe, and the resulting mental relaxation puts the mind into a 'broaden-and-build mode' (Fredrickson & Branigan, 2005). This state of mind facilitates flexibility, toying with ideas and 'What if …?' thinking. While it may foster constructive thought, it should be added that feeling happy can make people less critical of their understandings and constructions, and more ready to accept mediocre solutions (Newton, 2016). On the other hand, being gloomy, nervous, worried, or irritated can prevent thinkers entering the broaden-and-build mode or bring them out of it, and focus attention on the cause of the mood, or switch to methodical thought. Similarly, bringing strangers together for joint creative thinking is unlikely to have a productive start as their caution can put them into a methodical mode of thought (Newton, 2014a; Todd, Forstmann, Burgmer, Wood Brooks, & Galinsky, 2015).

This illustrates complementary effects of moods and emotions. Of course, neither methodical nor constructive thought are likely to be entirely pure from beginning to end; each may draw on other kinds of thinking as they progress, but careful thinking and carefree thinking are, respectively, at their core. It will have been noted that the theory of Dijksterhuis & Nordgren (2006) gives conscious thought the function of step-by-step thinking, and unconscious thought that of associative thinking; biases found in the families described.

Steering effects

Productive progress

Moods and emotions may help or hinder particular kinds of thought, but, when generated while working on a task, they may also offer potentially useful advice about its progress. In general, if our thinking makes progress, we feel some satisfaction and anticipation, and we are inclined to continue with that line of thought. Clore & Palmer (2009) described this phenomenon as an instance of emotion-as-information. Here, the emotion generated by progress tells us that the approach is promising. On the other hand, when progress stalls we become frustrated, even annoyed. This is like a signal telling us we need a different approach. Such information is potentially useful, particularly in problem-solving where promising ideas do not always bear fruit. Some students, however, do not seem to notice the message, and persist with a fruitless approach. Others bring emotions to the situation and react as though they were produced by the task in hand.

Decision-making

This role of emotions as a source of information about preferences is central to personal decision-making (Peters, 2006; Slovic, Finucane, Peters, & MacGregor, 2002). Decision-making is the selection of an action, mental or physical, from alternatives in order to achieve a goal. Arguably, it is a momentous kind of purposeful thought as it can determine life's trajectory (Newton, 2016). In personal decision-making, goals are often underpinned by personal values, beliefs and constraints which frequently have their origin in the past but have become submerged in the unconscious mind. Logic alone may point to one alternative, but a feeling of unease grows as the unconscious mind notes a threat to 'hidden' matters of personal concern. At the same time, options and their consequences can be difficult to compare in a rule-driven way. The unconscious mind, however, is able to give these incommensurable threats and benefits a common currency, and indicate a preference through comfort with or aversion to the options (Dijksterhuis & Nordgren, 2006; Leblanc, McConnell, & Monteiro, 2015). The emotional response is, in itself, rational, but it rests on goals, values and beliefs which may be anachronistic, anti-social or somehow maladaptive, rendering the decision inappropriate. Lerner, Li, Valdesolo, & Kassam (2015) accordingly propose an 'emotion-imbued choice model' in which emotions have their say, but their preference is interrogated closely for relevance and soundness.

The classical model of decision-making, primarily developed for use in, for example, economics, commerce and medicine, relies heavily on material and mental resources, information, computation and the calculation and weighing of probabilities. It is often a methodical process aimed at producing a logical preference to achieve the goals of the workplace. First, it is usually not practical to make personal decisions in this way. Time is often short, resources are limited and the methods of formal computation may be outside the decider's experience (Gigerenzer & Goldstein, 1996). Second, it risks overlooking personal values, beliefs and goals which lie in the unconscious mind. Third, the unconscious mind may not question assumptions about beliefs, goals and options: adolescents deciding on careers, for instance, may be unwittingly constrained by the habitus (Bourdieu, 1984). Hodkinson & Sparkes (1997) describe how cultural norms, beliefs, values and goals are assimilated through experience in the local subculture and become deeply embedded in a person's identity, often unconsciously circumscribing choices. Such tendencies, however, are open to change if subject to conscious evaluation (Baum & Davison, 2009; Navarro, 2006).

Teaching students to make personal decisions like machines risks outcomes that are logically sound but personally inappropriate. Students need to be able to use the products of both the unconscious mind (to allow unconscious matters of concern to make themselves felt) and the conscious mind (to take advantage of methodical processing by, for instance, checking the relevance of exposed values). Thagard (2001) advises that complex decisions are best taken by 'informed intuition', in which much is left to the unconscious mind (see also Lerner, Li, Valdesolo, & Kassam, 2015; Salvi, Bricoli, Koumios, Bourdon, & Beeman, 2016). Decision-making does need methodical thought, as when teasing out consequences, but attempting to purge it of emotion increases the likelihood that it will insufficiently reflect matters of personal concern.

Particular effects

There are specific emotional effects which seem contrary to general expectations. For example, love, commonly seen as a positive emotion, can, on occasions, reduce creativity (Yang & Hung, 2015). Here, what is important is the perceived benefit or threat to the current situation. Love is likely to seek to perpetuate the status quo; being creative could threaten that. Similarly, being sad is not normally associated with creativity, but those who suffer from bipolar disorder and clinical depression are over-represented in artistic occupations (Simeonova, Chang, Strong, & Ketter, 2005). It may be that the benefits offered by such activity, perhaps through distraction or externalised expression, are sufficient to induce engagement in this kind of creative pursuit. In both cases, the nature of the current situation is important – is it to be maintained or changed? Teenagers, however, take risks when the choice is not (to us) to their advantage. In the teenager's mind, the benefit (thrill) is heightened by the threat (danger), an interaction which may be heightened by hormonal changes (Peper & Dahl, 2013). At the same time, an incidental emotion brought to a decision may be mistaken for that produced by an option (Phelps, Lempert, & Sokol-Kersner, 2014). This is, of course, the role of soft music in a supermarket where it is used to produce stress-free moods and less critical and analytical thought (Milliman, 1982).

Pekrun, Goetz, Titz, & Perry (2002) have concluded that emotions in the classroom bear upon motivation, learning strategies, cognitive resources, self-regulation, and academic achievement. Such studies led Immordino-Yang & Damasio (2007) to point out that disregarding this interaction is a serious omission in education.

Educational implications

For teachers

Students' emotions can change markedly from one lesson to another according to the subject, the teacher, the topic, the activity and its level of demand. At the same time, students are different and their responses vary (Ahmed, van der Werf, Minnaert, & Kuyper, 2010). Are teachers aware of such effects and able to manage them? Emotional labour, 'the labour involved in dealing with other peoples' feelings', is now recognised as a significant aspect of the workplace (Berry & Cassidy, 2013; James, 1989, p. 15). Teachers may acquire some intuitive grasp of the interaction of emotions and cognition through classroom experience, and, perhaps, unconsciously accommodate it in their teaching (e.g. Williams, Cross, Hong, Aultman, Osbon, & Schutz, 2008; Wyness & Lang, 2016). For example, some teachers recognise the value of enthusiasm and its effects on students' interest (Scheve & Ismer, 2013). They may learn to adopt a calm, quiet demeanour to lessen excitement to facilitate methodical thinking, or they may try to relax a class in preparation for constructive, creative thought. Such behaviours, however, are probably unplanned and, at best, apply only to the broader effects of the interaction (e.g. Brookfield, 2015). Awareness, forethought and planning could significantly strengthen these behaviours.

Um, Plass, Hayward & Homer (2011) used the term 'emotional design' to describe planning aimed at making the most of the interaction between emotions and cognition to support learning from multimedia. For instance, they demonstrated that anthropomorphic graphics using warm colours can induce positive moods which, directly or indirectly, foster understanding and retention. It is likely that there are other ways of making teaching and learning materials emotive and so more capable of supporting particular kinds of purposeful thought. But the notion of deliberate emotional design can also apply to face-to-face teaching. At its simplest, a teacher could plan to use electronic 'clickers' so that a new class can respond to options by anonymous voting, avoiding exposing their thinking to others. Such devices can also offer immediate but private feedback (Yourstone, Kraye, & Albaum, 2008). Digital technology offers various ways of shielding susceptible students from the adverse effects of public performance until they have developed sufficient expertise to do so with less anxiety or embarrassment (Evans, 2009). But, to make the most of the interaction, such forethought needs to extend over a lesson in a more comprehensive way. By that, I do not mean inducing strong or maladaptive emotions, but influencing them as we do to lubricate social interaction; we more or less routinely try to lift overly sad moods in others, or calm those who are over-excited, so that the interaction is productive. For example, a teacher begins a lesson aware that there will be a need for methodical thought to focus attention on the nature of the task, followed by constructive, creative thought to develop ideas, and then a return to methodical thought to evaluate those ideas. Initially, this could benefit from calm, focused states of mind to foster attention on detail, then relaxed states to encourage wider-ranging thought, and then a return to focused states to evaluate that thought. Inappropriate moods in each of these phases could reduce the overall quality of the outcome. Note also that there is a tension between analytical and creative thought: if the former is induced too soon, it suppresses and crushes the latter (Newton, 2016).

How might moods be changed? A teacher's body language and facial expressions signal the tone, and is understood in a fraction of second. For example, a slumped posture can lower the mood, sympathetic listening can improve it, while covering the face with the hands can induce fear (Laird & Lacasse, 2014). The pace, rhythm and pitch of talk adds to the effect. A relatively even, quiet, slow enunciation lessens the intensity of emotions and makes them more neutral. Injecting enthusiasm, however, can raise interest and anticipation (Hatfield, Cacioppo, & Rapson, 1993). Of course, what is said also matters: praise, jokes and highlighting positives tend to lessen negative moods (Goodwin & Judd, 2005). On the other hand, negative feedback and criticism tend to produce them (Niven, Totterdell, & Holman, 2007), and all contribute to the emotional climate, the overall affective tone in a classroom, for better or worse. It should be added that there can be gender differences in responsiveness to particular strategies. For instance, men tend to prefer distraction to change their moods, whereas women prefer social activity (Thayer, Newman, & McClain, 1994). Such differences may be innate, cultural, or both.

For students

Ideally, students would adjust their own states of mind to suit the current need. Some will have acquired strategies for managing strong emotions, and those who have not could receive instruction (Ochnser & Gross, 2005). It is likely, however, that students, and particularly those who are young, will not be aware of the benefits of emotion management. There is no reason to keep it secret, and enlisting students in the activity could be a useful lesson in itself. Young children, for example, may be taught to manage emotions through role play (Lillard, Lerner, Hopkins, Dore, Smith, & Palmquist, 2012). Physical exercise can make moods more positive, relaxation and writing can lessen negative emotions, and detailed craftwork can lift moods from deep sadness (Garfield & Brockman, 2000; Hogan, Kiefer, Kubesch, Collins, Kilmartin, & Brosnan, 2013; Reynolds, 2000; Thayer, Newman & McClain, 1994). Of course, many factors bear upon states of mind and, in turn, on thought. Being tired, for instance, can make moods and emotions more difficult to control (Baum, Desai, Field, Miller, Rausch, & Beebe, 2014), so raising students' awareness of such effects may be useful. Music may help children change moods, and self-regulation of emotions is, in turn, associated with school success (Foran, 2009; Ivcevic & Brackett, 2014). This may bring to mind the sometimes controversial notion of 'emotional intelligence' (Salovey & Mayer, 1990). Where this means developing an ability to recognise and regulate emotions (e.g. Zeidner, Roberts, & Matthews, 2002), and to interpret and use the information provided by them (e.g. Yadav, 2011), it has some relevance here. Having this ability can also be an asset for a teacher (Hassan, Jani, Som, Hamid, & Azizam, 2015).

For teacher trainers

Those who train teachers should consider developing trainees' understanding of the interaction of emotions and cognition, and of how they might take advantage of it through forethought, emotional design and the management of emotional climate. The teacher should also be able to teach in ways which do not bring cognition and emotion into conflict (instead of, for example, setting a creative task and, simulta-neously, expecting evaluative thinking), or generating stress through time pressure (Newton, 2014a; Siu & Wong, 2016). At the same time, trainees should be aware that there is no need to tinker continuously with the emotional climate: interven-tion is only needed when it will adversely and significantly affect thinking and learning. Novice teachers may also benefit from reflection on the emotional nature of teaching, how it affects them, and how they might lessen unwelcome effects on themselves.

Teaching is not static. Digital technology, for example, continues to change practices. Of particular relevance are developments in humanoid robots. Kanda, Hirano, Eaton, & Ishiguro (2004) and Shin & Kim (2007) provided early demon-strations that, as teaching assistants, they can support learning. They can respond to students, elicit actions and answers, provide practice and offer feedback, and, in foreign language learning, they can enable a student to practice without undue anxiety (Chang, Lee, Chao, Wang, & Chen, 2010). While their current inability to portray emotions convincingly has been noted, teachers may need to reflect on more fundamental matters (Mubin, Stevens, Shahid, Al Mahmud, & Dong, 2013). For instance: How do these robots affect the classroom's emotional climate? Can they 'sense' the climate or a student's mood? If this ability is developed, will they respond in ways which make the students' emotions and cognition mutually sup-portive? Equally, is praise from a robot as effective or valued as much as praise from a human? Humanoid robots may prove themselves able to support cognition, but teachers must remember that cognition alone is not everything.

For researchers

The interaction of moods, emotions and cognition has several implications for those who seek to enhance the products of the intellect. First, the relevance of this major variable in the thinking processes should be considered in theories and tests of teaching strategies. Take, for example, the effect of music on learning: results are mixed and often contradictory. But, the effect of music on mood and its match (or mismatch) with the nature of the thinking may be overlooked. It is not a matter of, does music affect thinking, but do particular kinds of music produce particular states of mind which affect particular kinds of thinking. Second, ways of inducing particular emotions are well-known in psychological research but are often not appropriate in the classroom. Other ways of adjusting moods would be useful. Furthermore, the demands of a lesson are often complex, with methodical thought alternating with constructive thought. Third, the development of strategies to teach students to regulate their emotions to suit the learning needs of the situation may prove useful, particularly when they see the need for it and the pre-requisites are within their grasp. Experience may have taught some students some such skills. Are they optimal? Fourth, moods and emotions are not the sole province of the student; the teacher is equally subject to affect, something which can make teaching stressful and mentally exhausting (Doré, Silvers, & Ochsner, 2016; Troy, Shallcross,

& Mauss, 2013). Students' perceptions of teachers' emotional responses also affect the emotional climate. How these might be managed for the teacher's well-being, as well as for useful effect, may need some attention. Appraisal theories can help us understand how teachers and students respond to events and point us towards potential ways of alleviating problems and of enhancing useful effects.

Conclusion

The interaction of emotions and cognition serves as a reminder that teaching and learning are complex. In a particular classroom, on a particular day, this complexity can easily undermine sweeping claims for the effectiveness of strategies meant to develop the intellect (Cartwright & Hardie, 2012; Pawson, 2006; Simpson, 2017). Teachers, their trainers and researchers need to be aware of the interaction's central importance. Even an unsophisticated appraisal theory can offer some useful understanding of the generation and role of moods and emotions, and prepare the way for their effects. It might usefully underpin teacher training. While teachers may manage students' moods and emotions, students themselves could find long-term benefit in learning to adapt their moods to the needs of thinking. Raising students' awareness of the effects, therefore, and including students in their management could be worthwhile. Students with major emotional problems, however, need the care of specialists.

With good intentions, we may treat students as thinking machines: perhaps to develop their critical thinking skills, or to help them be less egocentric, or to notice unwarranted bias. These are worthy goals with the potential for rich rewards, material and otherwise, but ignoring moods and emotions in the process is like ignoring an elephant in the classroom (Newton, 2014b). The elephant is always there, sitting upon what purports to be dispassionate thought, and, contrary to popular belief, without always being bad for it. This is not an argument against rational thought, or a suggestion that moods and emotions should be allowed a free rein. Instead, moods and emotions need to be recognised, understood and managed to the thinker's advantage so that, as Larsen (2000) eloquently put it, 'We want people to have moods, but we don't want moods to have people'. The aim is for cognition and affect to work together productively.

References

Ahmed, W., van der Werf, G., Minnaert, A., & Kuyper, H. (2010). Students' daily emotions in the classroom. *British Journal of Educational Psychology, 80*, 583–597.

Andrews, P. W., & Thomson, J. A. (2009). The bright side of being blue. *Psychological Review, 116*(3), 620–654.

Badcock, P. B. T., & Allen, N. B. (2003). Adaptive social reasoning in depressed mood and depressive vulnerability. *Cognition & Emotion, 17*(4), 647–670.

Barry, E. S., Baus, M. J., & Rehm, L. P. (2004). Depression and implicit memory. *Cognitive Therapy and Research, 28*, 387–414.

Baum, K. T., Desai, A., Field, J., Miller, L. E., Rausch, J., & Beebe, D. W. (2014). Sleep restriction worsens mood and emotion regulation in adolescents. *Journal of Child Psychology and Psychiatry, 55*(2), 180–190.

Baum, W. M., & Davison, M. (2009). Modelling the dynamics of choice. *Behavioural Processes, 81*(2), 189–194.

Berry, K., & Cassidy, S. (2013). Emotional labour in university lecturers. *Journal of Curriculum and Teaching, 2*(2), 22–36.

Blanchette, I., & Nougarou, F. (2017). Incidental emotions have a greater impact on the logicality of less proficient reasoners. *Thinking & Reasoning, 23*(1), 98–113.

Blanchette, I., & Richards, A. (2010). The influence of affect on higher level cognition. *Cognition & Emotion, 24*(4), 561–595.

Bourdieu, P. (1984). *Distinction: A social critique of the judgement of taste.* London: Routledge.

Brennan, T., Martinussen, M., Hansen, B. O., & Hjemdal, O. (1999). Arctic cognition. *Applied Cognitive Psychology, 13*, 561–580.

Brookfield, S. D. (2015). *The skillful teacher.* San Francisco, CA: Jossey-Bass.

Brosch, T., & Sander, D. (2013). The appraising brain. *Emotional Review, 5*(2), 163–168.

Carbonell, J., Sánchez-Esguevillas, A., & Carro, B. (2016). The role of metaphors in the development of technologies. *Futures, 84*, 145–153.

Cartwright, N., & Hardie, J. (2012). *Evidence-based policy.* New York, NY: Oxford University Press.

Chang, C.-W., Lee, J.-H., Chao, P.-C., Wang, C.-Y., & Chen, G.-D. (2010). Exploring the possibility of using humanoid robots as instructional tools for teaching a second language in primary school. *Journal of Educational Technology & Society, 13*(2), 13–24.

Clark, C., Head, J., & Stansfeld, S. A. (2013). Longitudinal effects of aircraft noise exposure on children's health and cognition. *Journal of Environmental Psychology, 35*, 1–9.

Clobert, M., van Cappellen, P., Bourdon, M., & Cohen, A. B. (2016). Good day for Leos. *Personality and Individual Differences.* doi:10.1016/j.paid.2016.06.032

Clore, G. L., & Palmer, J. (2009). Affective guidance of intelligent agents: How emotion controls cognition. *Cognitive Systems Research, 10*, 21–30.

Cooper, S. B., Dring, K. J., & Nevill, M. E. (2016). High intensity intermittent exercise. *Current Sports Medicine Reports, 15*(4), 245–251.

Corbett, M. (2015). From law to folklore. *Journal of Managerial Psychology, 30*(6), 741–752.

Cram, H. G., & Germinario, V. (2000). *Leading and learning in schools.* Lanham, MD: Scarecrow.

Damasio, A. (1994). *Descartes' error.* New York, NY: Avon Books.

Dielenberg, R. A. (2013). The speculative neuroscience of the future human brain. *Humanities, 2*(2), 209–252.

Dijksterhuis, A., & Nordgren, L. F. (2006). A theory of unconscious thought. *Perspectives on Psychological Science, 1*(2), 95–109.

Dirkx, J. (2001). The power of feelings. *New Directions for Adult and Continuous Education, 89*, 63–72.

Doré, B. P., Silvers, J. A., & Ochsner, K. N. (2016). Towards a personalized science of emotion regulation. *Social & Personality Psychology, 10*(4), 171–187.

Evans, M. (Ed.). (2009). *Foreign language learning with digital technology.* London: Continuum.

Fletcher, A. (2005). *Meaningful student involvement.* Olympia, WA: CommonAction.

Foran, L. M. (2009). Listening to music. *Educational Horizons, 88*(1), 51–58.

Fredrickson, B. L., & Branigan, C. (2005). Positive emotions broaden the scope of attention and thought-action repertoires. *Cognition & Emotion, 19*(3), 313–332.

Garfield, S. E., & Brockman, S. E. (2000). Students find their voices in writing. *Journal of Adolescent & Adult Literacy, 43*(5), 484–487.

Gigerenzer, G., & Goldstein, D. G. (1996). Reasoning the fast and furious way. *Psychological Review, 103*(4), 650–669.

Goodwin, M. W., & Judd, L. (2005). Ensure success as a novice teacher. *Intervention in School and Clinic, 41*(1), 24–29.

Greenleaf, R. K. (2005). *Brain based teaching.* Newfield, ME: Greenleaf & Papanek.

Hassan, N., Jani, S. H. M., Som, R. M., Hamid, N. Z. A., & Azizam, A. (2015). The relationship between emotional intelligence and teaching effectiveness among lecturers at Universiti Teknologi MARA, Puncak Alam, Malaysia. *International Journal of Social Science and Humanity, 5*(1), 1–5.

Hatfield, E., Cacioppo, J. T., & Rapson, R. L. (1993). Emotional contagion. *Current Directions in Psychological Science, 2*(3), 96–99.

He, D. (2013). What makes learners anxious while speaking English. *Educational Studies.* doi: 10.1080/03055698.2013.764819

Hillman, C. H., Kamijo, K., & Pontifex, M. B. (2012). The relation of ERP indices of exercise to brain health and cognition. In H. Boecker, C. H. Hillman, L. Scheef, & H. K. Strüder (Eds.), *Functional neuroimaging in exercise and sport sciences* (p. 419). New York, NY: Springer. doi:10.1007/978-1-4614-3293-7_18

Hodkinson, P., & Sparkes, A. C. (1997). Careership: A sociological theory of career decision making. *British Journal of Sociology of Education, 18*(1), 29–44.

Hogan, M., Kiefer, M., Kubesch, S., Collins, P., Kilmartin, L., & Brosnan, M. (2013). The interactive effects of physical fitness and acute aerobic exercise on electrophysiological coherence and cognitive performance in adolescents. *Experimental Brain Research, 229*, 85–96.

Immordino-Yang, M. H., & Damasio, A. (2007). We feel, therefore we learn. *Mind, Brain and Education, 1*(1), 3–10.

Ivcevic, Z., & Brackett, M. (2014). Predicting school success. *Journal of Research in Personality, 52*, 29–36.

James, N. (1989). Emotional labour. *The Sociological Review, 37*(1), 15–42.

Johnson-Laird, P. N. (2010). Mental models and human reasoning. *Proceedings of the National Academy of Science, 107*(43), 18243–18250.

Kanda, T., Hirano, T., Eaton, D., & Ishiguro, H. (2004). Interactive robots as social partners and peer tutors for children: A field trial. *Human–Computer Interaction, 19*(1), 61–84.

Keller, M. C., Fredrickson, B. L., Ybarra, O., Côté, S., Johnson, K., Mikels, J. Conway, A., & Wager, T. (2005). A warm heart and a clear head. *Psychological Science, 16*(9), 724–731.

Keltner, D., & Horberg, E. J. (2015). Emotion-cognition interactions. In M. Mikulincerm, P. R. Shaver, E. Borgida, & J. A. Bargh (Eds.), *APA handbook of personality and social psychology* (Vol. 1, pp. 623–664). Washington, DC: American Psychological Association.

Labouvie-Vief, G. (2015). Emotions and cognition: From myth and philosophy to modern psychology and neuroscience. In G. Labouvie-Vief (Ed.), *Integrating emotion and cognition throughout the lifespan* (pp. 1–16). Geneva: Springer.

Laird, J. D., & Lacasse, K. (2014). Bodily influences on emotional feelings. *Emotional Review, 6*, 27–34.

Larsen, R. J. (2000). Towards a science of mood regulation. *Psychological Inquiry, 11*(3), 129–141.

Lazarus, R. S. (1991). *Emotion & adaptation.* New York, NY: Oxford University Press.

LeBlanc, V. R., McConnell, M. M., & Monteiro, S. D. (2014). Predictable chaos: A review of the effects of emotions on attention, memory, and decision-making. *Advances in Health Science Education, 20*(1), 265–282.

LeBlanc, V. R., McConnell, M. M., & Monteiro, S. D. (2015). Predictable chaos. *Advances in Health Science Education.* doi: 10.1007/s10459-014-9516-6

Lerner, J. S., Li, Y., Valdesolo, P., & Kassam, K. S. (2015). Emotion and decision-making. *Annual Review of Psychology, 66*, 799–823.

Lillard, A. S., Lerner, M. D., Hopkins, E. J., Dore, R. A., Smith, E. D., & Palmquist, C. M. (2012). The impact of pretend play on children's development. *Psychological Bulletin, 139*(1), 49–52.

Lindström, B. R., & Bohlin, G. (2011). Emotion processing facilitates working memory performance. *Cognition & Emotion, 25*(7), 1196–1204.

Mann, D. (2002). *Hands-On systematic innovation.* Plumlaan: CREAX.

Milliman, R. E. (1982). Using background music to affect the behaviour of supermarket shoppers. *Journal of Marketing, 46*(3), 86–91.

Mubin, O., Stevens, C. J., Shahid, S., Al Mahmud, A., & Dong, J.-J. (2013). A review of the applicability of robots in education. *Technology for Education and Learning, 1*, 209–215.

Navarro, Z. (2006). In search of cultural interpretation of power. *IDS Bulletin, 37*(6), 11–22.

Newton, D. P. (1988). *Making science education relevant*. London: Kogan Page.

Newton, D. P. (2014a). *Thinking with feeling*. London: Routledge.

Newton, D. P. (2014b). The elephant in the classroom. *Research in Education, 2,* 1–10.

Newton, D. P. (2015). There's more to thinking than the intellect. In R. Wegerif, J. Kaufman, & L. Li (Eds.), *The Routledge international handbook of research on teaching thinking* (pp. 58–68). London: Routledge.

Newton, D. P. (2016). *In two minds*. Ulm: ICIE.

Niven, K., Totterdell, P., & Holman, D. (2007). Changing moods and influencing people. *Prison Service Journal, 173,* 39–45.

Ochnser, K., & Gross, J. J. (2005). The cognitive control of emotion. *Trends in Cognitive Science, 9*(5), 242–249.

Pawson, R. (2006). *Evidence-based policy: A realist perspective*. London: Sage.

Pekrun, R., Goetz, T., Titz, W., & Perry, R. P. (2002). Academic emotions in students' self-regulated learning and achievement. *Educational Psychologist, 37*(2), 91–106.

Peper, J. S., & Dahl, R. E. (2013). The teenage brain. *Current Directions in Psychological Science, 22*(2), 134–139.

Peters, E. (2006). The function of affect in the construction of preferences. In S. Lichtenstein & P. Slovic (Eds.), *The construction of preferences* (pp. 454–463). New York, NY: Cambridge University Press.

Phelps, E. A., Lempert, K. M., & Sokol-Kersner, P. (2014). Emotion and decision-making. *Annual Review of Neuroscience, 37,* 262–287.

Piaget, J. (1954/1981). *Intelligence and affectivity*. Palo Alto, CA: Annual Reviews.

Plamper, J. (2015). *The history of emotions*. Oxford: Oxford University Press.

Race, P. (2001). *Using feedback to help students learn*. York: HEA.

Reynolds, F. (2000). Managing depression through needlecraft creative activities: A qualitative study. *The Arts in Psychotherapy, 27*(2), 107–114.

Richardson, V. (2003). Constructivist pedagogy. *Teachers' College Record, 109*(5), 1623–1640.

Rothbart, M. K. (2012). *Becoming who we are*. New York, NY: Guilford Press.

Salovey, P., & Mayer, J. D. (1990). Emotional intelligence. *Imagination, Cognition and Personality, 9*(3), 185–211.

Salvi, C., Bricoli, E., Koumios, J., Bourdon, E., & Beeman, M. (2016). Insight solutions are correct more often than analytic solutions. *Thinking & Reasoning, 22*(4), 443–460.

Scheve, C., & Ismer, S. (2013). Towards a theory of collective emotions. *Emotional Review, 5*(4), 406–413.

Schmidt, C. (2015). Mental health from the gut. *Nature, 518,* S12–S15.

Shin, N., & Kim, S. (2007). *Learning about, from, and with robots: Students' perspectives*. 16th IEEE International Conference on Robot & Human Interactive Communication, August 26–29, Jeju, Korea.

Sieber, J. E., O'Neil, H. F., & Tobias, S. (2013). *Anxiety, learning and instruction*. New York, NY: Routledge.

Simeonova, D. I., Chang, K. K., Strong, C., & Ketter, T. A. (2005). Creativity in familial bipolar disorder. *Journal of Psychiatric Research, 39,* 623–631.

Simpson, A. (2017). The misdirection of public policy: Comparing and combining standardised effect sizes. *Journal of Education Policy*. Retrieved March 20, 2017, from http://dx.doi.org/10.1080/02680939.2017.1280183

Siu, K. W. M., & Wong, Y. L. (2016). Fostering creativity from an emotional perspective. *International Journal of Technology Design Education, 26,* 105–121.

Sliwinski, M., Smyth, J. M., Hofer, S. M., & Stawski, R. S. (2006). Intraindividual coupling of daily stress and cognition. *Psychology and Aging, 21*(3), 545–557.

Slovic, P., Finucane, M., Peters, E., & MacGregor, D. G. (2002). Rational actors or rational fools. *The Journal of Socio Economics, 31,* 329–342.

Stickgold, R. (2013). Early to bed. *Trends in Cognitive Sciences, 17*(6), 261–262.

Swain, M. (2013). The inseparability of cognition and emotion in second language learning. *Language Teaching, 46*(2), 195–207.

Thagard, P. (2001). How to make decisions. In E. Millgram (Ed.), *Varieties of practical reasoning* (pp. 355–371). Cambridge, MA: MIT Press.

Thayer, R. E., Newman, J. R., & McClain, T. M. (1994). Self-regulation of mood. *Journal of Personality and Social Psychology, 67*(5), 910–925.

Todd, A. R., Forstmann, M., Burgmer, P., Wood Brooks, A., & Galinsky, A. D. (2015). Anxious and egocentric. *Journal of Experimental Psychology, 144*(2), 374–391. doi:10.1037/xge0000048

Troy, A. S., Shallcross, A. J., & Mauss, I. B. (2013). A person-by-person situation approach to emotion regulation. *Psychological Science, 24*(12), 2505–2514.

Um, E., Plass, J. L., Hayward, E. O., & Homer, B. D. (2011). Emotional design in multimedia learning. *Journal of Educational Psychology, 104*(2), 485–498.

Williams, M., Cross, D., Hong, J., Aultman, L., Osbon, J., & Schutz, P. (2008). There are no emotions in math. *Teachers College Record, 110*(8), 1574–1612.

Wyness, M., & Lang, P. (2016). The social and emotional dimensions of schooling. *British Educational Research Journal, 42*(6), 1041–1055.

Yadav, N. (2011). Emotional intelligence and its effects on job performance: A comparative study on life insurance sales professionals. *International Journal of Multidisciplinary Research, 1*(8), 248–260.

Yang, J.-S., & Hung, H. V. (2015). Emotions as constraining and facilitating factors for creativity. *Creativity and Innovation Management, 24*(2), 217–230.

Young, P. (2000). 'I might as well give up': Self-esteem and mature students' feelings about feedback on assignments. *Journal of Further and Higher Education, 24*(3), 409–418.

Yourstone, S. A., Kraye, H. S., & Albaum, G. (2008). Classroom questioning with immediate electronic feedback. *Decision Sciences Journal of Innovative Education, 6*(1), 75–88.

Zarrinabadi, N. (2014). Communicating in a second language. *System, 42*, 288–295.

Zeidner, M., Roberts, R. D., & Matthews, G. (2002). Can emotional intelligence be schooled? *Educational Psychologist, 37*(4), 215–231.

3

THINKING BEYOND RATIONALISM

Emma Williams

Introduction

My claim is that we need to think more about what is called thinking in education. We need to think more, that is, about what happens when we think, about the things we think about, and about the nature of the human being *who* thinks. I claim that the theory of thinking is currently dominated by a limited conception of thinking, which I designate by the term of art 'rationalistic'. However, I also argue that a way beyond this conception can be opened via a phenomenological exploration of thinking, which does more justice to the possibilities of the *ways* we think.

In the later sections of this chapter, I will say more about this phenomenological account of thinking. I will also illustrate what an education for the development of thinking might look like following this kind of approach. However, I will begin by examining the current theories of thinking in education – in particular, the areas of critical thinking, thinking skills and philosophy for children. I will do so with a view to exemplifying that a shared conception of the nature of thinking is at work in such accounts.

Today's thinking

Critical thinking

I begin with the critical thinking movement: a major field of theory and a key place in which thinking has been conceptualised within education in recent years. The genesis of the philosophical literature on this topic can be traced back at least as far as the 1960s and the work of Robert Ennis, who defined the concept of critical thinking as 'the correct assessing of statements' and, more fully, as 'reasonable, reflective thinking, focused on deciding what to believe or do' (Ennis, 1989, p. 4). While subsequent conceptions of critical thinking were developed by theorists Richard Paul and John McPeck, perhaps the most influential account of critical thinking is that advanced by the American philosopher Harvey Siegel. For more than three decades, Siegel has defended a highly developed 'reasons conception' of critical thinking. This resumes the idea that a critical thinker is one who is 'appropriately moved by reasons' and has the ability to 'believe and act on the basis of reasons' (1988, p. 3). A distinctive feature of Siegel's account, however, is the link it asserts between such reason assessment and the fields of *logic* and *epistemology*. For Siegel, logic affords subject-natural laws and models ideal forms of argument, and these constitute generic principles that are indispensable for the assessment of reasons and beliefs. Epistemology, meanwhile, provides critical thinkers with 'some understanding of why a given putative reason is to be assessed as it is'; that is, epistemology enables critical thinkers to have 'a theoretical grasp of the nature of reasons, warrant and justification' (1988, p. 35).

Thinking skills

In the last decade, focus in the theory of thinking has also turned to a discussion of 'thinking skills'. This notion first made its appearance within educational policy, and has been around at least since the British National Curriculum of 2004. Within the policy literature thinking skills were characterised as certain kinds of procedural knowledge ('know-how') – functional capacities that were generalisable across a number of contexts. A number of different types of skills were identified. For example, QCA defined thinking skills in terms of 'information-processing', 'reasoning skills', 'enquiry skills', 'creative thinking skills' and 'evaluation skills' (QCA, 2004, pp. 22–23).

   Thinking skills was thus a concept that covered a somewhat broader range of thinking than that in focus under the concept of critical thinking. As a result, some critical confrontation between theorists of critical thinking and thinking skills occurred. Thinking skills theorists claimed that their concept goes further than that of critical thinking, and charged the latter with perpetuating a too narrow focus on reasoning (see for example Smith, 2002). Nevertheless, it is also the case that a number of theorists of thinking skills have themselves been concerned at the potentially loose nature of the concept. One attempt to combat such a problem comes from Gerald Smith, who sought to provide a clearer analysis of what can be meaningfully identified as a 'skill' in thinking. Specifically, Smith has argued that skills in thinking should be understood like physical skills – hence we should call thinking skills only those mental acts that have 'procedural content' or a 'procedural structure' (pp. 663–664). In this way, Smith characterises thinking skills as cognitive acts that are (or are in principle capable of being) 'schematised or purposively sequenced' (p. 661). Such procedures, Smith claims, are generic and transferable.

   Smith finds his analysis of the concept of thinking skills to 'strongly support the practice of teaching thinking apart from the domain-specific content' (p. 676).

On this point, Smith's theory bears some comparison with what is happening in many educational programmes dedicated to the teaching of thinking in schools today. To take an example of a formal qualification currently on offer in the British curriculum, the Cambridge International Examination (CIE) A Level in Thinking Skills conceives its purpose similarly in terms of developing 'a specific set of intellectual skills, independent of subject content' (CIE, 2013). Such an agenda is stated to be 'reflecting the need voiced by universities and employers for more mature and sophisticated ways of thinking'. Another formal qualification in thinking, the Oxford, Cambridge and RSA (OCR) A Level in Critical Thinking, claims to 'provide candidates with a framework, which can be applied in a practical manner to a range of materials, situations, problems and issues' (OCR, 2013). On this course, the Specification asserts, 'there is no obvious major body of content to deliver', and the focus is instead on 'a set of skills that candidates should be enabled to acquire' (OCR, 2013).

Philosophy for Children

Holding out on an analysis of these theories and practices a little longer, let us consider a third, related branch of educational theory of thinking: Philosophy for Children. This is a diverse field with many factions. Yet an emphasis on the development of thinking has been present within this movement since its inception in the 1970s. Patricia Hannam and Eugenio Echeverria's book *Philosophy with Teenagers* (2009), provides a representative example of this kind. A distinctive aspect of this field is the appeal to the pedagogical technique of a 'community of inquiry'. This is an arena for discussion and, as Hannam and Echeverria put it, a tool to 'promote cooperation in illuminating a path to come closer to the truth of things' (p. 8). Notably, however, when adding more detail to what is involved in such a process, Hannam and Echeverria cite the activities of 'constructing, defining and clarifying concepts', and conceive the goals of such a process as the 'gradual development of thinking and reasoning skills' (p. 8).

In recent years, a series of broader arguments have been made in defence of the role of philosophy in schools – some of which have also asserted a link between philosophy and the development of thinking (see for example the collection by Hand and Winstanley, 2008). For example, Carrie Winstanley (2008) has defended two theses regarding the connection between philosophy and thinking: firstly, that 'critical thinking is the essence of philosophy' and, secondly, that philosophy is a subject that is not dependent upon any 'substantial empirical knowledge base' (p. 92). The first claim turns on the idea that philosophy is a discipline principally concerned with the 'validity of inferences, the quality of arguments, and the meaning of words', and is 'the embodiment of the abilities of exploring ideas with logic and rationality' (p. 87 and p. 92). The second thesis suggests that philosophical discussion focuses on 'concepts, ideas, and the logic of arriving at the views held', and that discussion of the 'reasons, coherence of argument and the rationality of the notions under examination' can be achieved without recourse to any substantial knowledge base (p. 92). Philosophy is seen as a tool for developing thinking, then, because it is taken to be a subject principally concerned with how to 'assess reasons, defend positions, define terms, evaluate sources of information, and judge the value of arguments and evidence' (p. 93).

Lines of rationalism

I want to claim that there is a *family resemblance* – a series of overlapping similarities – between the theories of thinking just rehearsed. While it is not possible to offer a full picture of this here (though see Williams, 2016, 2015), in what follows, I will draw out two central resemblance structures and seek to expose the philosophical assumptions that stand behind such structures, validating their idea(l)s.

Narrow argument

The first set of resemblances regards the foregrounding of *particular conceptions* of rationality, reasoning and argument. On the basis of what has been sketched above, it is not too hard to see that the notions of reasoning and argument are central constituents of accounts of critical thinking and Philosophy for Children. Moreover, it is not too hard to get a sense of what reasoning and argument are themselves being taken to consist of – usually, processes or activities such as conceptual analysis, inferential reasoning, and the production of logically sound syllogisms. Although theorists of thinking skills on one hand sought to get beyond an emphasis on reasoning, it can also be seen that similar notions of reasoning and argument also play a part in this tradition. Indeed 'reasoning skills' are featured in the inventory presented by the policy literature. Furthermore, and on reflection, it might also be said that a number of the supposedly *additional* cognitive capacities invoked in the thinking skills literature themselves may not be all that far removed from what goes under the banner of 'reasoning', especially in the way it is conceived within the critical thinking movement. Are 'evaluation skills' and 'enquiry skills' not themselves part and parcel of what good reasoning consists in? Perhaps, then, it is not all that surprising that Gerald Smith's more sophisticated analysis ends by specifying that 'deductive reasoning, causal diagnosis, argument construction and conceptual analysis' are the only candidates to which the concept of 'thinking skills' can be meaningfully applied (2002, p. 665).

It is important to be clear about where I am going with the reference to this resemblance structure here. What I am not working towards is the simple suggestion that just because all predominant theories of thinking show a commitment to rationality, reasoning and argument, they are problematic. Indeed, it would be absurd to say this and it would be quite contrary to what I wish to suggest. For I take it that reasoning, rationality and providing arguments are key to thinking education – but, and this is a crucial caveat, *there are different ways of reasoning and of exemplifying rationality.* The problem with the predominant accounts of thinking in education, as I want to contend, is not, then, that they foreground the importance of rationality or of reasoning, or even of arguments. *It is rather with the determined conception of reasoning and argument that is at work in the predominant accounts.*

What conception is this? As I see it, the predominant accounts of thinking education all buy into a particular philosophical model, whereby effective reasoning is taken to be tantamount the presence of an 'argument' – itself understood in a highly specific way as (ideally) a discussion that moves through a series of explicit and articulated inferences (using what philosophers call 'propositions'), with a view to reaching a conclusion. I say 'highly specific' so as to highlight how this conception is depending on a particular philosophical commitment – for having an 'argument' in ordinary life often does not proceed in this kind of way. Simon Glendinning has used the term 'narrow argument' to characterise this 'step-by-step' or 'plain-speaking argumentative mode', which is held up as being exemplary in certain areas of philosophy today (2007, pp. 20–22). This is a view that is further connected to the idea (1) that it is our *ratiocinative capacities* that are 'of first importance' when it comes to formulating arguments and offering reasons (p. 20). We shall come back to this point shortly.

Formal mapping

Let me now bring in the second resemblance structure I wish to highlight. This connects in important ways to the special conception of reasoning and argument we have just been unfolding. The structure in question relates, specifically, to the valorisation of *generic* and *universal* procedures of thinking within predominant discussions of thinking in education and the nearly ubiquitous reference to *non-domain specificity*. The very coinage 'thinking skills' enshrines such a standpoint most evidently – rendering as it does the idea that there are formal operations of thinking that can be mapped, sequenced and exercised in a number of different contexts. Yet it is worth noting that the conception of 'skills' such a picture hereby invokes – as bundles of knacks whose exercise does not involve any specialised knowledge – is something that has been elsewhere called into question as itself a false and reductive view of skills. It is not possible to attend to this argument in full here (see for example, Winch, 2010). Yet my claim is that an emphasis on generality and universality is not a feature of the thinking skills literature alone. It is perhaps worth noting here that, as we saw above, in the realm of educational practice where the teaching of thinking has come to be formally included on the school curriculum, it has tended to take the form of qualifications that emphasise the teaching of 'skills' and 'frameworks' rather than 'independent subject content' or a 'major body of content.' Yet a similar commitment is also exemplified in the other predominant theoretical discussions of thinking in education. Hence, as we saw above, recent defences of the role of philosophy in schools have asserted a link between philosophy and the development of thinking on the grounds that the discipline has no 'substantial empirical knowledge base' of its own – a sentiment that appears to be echoed in the way that philosophy is employed by certain factions of the Philosophy for

Children tradition. Meanwhile, the tradition of critical thinking also exemplifies a commitment to the idea(l) that reason assessment can hold consistently across a number of domains. As Siegel argued, criteria governing reason assessment are not subject-specific, but are rather the subject-neutral laws or principles of logic. For Siegel, moreover, such principles are generated by the philosophical tradition of *epistemology* – a universal tool for acquiring 'a theoretical grasp of the nature of reasons, warrant and justification'.

What can we make of all this? I once again want to suggest that this shared commitment to generic and universal processes of thinking is grounded in specific *philosophical assumptions* – about the nature of thinking and the way thinking happens. At this point, it will be useful to draw upon what Charles Taylor has identified as the 'representational' conception of thinking. Representational views of thinking are the product of a particular philosophical tradition that can be traced back to Descartes. Descartes' time was one of scientific revolution, and new aims for thinking at this time came to prominence. One in particular was the construal of thinking in terms of a project of *knowledge* – itself determined as 'the correct representation of an independent reality'; 'a certain relation holding between what is "out there" and certain inner states that this external reality causes in us' (Taylor, 1997, pp. 3–4). In connection with this, a new emphasis came to be placed on the discovery of reliable *methods* – adherence to which was thought to generate confidence in our mental operations and produce certainty in knowledge (pp. 4–5). Taylor argues that, as a result, thinking came to be understood *mechanistically* – the content of our thoughts needed to be analysed and ordered explicitly 'according to clear and distinct connections' (p. 5). Moreover, in line with the 'representational' characterisation Taylor presents, thinking came to be understood as a *depiction* of the outer world. And these, in turn, have certain consequences for understandings of the thinking being or the picture of the mind-in-world.

The point of Taylor's analysis of the representational view is to open up the realisation that, even when the particular enterprise for knowledge instigated by Descartes came to be repudiated (by contemporary work in analytical epistemology that rejects his foundationalism, for example), certain wider and deeper assumptions this project gave rise to – particularly about the nature of thinking and the human being *who* thinks – have been retained. Taylor specifically pinpoints such retention within the 'strong draw towards distinguishing and mapping the *formal* operations of our thinking' enshrined by computer models of the mind (1997, pp. 5–6). For Taylor, such domains manifest a 'widespread faith that our intelligent performances are ultimately to be understood in terms of formal operations' – a faith whose strength derives from 'the depths of our modern culture and the … model anchored in it' (p. 6). I would suggest that a similar faith pervades the predominant theories of thinking today. For via the notions of generalisability and universalisability, such accounts promulgate a mechanistic and representational picture of thinking. They manifest a similar draw towards the mapping and sequencing of thinking in formal and controlled procedures – a similar unquestioned belief in methods as the means for generating confidence in oneself and the ways one thinks.

Subjects and objects

I should like to go a little further with the analysis at this point. For I also want to suggest that these resemblance structures – of reasoning and the narrow argument, and of generalisability and universalisability – themselves depend upon certain assumptions about the human being *who* thinks (and about the things we think about). We began to glimpse something of this above within Taylor's account, but let me now make this more explicit. For I would claim that a precondition for understanding thinking as the depiction of reality and as what is to be conceived in formal terms, is the positioning of the human being *who* thinks as somehow separate from the world and standing apart from it. That is, the representational view depends on the idea that the human being is *disengaged* from the world – and is not dependent or reliant on the world in any way. Such disengagement in fact appears to be logically necessary once the aim of thinking is conceived in terms of knowledge and the accurate representation of external reality. For this achievement involves the idea(l) of grasping the world 'objectively' – as it is in itself. And this means, as Charles Taylor (2013) has pointed out, grasping the world as 'a third person observer would'. For this to happen we must step away from the world of our ordinary everyday experience. We must disinvest the world of objects around us of any meaning – for example the everyday meanings of a light switch that is out of reach; a deadline for work that is pressing on me; or a person who attracts me (Taylor, 2013). Furthermore, we must divest ourselves of intuitions, sensibilities and affective endowments. This is a radical sense of disengagement – from our ordinary modes of existence and from things as we ordinarily find them. It is an exclusion of anything that is not capable of being mapped in formal, third personal terms – hence we come to think according to articulable, quantifiable, formalisable lines or principles. This enshrines a certain valorisation of the cerebral and cognitive endowments of the human being. Our relation to the world becomes, as David Wood puts it, 'in a real sense … *a priori*'. In doing this we come to occupy a position of mastery with respect to the world – like 'a god enthroned, surveying its territory' (Wood, 2002, p. 47). Hence we can impose the generalisable principles whenever we are called to think, and whatever we are thinking about.

The ways we think

A way beyond

Having now discussed what philosophical assumptions I take to be informing the current predominant approaches to thinking education, I want to start to question these assumptions. However, in what follows I will not be providing 'knock down' argument of these assumptions. Rather, I will appeal to a range of philosophical accounts of thinking to work, via a kind of a cumulative effect, to bring into view a conception of thinking that goes *beyond* such assumptions and such ideals.

It is perhaps worth saying something about what connects the philosophical accounts I will draw on here. I want to suggest that this approach to thinking can be broadly construed as *phenomenological*. Now, phenomenology is a development in philosophy that took place during the twentieth century. I should like to follow Simon Glendinning (and others) in reading this development as one that 'includes some of *the* major figures in contemporary philosophy' (2007, p. 5). More specifically, what I mean by 'phenomenology' not only names a specific philosophical tradition, but is rather exhibited in a *particular kind of commitment*. This is the commitment to *doing justice to what is given in experience* – to taking on the 'imperative of staying with experience, acknowledging experience' (Wood, 2002, p. 33). In the context of the present discussion, this translates into the attempt to set aside philosophical presuppositions and assumptions about the nature of thinking, and instead do justice to the *actual ways we think* – which includes doing justice to *the human being who thinks*, as well as the *things we think about*.

This is not to say that phenomenology can be taken as a unilateral philosophical method.[1] In fact, there are significant differences between individual philosophers' and philosophical traditions' phenomenological approaches. This means that certain evaluative work is called for within this project. I will reflect this in what follows where I will discuss two pairs of couplets, comprising thinkers from contrasting (and at times opposing) philosophical traditions.

'Ahead of all beaten tracks'[2]

The first couplet to explore are the British ordinary language philosopher Gilbert Ryle and the German philosopher Martin Heidegger. What is particularly significant about the Heidegger-Ryle relation is the way both philosophers seek to provide a serious philosophical analysis of what is at stake in our everyday, engaged ways of thinking and behaving. This leads them to consider, not primarily intellectual and abstracted episodes of thinking (which had often been taken as exemplary in previous philosophy), but rather everyday episodes ranging from riding a bike, to hammering a nail into a wall. Through this, crucially, both Ryle and Heidegger come to offer quite a different – and more wide-ranging – account of our rational behaviour. In Ryle, this takes place through the discussion of what is at stake in what he calls *knows how* – practical modes of knowledge that he contrasts to *knowing that* (theoretical knowledge).[3] Heidegger's philosophy, meanwhile, discusses how humans are primarily and the for the most part beings who are involved and engaged in a world of concerns and projects.

I read both Ryle and Heidegger as opening, through this, accounts of the conditions of thinking that go beyond philosophical traditions that construe human beings' relation to the world primarily in terms of a detached, contemplative, theoretical grasp of an object. Of course, this is not to say Ryle and Heidegger are in total agreement with one another. A source of critical confrontation is Ryle's review of Heidegger's early text *Being and Time* (2009a [1928]). Yet one way of interpreting Ryle's review is that Ryle is himself still too wedded to those conceptions of Subject and Object, discussed above, to fully appreciate the Heideggerian position. For Heidegger's account suggests that human beings come into a world that is already populated by a matrix of involvements, meanings and significances passed down to us by history and by culture. Such meanings are not wilfully and autonomously taken over by the human being, but are rather the background conditions that make all autonomous acting and behaving possible in the first place. This has implications for the ways we understand our practical modes of worldly comportment, but *also* for our contemplative and theoretical modes of thinking. For Heidegger, in fact, knowing as the contemplative grasp of a thing is itself 'a *founded way of being-in-the-world*, a way which is always possible only on the basis of a non-cognitive comportment' (Heidegger, 1985 [1925], pp. 162–164). Hence, Heidegger suggests, we are *always* thinking within frameworks and matrices – detached, neutral thinking is a false ideal. These frameworks cannot *themselves* be turned into objects for critical reflection – or rather, if they are, such reflection will always be partial and selective, for there will always be further meanings and significances that remain un-reflected upon.

What task emerges for thinking following this picture? It is interesting to note that, in their later work, both Heidegger and Ryle come to stress the *receptive* nature of thinking. Ryle, for example, characterizes thinking in terms of a gradual event of 'dawning', and as involving organic processes such as 'germinating' – and he contrasts this to academic conceptions of 'disciplined' thinking, which attempt to make thoughts move 'like soldiers on the barrack-square' (i.e. in highly regimented and controlled lines) (2009c [1958]). Heidegger, comparatively, speaks negatively about the propositional and calculative ways of thinking that enact a kind of appropriating *grasp* of what is thought about. Against this, Heidegger construes thinking as a 'handicraft' – which invokes a sense of responsiveness that is further brought out by discussing the etymological relation between thinking and thanking. Heidegger's term here also invokes the sense that learning to think is an apprenticeship. It is not, as Ryle also puts it, a 'five minutes task'. Rather, learning to think is learning to dwell with and amongst the things we think about. Through this, new possibilities are opened for thinking, which are closed down if we just consider things one time, for one purpose, with a one-track mind. Some commentators read Heidegger's later work as a misguided move in the direction of mysticism and romanticism. Yet I would see it as an attempt to carry through the exploration of the conditions of thinking that were already implicit in his early work. Through this Heidegger – and Ryle – bring us to see that thinking is not the act of an already constituted subject that presides over already constituted objects. The ways we think are made possible by structures of meanings and significances that are beyond us. In and through our reception of these structures, however, our thinking is inceptive and projective – it opens the possibilities of something new.

Following the sign

At this point, I want to cross over to a second philosophical couplet: John Austin and Jacques Derrida. For I would suggest that, through their particular attentiveness to language, these thinkers take further the account of thinking I have just been articulating. To understand why, it is important to recognise that, as Heidegger himself came to suggest in his later work, language is not simply a *tool* for human use – the 'outer external clothing' for inward private thoughts that are in themselves fully fixed and secure in their intentional content. This view of language, in fact, goes somewhat hand in glove in the history of philosophy with the tradition of Subject and Object discussed above. Against this, however, is an alternative conception of language: one that takes language as itself the horizon within which human beings live their lives. This means language is fundamental to our thought and action – in fact to our being human. Moreover, this is not just language in the abstract but the particular language(s) we speak, and it is clear that different languages reveal the world in subtly different ways. In the light of this, it is worth considering the nature of the words and other signs (gestures, etc.) that we use, a topic to which few philosophers have given sufficient attention. Yet Derrida and Austin are notable exceptions.

Austin's exploration of language led him to discuss the nature of what he terms the 'performative utterance' (2009 [1962]). A simple example of the 'performative utterance' is an utterance such as 'I declare this meeting open'. Such a phrase, as Austin puts it, does not *describe* a state of affairs in the world but rather *does* something – the utterance is itself the opening of the meeting. Moreover, what makes such an achievement happen is *not*, contrary to what is traditionally assumed, the fact that there is some hidden, internal intention in the mind of the speaker. Rather, as Austin points out, the success of a performative utterance is guaranteed by the specific nature of the *context* in which the phrase is uttered and the conformity of a phrase to a particular conventional procedure. Such a view tallies with Wittgenstein's famous dictum that 'meaning is use': words get their meaning not by being attached to objects or thoughts like labels are placed on items, but rather in the way they are used and put to use within communities and cultures.

Derrida shared Austin's rejection of the traditional picture of language and meaning. However, in an infamous essay, *Signature Event Context*, Derrida also argues that Austin's re-formulation of language has its own limitations (1988 [1972]). Derrida's argument was controversial for Anglo-American interpretations of Austin, and sparked critical, and some hostile, reaction. Yet Derrida's main concern was that Austin had held back from following through on a key insight about language that his discussion of the performative had, at the same time, opened. This is, in short, the way that it is a characteristic of the signs we use that they are 'unsaturated' with meaning. This means that the signs are always available to new connotations and connections, and to new interpretations: in other words, they always have effects beyond our full control, beyond our intentions. At first sight, this looks both unconvincing and disturbing: is this not a new expression of the scepticism that says 'we can never really know what we are doing?' That this is not the case is clear when it is seen that Derrida is describing the fundamental ways in which signs must function, the conditions within which we are sometimes clear about what we are doing and sometimes not. The signs that animals use are unlike the more or less mechanistic signs that characterise the behaviour of the higher animals: their signs function in a more or less predictable functional way, and they function without remainder: animals carry on behaving the same way from generation to generation. The signs that human beings use, by contrast, are not static: a word is open to new connections and associations, we make inadvertent puns and Freudian slips, and we can project words into new contexts of use. A clear example of this last point is the use of the word 'mouse' for the handy device that sits by the side of our keyboard. In poetic writing especially the possibilities of words and their potential connections, in sound and semantics, are explored in innovative ways. When small children speak they play with words, exploring new associations and connections. The fact that children, even in the earliest stages of language learning, produce original sentences is further testimony to this. This leads Derrida to a further claim, which again on the face of it is very surprising. This is that the unsaturatedness of the sign means that it depends upon something that is absent – upon connections and associations that have not yet been made. For the sign to be a sign it must be available to occasions of use that are not anticipated. We can imagine the unique construction of a tool for a particular purpose – a tool that existed for that purpose but then was never produced again. But a word *qua* word can never be like that. Even a neologism must be available to further contexts. Derrida's expression for this is that the sign is iterable. A related way of thinking of it is that any sign, in order to be a sign, must be quotable.

Hence, it is the idea of the human dependence on a necessary absence that has been so powerful in his work. But why is this of significance? It is important because it opposes any idea that good thinking brings the object of thought under control, grasping it fully. Once again, this is not to outlaw the idea that we can sometimes grasp things or to deny that we can ever be sure what we are doing. What is under attack is a more metaphysical assumption that typifies the epistemology in question: this is that the best kind of thinking is epitomised by my holding something fully present in my mind, here and now, in a way that is autonomous and independent. The fantasy of independence here – one seen at its extreme in both Descartes' *cogito ergo sum* and in logical positivism (where my experience, here, now, is the ultimate authentication of the real) – derives from the fact that I lose sight of my necessary dependence not only on a background world but on the fact that the very terms of my thought depend upon usages that precede me and extend beyond me in ways beyond my control. This emphatically does not mean that I am simply determined by them, for the unsaturated nature of signs means that in my own thinking too they constantly find new connotation and connections. This is the very engine of imagination and creativity and culture itself. Rigour and refinement in thinking will depend upon our attunement to these conditions.

Beyond rationalism

I have only provided a sketch of the alternative account of thinking I should like to propose here, and a number of threads that have been left hanging. However, we should already be coming to see how this conception moves beyond the lines of rationalism sketched above.

For one, curtailing thinking to narrow argument will not do justice to openness that is constitutive of human thinking. For another, focusing on generic procedures of thinking that can be formalised does not do justice to co-dependency between the ways we think and what we are thinking *about*. Moreover, and linked to this, the guiding assumption that thinking happens through a detached and disengaged subject does not do justice to the mediated and constituted nature of the human being *who* thinks. That is to say, when we think we do not simply represent things and make calculations: our thinking is productive in that, as receptive, it allows the world to open to us in new ways; in a sense it is productive of the what the world can be, which is evident not only in the products of writers and artists but in the achievements of science and engineering themselves. We are not masters of what we think; we think productively when we are receptive and responsive in these ways.

All of this is not, of course, to say that the rationalistic account is entirely redundant. It is not to say that we cannot do things like reason to reach a conclusion, use a technique for judging the credibility of evidence, or submit an idea to conceptual analysis. However, it is to warn against the unquestioning adoption of certain philosophical ideals that cause us to over inflate such practices and hence exclusively focus on them as the bread and butter of an education for thinking. Furthermore, we must recognise that the rationalistic way of thinking is itself an approach that is made possible on the basis of a certain disclosure or revealing of the world. This is an important point to make for, as we noted above, current conceptions of thinking, bolstered as they are by their underlying philosophical assumptions, have a tendency to overinflate themselves and set themselves up as *the* way in which thinking in education should operate. They thus have the corresponding effect of producing the idea that the way the world is disclosed under their guise is *the way the world essentially is*. Hence the relative ease and confidence, the sense of 'of course-ness' that marks so much of the literature on thinking education today. And yet such values are important only if we are approaching the world *in a certain way*. Of course there is a place for such approaches, but there is a danger if such approaches masquerade as the best kind of thinking or the most rigorous kind. Hence they *must be* placed within the broader understanding of thinking that I am advocating here.

Perhaps this discussion is taking place on too abstract a level. We want after all to say something about the education of thinking. Let me now turn to say something on this.

Lived experience

What would a phenomenologically inspired approach to thinking in education look like? In what follows I will appeal to an example from my own work experience as the philosopher-in-residence in a UK secondary school (2008–2015).

Thinking with Camus

About two years ago, I was invited by a colleague in the Foreign Languages Department to join one of her lessons, in which they had been reading the play by Albert Camus, *Les Justes,* which is based on the true story of a group of Russian socialist revolutionaries who plan and execute the assassination of the Grand Duke Sergei Alexandrovich. In the course of studying this text a number of themes for discussion had emerged within the class. Knowing my background in philosophy, my colleague invited me along to stimulate further discussion of some of the themes. The brief was quite open; the teacher simply wanted her students to have the chance to re-engage with some of the interesting themes that had arisen in the course of the lessons.

I hence decided to structure the lesson loosely around a number of themes that I had found prevalent within the text, offering a hand-out of five key quotes from the play as illustrative examples. I stated at the outset that the themes I had picked out were likely to have been largely informed by my prior knowledge of Camus as a philosopher. I thus invited the pupils to challenge my interpretations (and, it should be noted, they did not need too much encouragement!). We read and re-read the passages I had selected, opening up and negotiating new meanings and significances. One pupil, for example, drew the class's attention to the epigraph at the outset of the play, which had interestingly not been included in my English translation. It was a quotation from Romeo and Juliet, Act IV Scene 5: 'O love! O life! Not life but love in death'. Does this mean the play, which is often cast as having a political message, could be re-read as a love story? And what kind of 'love' is being invoked? We also pondered the differences between reading text in the English translation I had provided and the original French version the students had studied. One student felt that it seemed like a different play to her when she read it in English; this provoked discussion about whether one language can ever do justice to another, or whether there is a sense in which something is lost in translation. I do not think we got past the first two quotes I had selected in the forty-minute lesson.

This lesson did not end with a sense of self-satisfied contentment – as though we had got to the bottom of *Les Justes* and worked it all out. Rather we left realising the openness and richness of the text and the possibilities of interpretation that had emerged from our engagement with just a few sections of it.

Contrasts

This example does not serve to offer a complete picture of a pedagogical structure for teaching thinking. This has not been the aim. Rather it has been to appeal to a rich experience that can happen when we think – gesturing towards what thinking education might faithfully be. Often at present, the teaching of thinking is happening via *stand-alone* courses in their own right – qualifications that emphasise the teaching of 'skills' and 'frameworks' rather than 'independent subject content' or a 'major body of content'.

Moreover, I was struck at the end of this class by just how different such a lesson had been from my usual experience of teaching existentialism within the A level Philosophy course. Here, Sartre's philosophy is introduced as a version of 'Libertarianism', and is pitted against the 'other views' on the Free Will–Determinism debate, cast as 'Determinism' and 'Compatibilism'. Given the demands of the A level course (Free Will and Determinism is only one module out of four required to be studied in the first year), I am barely able to spend two forty-minute lessons discussing existentialism. The result is that there is no room for thinking about and responding to existentialism as there was in the above-cited Camus lesson. In fact, what my students (and we might recall here that these are philosophy students) often end up with is a sense that they know all there is to know about Sartre's philosophy, simply because they can cite his argument in nugget form, and are able to roll out stock 'criticisms' of it (that often largely comprise those listed in mark-schemes for previous exam questions). Of course, this is not necessarily my students' fault. It is a result of an exam system that is driven by quantitative assessment, by the tick-box culture that pervades over education as a whole. Rather than provide the space for open and rigorous thinking of the kind I have articulated in this thesis and would contend is in operation in the above-cited example of the Camus class, the A level Philosophy lesson on Sartre rather seems to enforce a thinking that works by way of closed regurgitation.

Final words

This example does not, of course, serve to offer a complete picture of a pedagogical structure for teaching thinking. This has not been the aim of the present chapter. Rather, I have tried to offer an account of a non-rationalistic conception of thinking—one that will overcome current closures and open new possibilities for thinking in education. If we are to take the non-rationalistic account seriously, it seems appropriate that we should not end with a fully spelled-out, definitive programme. It seems appropriate, indeed, that we should rather end by gesturing towards what thinking education might faithfully be. This will not be an education that would satisfy the rationalistic criteria for what counts as 'good thinking' or, indeed, the good *teaching* of thinking. For teaching thinking will not be a matter of developing technical skills in reasoning or argument. It is not an approach that advocates a standing back, and a judging of what is being thought about in terms of objectively defined criteria or standards. Neither is it an approach that seeks to make explorations of issues reach a stable and steady, fixed and firm conclusion. The ways of thinking I want to explore are not the activity of the self-secure, autonomous and independent subject. Rather, they are ways of receptivity and responsiveness – in other words, the possibilities of thinking beyond the narrow straits of rationalism.

Notes

1   Sometimes it is taken in this way, however. For more discussion see Glendinning (2007).
2   The phrase 'ahead of all beaten tracks' is used by Ryle in·to illustrate the nature of philosophical thinking (Ryle, 2009b [1953], p. 312). It bears relation to the way Heidegger

characterised philosophical thinking as the 'way' and the Holzweg. Heidegger's epigraph in *Off the Beaten Track* reads: 'Wood is an old name for a forest. In the wood there are paths, mostly overgrown, that come to an abrupt stop where the wood is untrodden. They are called Holzwege. Each goes its separate way, though within the same forest. It often appears as if one is identical to another. But it only appears so. Woodcutters and forest keepers know these paths. They know what it means to be a Holzweg' (Heidegger, 2002 [1950], p. 1). The Heideggerian motif of the 'way' informs my own notion of the *ways* we think.

3   Notably, Ryle's appearance within a project assessing the nature of thinking in education is not unprecedented. In fact, Ryle's philosophy is often drawn upon in educational discussions of thinking; and paradoxically his distinction between 'knowing how' and 'knowing that' is often drawn upon to articulate the nature of thinking skills. However, I wish to point towards an *alternative* reading of Ryle – one that brings out the potentialities within his philosophy for a re-description of thinking that seeks to do justice to what actually happens when we think (Ryle, 1945).

References

Austin, J. L. (2009 [1962]). *How to do things with words*. Oxford: Oxford University Press.

CIE. (2013). AS and A level thinking skills. *Cambridge International Examinations*. Retrieved June 4, 2013, from www.cie.org.uk/qualifications/academic/uppersec/alevel/subject?assdef_id=765

Derrida, J. (1988 [1972]). Signature event context. In J. Derrida (Ed.), *Limited inc* (pp. 1–21). Evanston, IL: Northwestern University Press.

Ennis, R. (1989). Critical thinking and subject specificity: Clarification and needed research. *Educational Researcher, 18*, 4–10.

Glendinning, S. (2007). *In the name of phenomenology*. Oxford: Routledge.

Hand, M. & Winstanley, C. (Eds.). (2008). *Philosophy in schools*. London: Continuum.

Hannam, P., & Echeverria, E. (2009). *Philosophy with teenagers: Nurturing a moral imagination for the 21st century*. London: Continuum.

Heidegger, M. (1985 [1925]). *History of the concept of time*. Bloomington: Indiana University Press.

Heidegger, M. (2002 [1950]). *Off the beaten track*. Cambridge: Cambridge University Press.

OCR. (2013). Critical thinking. OCR. Retrieved June 4, 2013, from www.ocr.org.uk/qualifications/as-a-level-gce-critical-thinking-h052-h452/

QCA. (2004). The national curriculum: Handbook for secondary teachers in England. *National Archives*. Retrieved April 4, 2013, from http://webarchive.nationalarchives.gov.uk/20130401151715/https://www.education.gov.uk/publications/eOrderingDownload/QCA-04-1374.pdf

Ryle, G. (1945). Knowing how and knowing that. *Proceedings of the Aristotelian Society, 46*, 1–16.

Ryle, G. (2009a [1928]). Heidegger's 'Sein Und Zeit'. In J. Tanney (Ed.), *Collected essays volume 1* (pp. 205–222). Oxford: Routledge.

Ryle, G. (2009b [1953]). Thinking. In J. Tanney (Ed.), *Collected essays volume 2* (pp. 307–313). Oxford: Routledge.

Ryle, G. (2009c [1958]). A puzzling element in the notion of thinking. In J. Tanney (Ed.), *Collected papers volume 2* (pp. 404–419). Oxford: Routledge.

Siegel, H. (1988). *Educating reason*. Worcester: Routledge.

Smith, G. (2002). Thinking skills: The question of generality. *Journal of Curriculum Studies, 34*(6), 659–678.

Taylor, C. (1997). Overcoming epistemology. In C. Taylor (Ed.), *Philosophical arguments* (pp. 1–19). Cambridge, MA: Harvard University Press.

Taylor, C. (2013). Retrieving realism. In J. Schear (Ed.), *Mind, reason and being in the world* (pp. 61–90). Oxford: Routledge.

Williams, E. (2015). In excess of epistemology: Heidegger, Taylor, Siegel and the conditions of thought. *Journal of Philosophy of Education, 49*(1), 142–160.

Williams, E. (2016). *The ways we think: From the straits of reason to the possibilities of thought.* London: Wiley-Blackwell.

Winch, C. (2010). *Dimensions of expertise.* London: Continuum.

Winstanley, C. (2008). Philosophy and the development of critical thinking. In M. Hand & C. Winstanley (Eds.), *Philosophy in schools* (pp. 85–95). London: Continuum.

Wood, D. (2002). *Thinking after Heidegger.* Oxford: Polity Press.

4

PHILOSOPHY WITH CHILDREN FROM PRAGMATISM TO POSTHUMANISM

Thinking through the Community of Philosophical Inquiry

Laura Kerslake

Introduction

This chapter will consider the theoretical basis of Philosophy with Children (PwC) practice from its origins in Deweyan pragmatism (Lipman, 1998, 2003; Lipman, Sharp, & Oscanyan, 1980) to its subsequent reconsideration as a posthuman education practice (Murris, 2016). In recent years, Lipman's *Philosophy for Children* programme has been critiqued as reducing PwC to a critical thinking programme (Weber, 2012), provoking a demarcation between 'first' and 'second' generation PwC thinkers, and leading to PwC being described as 'in transition' (Vansieleghem & Kennedy, 2012).

This shift is partly due to the reconceptualisation of childhood within the education system (Kohan, 2012, 2014) as well as a questioning of why PwC is a desirable practice. The latter issue has led to PwC being criticised as an 'instrumental' practice in schools (Biesta, 2011), as it can be seen as providing children with certain sought-after skills and attributes to meet educational ends. For example, there was a great deal of press surrounding the findings of a recent SAPERE (Society for the Advancement of Philosophical Enquiry and Reflection in Education) study which indicated that a year of weekly PwC sessions resulted in gains in English and Maths standardised testing scores at the end of primary school (EEF, 2015).

Others (for example Echeverria & Hannam, 2016) have argued that the methodology of PwC practice allows for children's development in broader terms than the instrumentalist view of progress toward prescriptive outcomes (see also Kerslake & Rimmington, 2017). This chapter will therefore examine the Community of Philosophical Inquiry (CoPI) as a method of PwC practice – indeed, described as its 'signature practice' (Gregory, Haynes, & Murris, 2016, p. 2) – and the arguments surrounding its use with children of primary school age (4–11). It will also explore the impact of PwC's shifting theoretical basis on CoPI practice, arguing that the

CoPI has a sound pedagogical basis for practical application in the classroom, and that its nature is congruent with posthuman theory, although there remain significant theoretical issues.

The Community of Philosophical Inquiry

The CoPI as an education practice originated with Lipman (2003), who set out five stages of the process (pp. 101–103):

1. The offering of the text [reading a philosophical story together]
2. The construction of the agenda [children raise questions prompted by the text]
3. Solidifying the community [children discuss the questions as a dialogue guided by an adult facilitator]
4. Using exercises and discussion plans [facilitator introduces further activities to deepen the inquiry]
5. Encouraging further responses [e.g. self-assessment of philosophy practice or artwork]

For Lipman (2003), the CoPI is a pedagogical strategy for remedying what he calls the 'stupendous category mistake' (p. 20) that Dewey had observed about educational practice: the end-point of inquiry is confused with the process of inquiry. The aim of traditional education is for children to acquire as many of these end-points as received facts as possible by the end of their schooling. This has also been referred to as the 'transmission' model of education (Freire, 1993), in which knowledge is transmitted from teacher to learner. As part of the rise of critical pedagogies since the 1970s, Freire and others (see Schwarz & Baker, 2017) critiqued this model for positioning learners as passive receivers not only of knowledge but also as subject to traditional power structures and cultural biases.

In contrast, what Lipman refers to as the 'reflective paradigm of critical practice' (p. 18) takes problematic material for its starting point as the material of inquiry. In the case of philosophy, this might be conceptual difficulties or contradictions; Lipman wrote a series of philosophical novels which deal with many of philosophy's traditional domains: ethics, aesthetics, metaphysics and so on, through the subject matter of animal rights, personal identity, divorce, racism and justice, etc. He claimed that it is through engagement with these problematic issues that children, led by the examples of the children in the texts, come to feel the 'twinge of doubt or puzzlement' (Lipman, 2003, p. 21) which is the starting point for any meaningful inquiry.

Of course, those moments of doubt and puzzlement are personal to the child – such an approach would not work as an inquiry if it were the teacher who decided which moments in the text were confusing or puzzling. This would be the transmission model of teaching in another guise rather than a reflective pedagogy. Therefore a key aspect of the CoPI process is that the children decide which questions they want to raise about a text. Following the sharing of the text, children share any questions they have which are typically written down by the facilitator.

For Lipman, this is a 'pivotal moment' in the inquiry. If the facilitator chooses the question to be discussed from the children's output, this will constitute a return to the 'old authoritarianism' (p. 98).

Not only is it the children who must choose the questions, but there must be a clear democratic process in making the choice: Lipman suggests asking someone who has not submitted a question or by voting for the question most people would like to answer. Following this, the discussion proceeds to take place with children articulating their viewpoints, challenging or supporting others' ideas and giving reasons: in other words, becoming competent participants in a community of 'cooperative reasoning' (p. 102). The commitment to the democratic process is maintained throughout with the introduction of talk rules at the beginning of the session to reinforce a shared commitment to turn-taking and listening to others.

Echeverria & Hannam (2016) therefore understand the CoPI as democratic education, making the distinction between that and 'education for democracy' (p. 4). In the latter, the model is akin to the transmission model of education, in which democracy is constituted as a set of normative values and beliefs which are to be learned about in school. By contrast, the CoPI process inducts children into deliberative democracy as co-constructors in a democratic process. The difference between the two may seem subtle, but as Butler (2005) remarks, 'it is one thing to say that a subject must be able to appropriate norms, but another to say that there must be norms that prepare a place within the ontological field for a subject' (p. 9). Whereas the CoPI is a practice in which 'the plurality of the group is taken seriously' (Echeverria & Hannam, 2016, p. 8), a pre-existing set of norms of what is worthwhile in education would anticipate children's development being in line with those norms and tolerate little deviation.

Cam (2014) also makes the point that, in terms of values education, learning what democratic values are will not necessarily help children to always make democratic decisions. In 'all the contingencies of life' (p. 1208) they will face situations for which a rote learning of democratic values will not help them make decisions. In fact, he argues, to rely on such a tool kit and believe that we are therefore as-a-matter-of-course democratic is dangerous, because we are less likely to make context-specific judgements. Any kind of values education should involve the cultivation of judgement-making so that we can identify our own biases, limitations and perspectives to arrive at the best course of action. While the links to civic life are clear here, as they are for Lipman and Dewey, this is a process that must be modelled from children's earliest years, which generally means within the education system.

Murris, too, values the democratic element of the CoPI, except she argues that our very concept of child and childhood has made it very difficult for children to be thought of as beings who can participate in such a process. Children's ontological place – the nature of their being – within the education system is a subject with which much of Murris's (2016) *The Posthuman Child* is concerned. For Murris, the Cartesian split between subject and object, or I and not-I, has led to binary concepts which have deeply penetrated our engagement with the world around us. One of these binaries is that of the human/non-human, and in a humanist framework precedence has been given to the human side of the split. Moreover, the category of 'human' has historically been determined by gender, class, geography, and, Murris contends, age. The binary of child/adult has led to the child being positioned as inferior when compared with the 'transcendental signifier' of the adult, which is received as 'mature, developed and complete' (p. 89). In addition, the path of development is normative and expressed in binary terms: the educative process transforms children from savage to civilized, concrete to abstract thinkers, a process which is complete only when the child has achieved a mind which is scientific and rational.

While postmodernism, in its various guises, has done much to question the politics of cultural, racial and gendered identities, the result is that child and childhood have come to be regarded as 'a variable of social analysis' (Murris, 2016, p. 85). The child therefore exists through its relationship with others in various cultural contexts which, Murris argues, has become the default perspective on childhood. However, the study of the child through binary lenses of rich/poor, black/white, male/female is a humanist perspective which relies on representation of the child only and still positions the child as object. By not giving sufficient consideration to age – the child/adult binary – in power differential studies, children are still acted-upon.

Murris therefore proposes a 'new ethicoontoepistemology' (p. 88) of posthumanism to reconsider how child and childhood are understood. Referencing Barad and Braidotti, she uses the term 'materialdiscursive' (p. 91) to describe how the entanglement of relations that is 'child' should be unbounded by humanist preconceptions of the human mind as maker of meanings *par excellence*, and instead incorporates the 'I' as part of the world – as matter of the world as much as a biological entity or a social construct. Only by considering the child in this unbounded way can the nature of their being, and by extension, the way in which they come to know, be fully realised.

Yet, while Murris claims the CoPI is a pedagogy which is commensurate with the ethicoontoepistemology of posthumanism (2016, pp. 179–181), Ellerton (2016) situates CoPI practice firmly within the epistemology of (humanist) pragmatism, claiming that this is also consistent with CoPI's links to both critical and scientific thinking. Given that there are a number of incompatibilities between pragmatism and posthumanism, for the CoPI to be claimed as a pedagogy in both cases is inconsistent. I therefore now turn to the theoretical underpinnings of inquiry practice to examine the possibilities and challenges for the CoPI within a posthuman education framework, asking whether or not posthumanism presents a viable theoretical perspective in which to situate the CoPI. To do so, I will initially consider each aspect separately: Community, Philosophy, and Inquiry, before returning to CoPI as a practice within the education system as a whole.

Community

For Splitter (2000), 'a community is not necessarily a community of inquiry' (p. 12). In some ways this is an obvious point: the word 'community' is colloquially used to mean 'a group of people', usually those who share some defining characteristic: Jewish community, gay community, local community. For children, the community is that of the classroom, fulfilling Vansieleghem and Kennedy's (2012) criterion of the community as constituting a 'relatively stable and regularly attending group of people' (p. 266). In other ways, and particularly in the classroom, it is an important point to note the separation of the terms community and inquiry. A 'learning community', for example, as Lipman (2003) points out, does not necessarily exhibit the self-critical, exploratory, inquisitive practices that constitute the CoPI.

The use of the word 'community' also serves to highlight the role of the teacher, as if a community shares a defining characteristic, then (as with traditional, transmission models of education) the teacher is excluded from that community because the children are seen as the 'learners' and he or she is there as the 'teacher'. It is no coincidence, therefore, that the 'leader' of a CoPI is known as the facilitator. For both Lipman and Murris, the role of the facilitator is that of the co-inquirer, with McCall & Weijers (2016) stipulating that 'in a successful CoPI session the chairing is not visible' (p. 84). Commentators since Lipman have seen his term 'Philosophy *for* Children' as indicative of the instrumentalising tendencies of education, and prefer Philosophy *with* Children (Vansieleghem & Kennedy, 2012) or Philosophy *alongside* Children (Murris, 2015) as preferable terms. For Murris, this is not merely a trivial point but one which expresses the ontoepistemological relations between adult and child, and is a term which can help to blur the adult/child binary.

The role of the facilitator – who in a classroom PwC session is likely to be the classroom teacher – is of note here. If the chairing is invisible, what does that mean for the role of the chair or teacher? Biesta raises this as he critiques social constructivism for being a theory of learning and not a theory of teaching. Therefore the role of the teacher can become obfuscated.

The other issue that is addressed with the word 'community' is that of the individual's relations to other individuals. Community can be seen as a reductive term, where all participants are defined by a given characteristic and reduced to it. While autonomy within the community is important in the CoPI, it is conceived of in a specific way. Lipman is clear that autonomy should not mean the 'rugged individualism' which he fears it has come to, with critical thinking being associated with the 'self-sufficient cognitive macho type' (2003, p. 25). Indeed, Hayes (2015) uses this notion of the critical thinker to argue against critical thinking pedagogies such as PwC because such individualism prohibits the willingness to receive others' ideas.

However, Echeverria & Hannam (2016, p. 3) position the CoPI as 'advancing communicative rather than individual notions of autonomy', which can be seen in Millett & Tapper's (2012) reference to inquiry practice as CPI, where the C stands for collaborative. The community of the CoPI is therefore one in which individuals come together in an 'intentional speech community' (Vansieleghem & Kennedy, 2012, p. 266) in which there is an inquiry into a specific issue at which the inquiry is aimed. For Murris (2016), the concept of autonomy is an outdated one – a 'metaphysical illusion' (p. 105) – because there is no 'I' in the sense of a bounded self. Instead the relations of a community are important, and indeed necessary for inquiry as they establish 'powerful bonds of trust, collaboration, risk-taking and a common purpose' (Splitter, 2000, p. 12). However, this is an extreme position to take, as Murris herself admits. She quotes Braidotti who has only recently been 'brave enough' to use the term 'inhuman' to refer to the unbounded (human) organism which is entangled with the world around it.

Philosophy

Just as not every community is one of inquiry, neither is every community of inquiry one of philosophy. As Lipman (2003) writes, when Peirce first juxtaposed 'community' and 'inquiry' in a relation he did so with the intention of it being a scientific community of inquiry. Those who extol the pedagogical potential of the CoPI do so across the curriculum; in argument redolent of Dewey's claim of category error in education practice, Burgh and Nichols (2012) argue for CoPI practice in science education as a prelude to any science teaching in order for children to learn what being scientific actually means. Kennedy & Kennedy (2011) posit the benefits of CoPI for maths education particularly, as well as offering suggestions for CoPI practice across the curriculum.

For White (2012), CoPI practice is divided into two strands: strand one is the more common, certainly in England with SAPERE, and is predicated on Lipman's original *Philosophy for Children* programme. The emphasis in this strand is on the inquiry rather than the philosophy, White argues, as the questions raised for discussion are raised by the children, and facilitated by the teacher who may only have a small amount of philosophical training (the SAPERE level one course lasts for two days). Strand two, which is less common (White cites McCall (2009) as a proponent of this strand, as well as Peter Worley's work with the Philosophy Foundation), requires that teachers have more extensive philosophical training, and it is the teachers who organise the CoPI topics for discussion.

White describes strand two as an 'embryonic version' of the 'yardstick' (p. 454) of university philosophy. He seems more critical of strand one, stating that although the CoPI may induce children to reasonableness, or democracy, people can be reasonable or democratic in everyday life without necessarily being philosophical; calling it a philosophical discussion would be stretching the use of the term. However, both Lipman and Murris would disagree with this view, as both would claim that the CoPI is *inherently* philosophical. As Lipman originally identified, and Murris, citing his view, followed, a philosophical discussion can be recognised by its progression towards a judgement but one which is meandering, not linear.

Even when children are discussing a different curriculum subject, such as science, in a CoPI they are still being philosophical as they are discussing not the subject itself but the concepts that underpin it – the philosophy of science. Although every community of inquiry may not be one of philosophy (in the sense of philosophy as an academic subject), every community of inquiry is philosophical (in the sense of thinking philosophically). McCall & Weijers (2016) state that 'philosophical assumptions underlie all aspects of both individual and collective social life' (p. 83), and it is perhaps the recognition of assumptions and the identification of troubling and contradictory subjects that make philosophy such a 'horn of plenty' for the CoPI.

Nevertheless, White has a point when he states that perhaps a better title for Philosophy for Children would be 'Various Sorts of Reasoning for Children' (p. 459). Although this sounds provocative, it is a sentiment which does actually seem to reflect the concerns of commentators such as McCall & Weijers (2016) who insist upon certain criteria being fulfilled, such as evidence of children's Socratic questioning, for PwC to earn the name. Critical thinking, democratic thinking and so on may be valuable, but they are not philosophy.

However, there is also a demarcation between academic philosophy being taught (as it sometimes is from age fourteen in the UK) and philosophising as a process, which teaches children from a much younger age to recognise and apply the hallmarks of philosophical thinking. Worley's (2015) approach to PwC is to introduce a stimulus and then to provide the children with a question in order to ensure that the resulting discussion has a philosophical basis. This is in contrast to Lipman's approach, expanded upon previously, as for Worley, it is the questions that the children have *of the original question* that are of key importance in unpacking the concepts of philosophical thinking.

I think that at the heart of this issue are questions of skills and knowledge (see Berieter & Scardamalia, Chapter 5, this volume). There is philosophical knowledge – that is, knowledge of issues that belong to certain strands of philosophy (e.g. metaphysics, ethics) – and the skills that are needed to further illuminate these issues, such as identifying conceptual contradictions, taking account of the ideas of others and expanding upon one's own position. Despite the difference in how questions are generated, Lipman's programme also introduces philosophical content to children in the form of the novels. By contrast, Murris (2015) values picture books as a stimulus.

Inquiry

As we have seen, for Lipman the CoPI is the pedagogical embodiment of reflective, self-critical inquiry education. It stands in opposition to transmission models of education in which children are passive receivers of knowledge from teachers. However, while opposed to transmitted knowledge, an inquiry is not an aimless conversation (Lipman, 2003), but it is aimed at a further-on point: there is something to be gained from the inquiry. I use the term 'further-on-point' rather than 'end-point' deliberately as it is a key point in the epistemology of pragmatism. Peirce denied the Cartesian duality of knowing for certain or relinquishing all claims to knowledge and instead perceived doubt as 'simply a necessary fact of being in the world' (Ellerton, 2016, p. 112).

Thus inquiry is a process of doubt, grounded in epistemic fallibilism, and it is this which in fact enables the inquiry to take place at all. Only by rejecting the duality of absolutism and relativism can beliefs be held cautiously, to be doubted, questioned and reformulated as further beliefs to be held tentatively. Dewey (1933) summed this up as: 'there is no belief so settled as to not be exposed to further enquiry' (pp. 8–9). Situating inquiry education within a pragmatist epistemology which blurs the boundaries of absolute/relativist knowledge claims and also mind/world boundaries (see Vansieleghem & Kennedy, 2012) is a position which presages posthuman ontoepistemology. Indeed, Murris (2016) aligns herself with this basis of inquiry education, asserting that in PwC 'beliefs are held tentatively' and knowledge is 'always incomplete' (p. 153).

Ellerton (2016) notes that inquiry education has both epistemological and pedagogical commitments; while the epistemological commitments have been considered above, there are also pedagogical issues, namely children's cognitive development through CoPI practice. According to Lipman, the cognitive process within the CoPI is the 'internalization of the overt cognitive behaviour of the community' (Lipman, 2003, p. 102). That the process of social activity becomes internalised to individual inner activity is clearly a Vygotskian (Vygotsky, 1978) idea and in further writings, Lipman (2008) expresses this debt. Kennedy & Kennedy (2011) further claim that CoPI practice 'exemplifies Vygotsky's notion of learning' (p. 271). Historically, as inquiry learning is epistemologically pragmatic, it is pedagogically social-constructivist.

Examining the constituent parts of the CoPI makes clear that a number of key features of the practice are not only situated in pragmatism but also have resonance with posthuman theory. The community aspect seems least contested, with both Lipman and Murris agreeing on the role of the facilitator, the necessity of the community aspect of inquiry, and the sense of communal autonomy which the CoPI aims to foster. Whether or not philosophy is constituted by taking part in a CoPI dialogue, or if it is a subject with its own content remains an important question, albeit one on which Lipman and Murris again agree, with other commentators raising questions regarding philosophical content. However, it is the underpinnings of inquiry education which, I aim to show, provide the most problematic issues for maintaining that the CoPI is commensurate with Murris's posthuman theory.

CoPI in the classroom

Social constructivism has been a shaping force in pedagogy for a number of decades (Biesta, 2013), and it is one which has shifted the focus in pedagogy from the teacher to the learner. For Biesta this has significant (negative) implications for the role of the teacher, who is a facilitator of learning, not only within the more specific context of the CoPI but in constructivist pedagogy in general. Indeed, Schwarz & Baker (2017) point out the impracticalities of a social constructivist model of education in a classroom where the teacher is responsible for thirty pupils: it is no easy task to facilitate the 'further-on point' of thirty different children.

Schwarz & Baker (2017) also comment that 'Vygotsky's ideas bring to the fore the role of the adult, who has already discovered what is to be learned' (p. 114), which is an important point in the compatibility of social constructivism and post-modernism and posthumanism. The role of the adult has been problematised in postmodern readings of education, with PwC seen as an instrumental tool in promoting critical thinking as an ideal (Weber, 2012 and see Gregory, 2012) which children are to attain. This normative model 'enforces a discipline of alleged clarity of reason on children' (Martens, 2013, p. 161), and the 'adult' in this case is not only the teacher in the classroom but also those who determine education policy and those, such as Lipman, who devise PwC programmes. According to Kennedy (2006), schools are sites of oppression, where the aim is to tame and make docile the child; the fear is that PwC will become another mechanism for doing this.

Although Vansieleghem & Kennedy (2012) name Murris as one of the 'second generation', and Gregory (2012) names posthumanism along with postmodernism and poststructuralism, with *The Posthuman Child* Murris herself would, I suspect, now name herself as more of a 'third generation'. She argues that even postmodernism is still committed to the 'anthropocentric gaze' (p. 6), caught up in binaries of adult/child and mind/body. The problematisation of the adult is due to the binary-enforcing practices of adults in the education system. She also names social constructivism as a perpetration of this practice. There are possible answers to this tension: either CoPI practice is more adult-driven than Murris and others would admit, or the CoPI is capable of being a pedagogy that so disrupts the usual adult/child, teacher/learner binaries that it is compatible with posthuman theorising.

In his discussion of talk rules, the child-led generation of which is the near-universal starting point of the CoPI, Lambrith (2009) agrees with the former of the options. He claims that talk rules are steered toward an already present agenda: the CoPI will be a democratic space in which children listen, take turns, and so on. No matter the rules the children actually generate, they will be steered toward a set of rules that espouses these principles, making the negotiation a farce. On the face of it, this is true: it would be an unusual community of inquiry in which talking over other people, not listening to others and not valuing each other's ideas was taken as the norm. However, this example provides an instance of how the CoPI allows beliefs to be held tentatively, to be questioned and explored. In such a case a child could vehemently object to the talk rules and insist on her own. A facilitator could agree to try those rules, and then engage the group in a critical discussion of them. It is true that it does require some acceptance of a shared set of values but rather than a fixed and unchanging imposed set of rules, the CoPI can allow for reflexive consideration of itself. As Cam (2014) argues, rules within the CoPI can be heuristic and strategic, dependent on context.

Hand (2015) critiques Murris's concern over the epistemological positioning of children, as he accuses her of a 'conflation of epistemic justice and epistemic equality'. Into the former category he places such injustices as choosing boys to answer rather than girls, or valuing the contributions of white over black pupils. However, in response to her claim that children are positioned as 'immature, ill-informed and endearing', Hand writes that children *are* immature, ill-informed and endearing' (p. 329). They *are* different from adults by virtue of being relative newcomers in the world, and to expect epistemic equality is foolish. In pedagogical terms, asking a child what they wanted to learn would make less sense than asking a teacher whose profession it is to help children to learn. Therefore a social constructivist approach is a sensible one because teachers do already know what has been learned.

However – and it is worth noting that Hand's article was written before Murris's *The Posthuman Child* – a materialdiscursive understanding of the child is not claiming that the child (or the adult) knows best. It is a humanist perspective, with the humanist binaries of immature/mature, ill-informed/well-informed, endearing/ not-endearing, that positions children as ontoepistemologically inferior. The implication of Hand's critique is that only those who are mature and well-informed should be considered as equal knowers, and this is only because Murris would contend that knowledge has been wrongly conceived of as 'representational' (Murris, 2016, p. 146) of a world outside the on-looking subject-knower.

Instead, a materialdiscursive understanding also considers the child as body (matter) in the world: 'it is impossible to say where the boundaries are of each child, or the teacher, or the parent, or the gecko on the wall, or the furniture, or the drawing, and so forth' (Murris, 2016, p. 156). It is more than that they are presented and represented as immature, ill-informed and endearing, along postmodern lines of power issues; it is that children's bodies in the world *are* immature, ill-informed and endearing, but the sort of knowledge that arises from that is not in any way deficient. For Murris, the posthuman ethicoontoepistemology is a way of 'theorizing the legitimacy' (p. 246) of the contributions of children to the CoPI, for all such contributions might not look like examples of traditional philosophical thinking.

As a growing number of studies attest and theories postulate (Millett & Tapper, 2012; Roche, 2011; Scholl, 2014), it is possible to reconfigure teacher attitudes to pedagogy through the CoPI. As Scholl (2014) writes, 'crucial' to this is that teachers 'genuinely view themselves as learners' (p. 90). While this is an example of Murris's posthuman boundary-blurring, it is also an echo of Lipman's earlier view that teachers must open themselves to reflection. According to Scholl, CoPI practice therefore also affects the theoretical framework of social constructivism. She offers the diagram shown in Figure 4.1 to illustrate her point (p. 100):

The Zone of Proximal Development (ZPD) is no longer a one-way development of student towards teacher, but the boundary on the teacher's side is conceived of as porous too. And of course there is not only one student in a CoPI but many, and many circles with porous boundaries, and a third space in the middle of them all (as a further diagram of Scholl's attests (Scholl, 2014, p. 101).

Scholl's comment on teachers' willingness to view themselves as learners raises a question about CoPI pedagogy: what if a teacher doesn't particularly want to do it? He or she may have to implement the CoPI as part of school policy without having any personal investment in it, for example. Both Lipman's focus on the dispositions required for the CoPI (reflexive, democratic), and Murris's insistence that adults need to position children epistemologically so that they can 'hear' them, cast doubt on whether or not this is possible. The role of the teacher is a key point, then: it will be difficult for children to engage in dialogue if they are not given opportunities

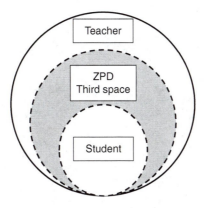

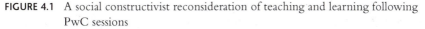

FIGURE 4.1 A social constructivist reconsideration of teaching and learning following PwC sessions

to do so; yet for teachers who do not engage in dialogic practice, presenting the need to do so can be challenging without also being didactic in the presentation of that need. As Freire (1993) writes, such an imposition when a need for it is not felt or known is counter to community of inquiry practices and will only serve to reinforce teacher/learner divisions and hierarchies.

Yet, if CoPI practice is as transformative as has been suggested, then the hope is that the very fact of carrying it out is likely to have an effect on teachers' practice. As Lipman writes: 'participants come to think as the process thinks' (2003, p. 21). Scholl's (2014) empirical study found that interviews with teachers after they had facilitated CoPI sessions indicated they had developed dispositions in line with those of CoPI pedagogy – what Scholl refers to as a 'critical juncture in pedagogical change' (p. 89). Therefore while on this reading the CoPI is social-constructivist pedagogy, it is not limited to the learner only, or rather, it can make all participants into learners.

Dialogue

Another feature the Community/Philosophy/Inquiry facets have in common is situating the CoPI as a dialogue, with a number of commentators referencing it as such (Cam, 2014; Daniel & Auriac, 2011; Wegerif, 2009, 2011) in addition to Lipman and Murris. 'Dialogue' has been used in a more pedagogical sense by Alexander (2004, 2010) to refer to good quality classroom discussion, and the sort of classroom environment in which learner talk is valued and encouraged. It has also been used in a more theoretical sense by Wegerif (2011), who uses it in the Bakhtinian sense of the dialogic relationship between people. Both senses of the term, but particularly Wegerif's, resonate with a posthuman understanding of the CoPI.

Alexander's (2004) view is that writing is seen as the only 'real' schoolwork. He also writes of a cultural lack of importance attached to educationally developmental uses of talk in the UK classroom, contrasting with Continental European countries where 'Oracy is no less important than literacy' (p. 19). In Germany, for example, states such as Nord-Rhine Westphalia and Mecklenburg-Pomerania have established philosophy with children as a school subject (Martens, 2009). It is of note that it was a study conducted on behalf of the German Ministry of Education in 1986 that led to its establishment as a school subject in 1992 (in Martens, 2009). The short time frame of the adoption of philosophy as a school subject stands in contrast to practice in the UK where, despite a now considerable amount of research, and the formation of various philosophy in education groups, including SAPERE, practice in schools remains patchy and quite often subject to the interest of individual teachers.

A focal reason for the comparison of the two countries is that the philosophical basis of PwC itself is different: while England has followed an Analytic philosophical tradition (from Lipman), Germanic PwC practice has developed from a Continental philosophy position. Weber (2012) is clear that the differences in these positions has led to German academics rejecting Lipman's conception of philosophy as that of a 'disembodied head' (p. 79), preferring the whole-child approach which, she argues, follows from that Continental position, and is augmented by a cultural acceptance of talk as a means of education.

Murris (2016) also critiques the focus on written language as the primary means of schoolwork. She uses the metaphor of Malaguzzi's 'The Hundred Languages' to highlight that writing is but one avenue of schooling and there are other 'languages' to 'learn'. These include meaning-making through the visual arts, scientific and mathematical language, oral tradition and the affordances of technology, as well as through philosophical language. By focussing on only one 'language', she argues, the potentiality for children to think and communicate in a variety of different ways is lost, and so 'we fail so many of the world's children' (p. 154).

A considerable part of this problem is ensconced in the language we use, for Murris, as she claims that the pronoun 'I' is used to bound the child in a relational ontology to others – 'I am this/I am not this', and so reinforces the distinctions between adults and children (or other binaries). This has a great deal of overlap with dialogic theory as intended in the Bakhtinian sense of 'dialogue', which is not about classroom discourse in Alexander's sense, but the meaning that is made between people, and the world that they are in. Holquist (1990) claims that this view of dialogue also means that 'I' assumes a different meaning, as 'I' becomes a 'word that has no referent' (p. 22). This is because a voice, in the dialogic sense, is not embodied in one single being. Instead, all dialogue is always in dialogue with previous dialogue, creating what Wegerif (2011) refers to as a 'dynamic continuous emergence of meaning' (p. 180).

Therefore dialogue is an ontology, one which assumes 'I' which is not fixed and unchanging in one body, but one which is dependent on context. In terms of education, if a child says something which a teacher would have taken as meaningful and insightful coming from an adult, but doesn't take it seriously on the grounds that a child said it, then the teacher has positioned the child as a fixed 'I', one which is not capable of having the same mature, informed voice as adults. In the PwC community, Johansson (2012) pointed out that adults position children as irrational based on specific examples, such as giving voice to inanimate objects in play. However, he claims, adults perform similar acts, such as when anthropomorphising in imaginative works (he cites Ted Hughes's poem *The Jaguar*). To cite one as an example of irrationality and immaturity, and the other as creative endeavour is to participate in the prejudice of age to which Murris refers. Just because children play does not mean they are not capable of philosophical thought – the child emerges as an 'I' in context-specific dialogue.

Murris's (2016) solution to the assumptions that are made by the pronoun 'I' is to introduce the neologism 'iii' (p. 90). This refers to the ontoepistemological assumption that children are not the 'I' of the bound organism, or the 'ii' of the socially constructed child, but an 'iii' which is entangled in an unbounded material and discursive way in and of the world. This conception of an 'iii' also resonates with dialogic theory; dialogue 'can be reduced to a minimum of three elements…an utterance, a reply, and a relation between the two' (Holquist, 1990, p. 38). The relation between the two is the key point, the dialogic 'gap' that 'keeps non-fused two autonomous consciousnesses' (Todorov, 1984, p. 22). This is akin to the 'third space' that Scholl identified as being created in the CoPI. There is also an ethical element, as if we seek to understand the 'other' in a non-I way, then the 'other' becomes the object of one's own narrative, reducing the other to its relation to ourselves.

Conclusion

This chapter has been an exploration of the ways in which the CoPI functions as a pedagogical structure, as well as the coherence of the theoretical framework supporting it. A successful CoPI seems to require a number of things:

1. A thought-provoking or problematic starting point to make the inquiry meaningful.
2. An acceptance that all beliefs are open to question (epistemic fallibilism).
3. A facilitator who positions children as ontoepistemologically capable of philosophical thinking.
4. A focus on dispositions as much as skills.
5. An inherent commitment to the inquiry by all participants.
6. A facilitator who positions herself as 'learner' as much as the other participants.

Despite the CoPI's origins in pragmatism, as pedagogy it does seem particularly apt for a posthuman or dialogic ontology (see Higham, in press). This in itself, however, raises a number of issues because of the theoretical differences between those positions.

A key problem that has been identified with CoPI practice is that we cannot know from what motivation the teacher is acting. Lipman (2003) is clear that the teacher should have the disposition of facilitation in order for a successful CoPI to take place. Murris (2016) does not seem to view this as a particular problem, claiming CoPI practice as a pedagogy entirely congruent with posthumanism. The act of participating in the CoPI expands the 'horizon of meaning' to be greater than that of only one perspective. It is enough to participate in this sort of pedagogy, as it 'generates and nurtures feelings of culture and solidarity, responsibility and inclusion' (p. 157). Presumably, even if a teacher does not particularly want to engage in CoPI pedagogy, by doing so he or she may change their views.

However, ultimately, it is difficult to know if a teacher is inherently positioning children as ontoepistemologically valid 'others' or instrumentally doing so. The same applies to the learners in a dialogue. Michaels, O'Connor, & Resnick (2008) reinforce this, cautioning that there is an ontological obligation to hear all of the voices in a dialogue, otherwise there can be no effective discursive practice. They use the example of a boy who is, in technical terms, highly competent at discursive practice: 'questioning premises, making claims, bringing counter-examples' (p. 294). However, what is also clear from the boy's speech is that the contributions made by the group don't matter. The authors go on to state that this is 'pervasive' (p. 294) in the examples at which they have looked.

A further problem is to be found in the inquiry process itself. Lipman situates the inquiry process within a social constructivist framework, which is part of a tradition that has a long provenance from Hegel to Marx to Vygotsky. Wegerif (2011), however, argues that, from a dialogic perspective, there is no sense to be made from the idea of 'overcoming' the social to develop rational, individual selves because the relationship with the other is paramount. Similarly, for Murris, the notion of such autonomy is not one which makes sense in a posthuman framework in which humans are entangled in the world.

The Community of Philosophical Inquiry has powerful pedagogical possibilities. It is not merely conceived of as a pedagogical tool, but as a transformative education practice. Its possibilities extend to the very ways in which teachers and learners are positioned as beings as well as knowers, as intrinsically valuable to the inquiry. There is also a strong ethical dimension in the ways in which the CoPI develops democratic dispositions, valuing the voices of all participants. It is not a surprise that such a form of pedagogy has been 'claimed' by a number of theorists as a key pedagogy. However, if it is to be the case that Murris and others 'adopt' the CoPI while distancing themselves from the theoretical basis on which Lipman (and Dewey) founded it, then there must be a clear and coherent justification for doing so.

References

Alexander, R. (2004). *Towards dialogic teaching: Rethinking classroom talk* (4th ed.). Cambridge: Dialogos.
Alexander, R. (2010). Speaking but not listening? Accountable talk in an unaccountable context. *Literacy, 44*(3), 103–112.
Biesta, G. (2011). Philosophy, exposure, and children: How to resist the instrumentalisation of philosophy in education. *Journal of Philosophy of Education, 45*(2), 305–319. doi:10.1111/j.1467-9752.2011.00792.x
Biesta, G. (2013). Receiving the gift of teaching: From 'learning from' to 'being taught by'. *Studies in the Philosophy of Education, 32,* 449–461.

Burgh, G., & Nichols, K. (2012). The parallels between philosophical inquiry and scientific inquiry: Implications for science education. *Educational Philosophy and Theory, 44*(10), 1045–1059.

Butler, J. (2005). *Giving an account of oneself.* New York, NY: Fordham University Press.

Cam, P. (2014). Philosophy for children, values education and the inquiring society. *Educational Philosophy and Theory, 46*(11), 1203–1211.

Daniel, M., & Auriac, E. (2011). Philosophy, critical thinking and philosophy for children. *Educational Philosophy & Theory, 43*(5), 415–435. doi:10.1111/j.1469-5812.2008.00483.x

Dewey, J. (1933). *How we think: A restatement of the relation of reflective thinking to the educative process.* Boston, MA: Heath.

Echeverria, E., & Hannam, P. (2016). A pedagogical proposal for advancing democracy. In M. Gregory, J. Haynes, & K. Murris (Eds.), *The Routledge international handbook of philosophy for children* (pp. 3–10). London: Routledge.

Education Endowment Foundation. (2015). *Philosophy for children: Evaluation report and executive summary* [online]. Retrieved June 1, 2017, from https://educationendowmentfoundation.org.uk/uploads/pdf/Philosophy_for_Children.pdf

Ellerton, P. (2016). Pragmatist epistemology, inquiry values and education for thinking. In M. Gregory, J. Haynes, & K. Murris (Eds.), *The Routledge international handbook of philosophy for children* (pp. 111–118). London: Routledge.

Freire, P. (1993). *Pedagogy of the oppressed.* New York, NY: Continuum.

Gregory, M. (2012). Philosophy for children and its critics: A Mendham dialogue. In N. Vansieleghem & D. Kennedy (Eds.), *Philosophy for children in transition: Problems and prospects* (pp. 30–51). Chichester: Wiley-Blackwell.

Gregory, M., Haynes, J., & Murris, K. (Eds.). (2016). *The Routledge international handbook of philosophy for children.* London: Routledge.

Hand, M. (2015). What do kids know? A response to Karin Murris. *Studies in Philosophy & Education, 34*(3), 327–330. doi:10.1007/s11217-015-9464-5

Hayes, D. (2015). Against critical thinking pedagogy. *Arts and Humanities in Higher Education, 14*(4), 318–328. doi:10.1177/1474022215592248

Higham, R. (in press). 'To be is to respond': Realising a dialogic ontology for Deweyan pragmatism. *Journal of Philosophy of Education, 51*(4), special issue on Dewey's D&E centenary.

Holquist, M. (1990). *Dialogism: Bakhtin and his world.* London: Routledge.

Johansson, V. (2012). 'In charge of the truffala seeds': On children's literature, rationality and children's voices in philosophy. In N. Vansieleghem & D. Kennedy (Eds.), *Philosophy for children in transition: Problems and prospects* (pp. 190–209). Chichester: Wiley-Blackwell.

Kennedy, D. (2006). *Changing conceptions of the child from the renaissance to post-modernity. A philosophy of childhood.* Lewiston, NY: The Edwin Mellen Press.

Kennedy, N., & Kennedy, D. (2011). Community of philosophical inquiry as a discursive structure and its role in school curriculum design. *Journal of Philosophy of Education, 45*(2), 265–283.

Kerslake, L., & Rimmington, S. (2017). Sharing talk, sharing cognition: Philosophy with children as the basis for productive classroom interaction. *Issues in Early Education, 1*(36), 21–32. Retrieved December 17, 2017, from www.pwe.ug.edu.pl/wp-content/uploads/2017/06/pwe-36.pdf

Kohan, W. (2012). Childhood, education and philosophy: Notes on deterritorialisation. In N. Vansieleghem & D. Kennedy (Eds.), *Philosophy for children in transition: Problems and prospects* (pp. 170–198). Chichester: Wiley-Blackwell.

Kohan, W. (2014). *Philosophy and childhood: Critical perspectives and affirmative practices.* New York, NY: Palgrave Macmillan.

Lambrith, A. (2009). Ground rules for talk: The acceptable face of prescription. *The Curriculum Journal, 20*(4), 423–435. doi:10.1080/09585170903424971

Lipman, M. (1998). *Philosophy goes to school.* Philadelphia, PA: Temple University Press.

Lipman, M. (2003). *Thinking in education* (2nd ed.). Cambridge: Cambridge University Press.

Lipman, M. (2008). *A life teaching thinking*. Montclair, CA: IAPC.

Lipman, M., Sharp, A., & Oscanyan, F. (1980). *Philosophy in the classroom* (2nd ed.). Philadelphia, PA: Temple University Press.

McCall, C. (2009). *Transforming thinking: Philosophical inquiry in the primary and secondary classroom*. London and New York: Routledge.

McCall, C., & Weijers, E. (2016). Back to basics: A philosophical analysis of philosophy in philosophy with children. In M. Gregory, J. Haynes, & K. Murris (Eds.), *The Routledge international handbook of philosophy for children* (pp. 83–92). London: Routledge.

Martens, E. (2009). Children's philosophy and children's theology – A family resemblance. In G.Y. de Iversen, G. Mitchell, & G. Pollard (Eds.), *Hovering over the face of the deep: Philosophizing and theologising with children* (pp. 107–116). Münster: Waxmann.

Martens, E. (2013). *Philosophieren mit Kindern. Eine Einführung in die Philosophie*. (Translated by Rimmington, S. (2017). *Philosophising with Children: An introduction to philosophy*. Stuttgart: Reclam. Full translation available: sarahrimmington66@gmail.com.)

Michaels, S., O'Connor, C., & Resnick, L. (2008). Deliberative discourse idealized and realized: Accountable talk in the classroom and in civic life. *Studies in Philosophy and Education, 27,* 283–297. doi:10.1007/s11217-007-9071-1

Millett, S., & Tapper, A. (2012). Benefits of collaborative philosophical inquiry in schools. *Educational Philosophy and Theory, 44*(5). doi:10.1111/j.469-5812.2010.00727.x

Murris, K. (2015). Posthumanism, philosophy for children and Anthony Browne's 'little beauty'. *Bookbird: A Journal of International Children's Literature, 53*(2), 59–65. doi:10.1353/bkb.2015.0030

Murris, K. (2016). *The posthuman child: Educational transformation through philosophy with picturebooks*. London: Routledge.

Roche, M. (2011). Creating a dialogical and critical classroom: Reflection and action to improve practice. *Educational Action Research, 19*(3), 327–343. doi: 10.1080/09650792.2011.600607

Scholl, R. (2014). Inside-out pedagogy: Theorising pedagogical transformation through teaching philosophy. *Australian Journal of Teacher Education, 39*(6), 89–106. doi:10.14221/ajte.2014v39n6.5

Schwarz, B. B., & Baker, M. (2017). *Dialogue, argumentation and education: History, theory and practice*. Cambridge: Cambridge University Press.

Splitter, L. (2000). Concepts, communities and the tools for good thinking. *Inquiry: Critical Thinking across the Disciplines, 19*(2), 11–26.

Todorov, T. (1984). *Mikhail Bakhtin: The dialogical principle* (Wlad Godzich, Trans.). Manchester: Manchester University Press.

Vansieleghem, N., & Kennedy, D. (2012). *Philosophy for children in transition: Problems and prospects*. Chichester: Wiley-Blackwell.

Vygotsky, L. S. (1978). *Mind in society: The development of higher psychological processes*. Cambridge, MA: Harvard University Press.

Weber, B. (2012). Childhood, philosophy and play: Friedrich Schiller and the interface between reason, passion and sensation. In N. Vansieleghem & D. Kennedy (Eds.), *Philosophy for children in transition: Problems and prospects* (pp. 66–81). Chichester: Wiley-Blackwell.

Wegerif, R. (2009). *What does it mean to teach thinking? Philosophy for children as an example of dialogic education* [Draft for ICPIC 2009 Conference Proceedings].

Wegerif, R. (2011). Towards a dialogic theory of how children learn to think. *Thinking Skills and Creativity, 6*(3), 179–190. doi:10.1016/j.tsc.2011.08.002

White, J. (2012). Philosophy in primary schools? *Journal of Philosophy of Education, 46*(3), 449–460. doi:10.1111/j.1467-9752.2012.00860.x

Worley, P. (2015, November 17). Thought adventure 41: Here and elsewhere – thinking about migration and identity. Bloomsbury Education Blog. Retrieved December 19, 2017, from https://bloomsburyeducation.wordpress.com/2015/11/17/peter-worley-thought-adventure-41-here-and-elsewhere-thinking-about-migration-and-identity/

5

FIXING HUMPTY DUMPTY

Putting higher-order skills and knowledge together again

Carl Bereiter and Marlene Scardamalia

Introduction

Students must be prepared for a rapidly changing world; that much is clear. But what does this mean when translated into pursuable educational goals? One thing it has meant is a rising emphasis on personal attributes—such as skills, attitudes, and values. In education, this trend has taken its most conspicuous form in the "21st century skills" movement and its emphasis on soft skills (Johnson, 2009). At the same time there is declining emphasis on knowledge. It is not that knowledge itself has been devalued: "alternate facts," "fake news," anti-science, and related trends do not deny the value of knowledge, no matter how much they distort it. Rather, what has declined in value is having quantities of knowledge stored in memory. The new concept, heavily promoted for instance in health care, is "just-in-time" information (Johnmar, 2013). The common line of argument is that stored knowledge becomes rapidly obsolete, that new knowledge is constantly being added, and that the web makes the latest knowledge available at the moment it is needed. Something is missing in this line of thought, however. Surely health care professionals, like people in many other rapidly moving fields, need access to up-to-date information; but this presupposes that they are able to understand it. And a decade of intensive research on reading comprehension showed that the best predictor of new learning is what one already knows (Schallert, 1982). In other words, understanding depends on *knowledgeability*, a coherent background of knowledge acquired over an extended period of time. Just-in-time information is undoubtedly an important resource for intelligent action in today's world, but only if it is understood; and there is no such thing as just-in-time understanding.

In this chapter we look historically at how the prevailing conception of thinking came to separate knowledge from skills in working with it. Recognizing that both are important is not enough. A richer conception of knowledge calls for rethinking what it means to be a good thinker, reconsidering the whole notion of thinking skills. This in turn leads to reconsidering what it means to teach students to think. Skills may still have a role, but not a magisterial one. Teaching thinking becomes helping students develop as thinking people and socializing them into a knowledge-creating society.

Background: how did thinking skills get separated from knowledge?

The concept of "higher-order thinking skills" (Brookhart, 2010), along with its re-emergence in "21st century skills," rests on a separation between knowledge and the ability to apply and operate on that knowledge. This separation is a relatively recent development in educational thought and has no secure theoretical or scientific basis. Sometime in the second half of the 20th century, "teach them to think" became "teach them thinking skills." Correspondingly, knowledge became no longer an inseparable part of ability to think but instead provided material for thinking skills to work upon. Calls for teaching students to think date from way back (at least as far back as Plato), and they have frequently come not from trend-followers but from proponents of traditional liberal education. But the older advocates of teaching students to think did not treat thinking as a matter of skill distinct from knowledge. A statement appearing frequently on the web and attributed to Bertrand Russell (but without identifying a source) expresses the more classical view:

> When you want to teach children to think, you begin by treating them seriously when they are little, giving them responsibilities, talking to them candidly, providing privacy and solitude for them, and making them readers and thinkers of significant thoughts from the beginning. That's if you want to teach them to think.

There is no mention of skill here. Instead, teaching children to think is treated broadly as a sort of character development: helping children develop into thinking persons. Knowledge, acquired through the reading of "significant thoughts," plays an important part.

Even more explicit on the intimate connection between content and process was A. N. Whitehead, who wrote "Nobody can be a good reasoner unless by constant practice he has realized the importance of getting hold of the big ideas and of hanging on to them like grim death" (1929, p. 91).

Friedrich Nietzsche presented a more light-hearted account of the place of ideas in education "…dancing in all its forms cannot be excluded from the curriculum of all noble education; dancing with the feet, with ideas, with words, and, need I add that one must also be able to dance with the pen?" (2007/1889, p. 47).

The rise of behaviorism and the emphasis on behavioral objectives may have encouraged the shift to treating thinking as a set of skills, although thinking skills have never leant themselves well to behavioral objectification. But the signal event in mid-century pedagogical thought in America was the publication of what came to be known as Bloom's *Taxonomy* (Bloom, 1956). The *Taxonomy* proposed a hierarchy of educational objectives, with Knowledge occupying the lowest level. Arranged in ascending order above it were Comprehension, Application, Analysis, Synthesis, and Evaluation. To judge by what had gone before and what has come after, this hierarchy marks the birth of "higher-order thinking skills," the separation of process from content, and the subsequent devaluing of knowledge.

In 2001 a major revision of Bloom's *Taxonomy* appeared (Anderson and Krathwohl, 2001). Although it modernized the original taxonomy in several ways, its overall effect is to further separate skills from knowledge. Whereas the original taxonomy posited a one-dimensional ladder of skills and abilities, with Knowledge occupying one of the rungs, the revised version offers a two-dimensional array, with Knowledge as one of the dimensions, orthogonal to the skills dimension.

The classical and, one might say, "natural" affinity of knowledge and thinking lives on in liberal education generally—for instance, in the International Baccalaureate—and in a variety of educational approaches heavily involved with ideas, discourse, and understanding (e.g., Gardner, 1999; Lipman, 1988; Scardamalia & Bereiter, 2006; Wegerif, 2010). More generally, the many strands of research and educational development carried out within the learning sciences have taken for granted a close association between learning and thinking and have tended to strengthen it (Bransford, Brown, & Cocking, 1999; Bransford & Donovan, 2005; Sawyer, 2006, 2014). Learning science research has expanded to give more attention to social and emotional issues such as well-being, diversity, and equity, but learning science researchers have shown little interest in thinking skills as a separate focus. If, however, one looks at major reforms of tests, curricula, and standards, the focus is on moving skills toward the center. In its broadest sense this not only separates skills from knowledge, it separates them from considerations of culture and acculturation.

Russell and Whitehead did more than offer a few pithy observations about education. They were recognized thought leaders of an intellectual culture that placed high value on disciplined knowledge and reason and in which teaching the young to think meant socializing them into that culture. Although from today's standpoint it is easy to criticize it as Eurocentric, androcentric, and overly rationalistic, it must also be recognized that their cultural view is in tune with contemporary thought and that the culture of rational and evidence-based knowledge advancement has become global and normative. Today all the major journals in all the disciplines are international journals, with authors from all over the world striving to meet the same standards as to what will be counted as a contribution to knowledge. If we are serious about enabling more people to find a place in a world of accelerating innovation and knowledge creation, we must look beyond skills to acculturation.

The infusion delusion

The 1970s saw a wave of thinking skills programs. Strategy instruction and practice were their main ingredients, leaving them essentially content-free or content-irrelevant. During the 1980s, however, the emphasis began to shift toward integrating or "infusing" thinking skills development into subject-matter courses (Swartz, 1987). Although content-free thinking skills instruction is still to be found, especially in computer software, the mainstream educational literature is now solidly on the side of doing skill teaching within regular school subjects.

From this it might appear that process and content have come back together, but that is an illusion. The essential idea of infusion is that content learning serves as a vehicle for skill learning (see, for instance, Swartz & Parks, 1994). In practice this means the incorporation of specific thinking activities into subject matter instruction that otherwise retains its customary form. Infusion thus stands in contrast to approaches such as the "thinking curriculum" of Resnick & Klopfer (1989), which transform the curriculum to achieve a more thoughtful form of engagement with subject content. Good teachers who adopt infusion may combine thinking skills activities with thoughtful engagement with disciplinary concepts—but this is combination, not synthesis. The thinking activities remain add-ons, possibly contributing something to the growth of disciplined knowledge but also quite possibly trivializing content and fragmenting it into bits attached to different activities. The web offers an abundance of thinking activities for every school grade and subject. While individually many of these may have merit, they do not fit together to build a deep and coherent understanding of the world nor a thinking person's outlook on it.

Not all abilities are skills

No one is likely to deny that creativity, problem-solving ability, critical thinking, effective oral communication, and ability to collaborate are good qualities to possess. But it does not follow that these attributes are skills. There are many human qualities besides skills that may be conditioned by experience: for instance, virtues, attitudes and values, traits of personality, aptitudes, and habits. Educational design has been influenced, however, by a confusion of skills with abilities. This confusion promotes the illusion that there is scientific evidence for the existence of generic intellectual skills of the kind that many "21st century skills" programs intend to teach. Not all abilities are skills; the authors of the original *Taxonomy* recognized that there was an ontological issue here, but they elected to dodge it (Bloom, 1956, pp. 38–39). Put simply, skills are the subset of abilities that are to a substantial degree learnable and improvable through practice. Claims that such skills are teachable require evidence of learnability and transfer of learning.

The distinction between skills and abilities becomes complicated by the extraordinary human capacity for improvement through practice—for the development of expertise. As a rough generalization, we can say that if you keep repeating any task you will keep getting better at it (Newell & Rosenbloom, 1981). Even such an apparently hard-wired ability as memory can be affected by training. The most dramatic demonstration of this has been huge increases in digit span (repeating back strings of digits) stretching the normal limit of around seven digits to as high as 80 (Chase & Ericsson, 1982). Although usually less dramatic in its effects, skill learning pervades all our purposeful activity. Doesn't this, then, vindicate an emphasis on training higher-order thinking skills?

Unfortunately for the 21st century skills movement, there is a downside to the skill-learning story. The skill developed through training and practice on a task is specific to the task. The digit-span prodigy not only did not show any general improvement in memory but did not even show improvement in letter span—the same memory task but using letters of the alphabet instead of numbers (Ericsson & Chase, 1982). Skill learning results in acquiring strategies—sometimes conscious, sometimes not, sometimes at a neuromuscular rather than a cognitive level—that become increasingly specialized to repetitive aspects of the task. Problem solving instruction can improve performance, but it generalizes so little beyond the kinds of problems used in instruction that experts have shifted to teaching domain-specific skills (Mayer & Wittrock, 2006). But the question then becomes, what are the domain-specific thinking skills good for? Where, outside of school, does one ever encounter those peculiar entities known as mathematical word problems? Similarly, creativity training may show gains on a test calling for listing novel uses for a brick or a coat hanger. By a stretch one might claim that this sort of idea generation does occur in real-life creative work; but where in real life does the *number* of ideas one can generate constitute a measure of one's contribution to a creative product—to an invention, theory, plan, or problem solution? This is not to deny that, as test items, arithmetic word problems and listing uses for a brick may have value as indicators of more general abilities, but it is to question whether teaching students how to do better on such tasks is of any real-life value.

The problem of transfer (McKeough, Lupart, & Marini, 1995) receives little attention in the thinking skills literature. The implicit, never stated assumption is that skill learning will automatically transfer to any situation where the same skill label can be applied. But this is word magic, not science. The burden of proof ought to be on thinking skills advocates to demonstrate that the effects of skill teaching transfer to significant real-world behavior rather than expecting skeptics to prove that transfer does not occur. Given the generally discouraging results of decades of research on transfer (Detterman & Sternberg, 1993), the default assumption should be that transfer of thinking skill teaching will be weak and narrow. One of the most optimistic theoretical treatments of transfer is that of Bransford & Schwartz (1999), who suggest that the place to look for evidence of transfer is in "savings" in future learning. This seems to be what employers are actually looking for when they urge an educational emphasis on 21st century skills. They do not expect the schools to train people for the particular jobs they will enter. Specific job skills are learned on the job or in company training programs. What the employers want are people whose on-the-job learning will be quick and successful. To that end, they call on the schools to teach learning skills and thinking skills. The employers' need is real and understandable, but the prescription is grounded in a naïve psychology that assumes unlimited transfer of learning.

The normal term for readiness to develop a certain class of skills is "aptitude." To say that someone has exceptional athletic ability is not to say that they are good at golf, for instance, but it is to say that they have an aptitude for athletics such that if they took up golf they would learn it readily and would eventually become better than average at it. Accordingly, discussions of 21st century educational needs might proceed on a more realistic basis by striking out the word "skills" and replacing it with "aptitudes," so that the educational goal becomes teaching "21st century aptitudes." This is no mere relabeling, however; it immediately raises doubts as to whether the goal is attainable. Those doubts are well justified. Increasing an aptitude is a much more complex undertaking than teaching a skill. Whether it can be done at all is uncertain, but if it can it will surely depend on a very broadly based program of human development, which may include different kinds of skill development, but only as a part.

The correlation illusion

Most people who know what a correlation coefficient is also know that "correlation does not prove causation" (despite which, every newsworthy correlational finding is reported somewhere in the media as if it shows a causal relationship). But that is not the only way correlations can be misleading. There is, for instance, a moderate positive correlation between scores on creativity tests and creative achievement in later life (Cramond, Matthews-Morgan, Bandalos, & Zuo, 2005). Here, because of the time lag, the causal relation cannot run backward (creative achievement affecting earlier test scores). There could be a common cause, for instance something about brain anatomy that affects creativity test scores in the young and creative achievement in adulthood. This is where the aforementioned confusion between skills and abilities enters in. Creativity skills trainers will want to say that the common element is teachable skills, whereas an alternative is that the common element is brain structure—or perhaps temperament, energy level, self-concept, cognitive style, or more likely a combination of many factors. But wait, isn't there plenty of evidence that creativity training works? Yes, but the evidence is that it can raise scores on creativity tests. It is not evidence that creativity training increases creative achievement in later life.

A common way of expressing a correlation such as that between creativity test scores and later creative performance is a statement on the order of "For every 10-point increase in creativity test score you get an increase of one level on a scale of creative achievement." This would be an accurate but misleading statement. It strongly suggests that if you can by some means increase a person's creativity test score by 10 points the result will be an increase of one level in creative achievement. The correlation actually says nothing of the sort. It merely represents a relation between two sets of data on the same people and says nothing whatsoever about the effect of modifying one set of data by instruction or any other means. The effect could be to reduce or increase the correlation, there might be no effect at all, or the effect could even be negative—by inducing a way of thinking that was good for test performance but detrimental in real creative work. The only way to find out about the effect of creativity training on later creative achievement is to do experiments directly testing for such effects. As long as the evidence for the teachability of 21st century skills is limited to evidence of increases in scores on tests intended to measure the skills, any claims of long-term personal or social benefits have to be taken as unproven.

The claims of long-term benefits are not disproven either, of course. In some cases, such as with basic literacy and numeracy, a case for skill teaching may be reinforced by correlational data but does not rely on it. Modern assessments, for instance, often define levels of literacy in terms of what they enable people to do: one level represents literacy sufficient for the ordinary demands of modern life, a level below that is deemed insufficient for meeting these demands, and levels above it are deemed essential for higher education and for doing knowledge work. A similar set of meaningful levels can be defined for mathematical abilities. Evidence supporting or disputing the definitions of levels would need to go beyond statistical analysis of correlations and present data on the actual life and work experience of people with different tested levels of literacy or numeracy. But meaningful levels of competence cannot be similarly defined for creativity, critical thinking, oral communication and other such soft skills. What level of score on a critical thinking test do you need in order to vote intelligently and not be duped by politicians' lies and false news? Not only do we not know, we do not even have any basis for believing that such a test score level exists.

Needed: a richer conception of knowledge

The authors of Bloom's *Taxonomy* suggested that we think of knowledge as the contents of a filing cabinet and the higher-order skills as constituting our ability to make use of the filing cabinet's contents. But only in extreme and essentially trivial cases can the *Taxonomy*'s higher-order ability, Comprehension (or in the revised version, Understand), be separated from the lowly Knowledge category, now labeled Remember. As we move to more complex knowledge, other supposed higher-order abilities become part of the knowledge itself rather than skills applied to the knowledge. Consider the following, which are on every 21st century skill list:

- **Critical thinking:** Any time the online news highlights some example of public gullibility or bad judgment, there will be commenters blaming the schools for failing to teach critical thinking. But what kind of skill teaching would have set people on the path of right thinking? On any controversial issue, large or small, it is fair to ask: If you fully understand the opposing sides, is there anything left that calls for some special thinking skill? We don't mean knowledge about common propaganda and sales tricks, which is knowledge any citizen ought to have. And we don't mean critical thinking disposition— that is a habit of mind or a virtue that deserves serious attention. But skill?
- **Problem solving:** Research on mathematical problem solving shows that teaching students problem solving strategies improves performance on this task—although, as already noted, it does not transfer to other kinds of problem

solving (Mayer & Wittrock, 2006). There is no evidence, however, that students actually use the taught strategies except on demand. The first strategy is always *understand the problem*. Studies comparing expert and novice problem solvers show that they differ mainly on this point. Experts invest effort in understanding the problem and connecting it to their knowledge whereas novices tend to plunge in blindly. Investing in problem analysis isn't a strategy; it's a habit of mind. The most likely explanation of the effects of problem solving instruction is that it gets students to think more about what they are trying to solve and bring their knowledge of the domain to bear on the problem.

- **Creativity:** The theory of evolution by natural selection was independently invented by the two people in the world—Darwin and Wallace—who had the most (and very similar) relevant knowledge (Quammen, 1996). In many other examples, once we take full account of the knowledge involved, the scope for creativity as a distinct trait is considerably reduced (Weisberg, 1999). It is not eliminated, however. The challenge of educating people to work creatively with knowledge is a top-level challenge for 21st century education, and one we discuss further in the next section.

In summary, a separation between knowledge and skill makes sense only with an extremely restricted conception of knowledge. As knowledge becomes more complex, skills become inseparable from the knowledge itself. At the behavioral level, there is no such thing as thinking unaffected by knowledge. Central to efforts to adapt education to 21st century needs should be an effort to design educational programs that close the breach between knowledge goals and skill goals. Instead of treating skills and subject matter knowledge as distinct objectives, the challenge for curriculum developers should be to foster knowledge that is of maximum value in thinking. This is not the same as the "infusion" strategy discussed earlier. It is not inserting thinking problems and challenges into subject-matter courses; it is focusing on knowledge worth thinking about. (The two are not incompatible, but they certainly compete for time and attention.) The main application of schooled knowledge is in acquiring further knowledge. And it is not only the quality of knowledge that helps us think. Quantity also makes a difference. It increases the likelihood of finding productive analogies and finding relevant cases in case-based reasoning (Kolodner, 2006). Perhaps most importantly, it enables us to get a foot in the door of discourse that will lead to deeper knowledge.

Creativity

The most noticeable change to Bloom's *Taxonomy* in a revised edition is the addition of Creativity to the hierarchy of abilities—the highest higher-order thinking skill (Anderson & Krathwohl, 2001). If knowledge creation is the defining work of the 21st century, then creativity—as a talent, skill, personality trait, or however one chooses to categorize it—would seem to deserve a top position among educational priorities. It is already highly prized. However, everything we say and do is in some degree creative, and so what needs to be understood and fostered is creativity that produces significant results—known in the literature as "big C creativity" (Piirto, 2004).

Two factors divert schools from fostering "big C" creativity. One is a tendency, especially strong in elementary schools, to equate creativity with creative writing and performing arts. Although artistic creativity is as valuable as ever, the creativity deemed to be in short supply in 21st century conditions is ideational creativity—creativity in work with ideas. The other factor is the tendency, common in adult creativity workshops as well as in schools, to focus on generating singular bright ideas. In real world enterprises (and in lively classrooms, too) there is usually an abundance of bright ideas. But as the design group Fahrenheit 212 has emphasized, "Ideas are the easy part" (Maulik, 2010). The challenge is to develop them into something significant, and this requires sustained creativity over weeks, months, and sometimes years. Educational timetables seldom allow for sustained creativity; in fact, curriculum guidelines and course outlines seem not to acknowledge that such a thing even exists. Little would be lost and much might be gained if schools simply abandoned teaching ideational creativity and focused instead on engaging students in authentic pursuits and problems of understanding that are by their very nature creative.

Technology skills

Every 21st century skill list gives a prominent place to computer and digital media skills. At one time "knowing how to use a computer" denoted a fairly limited and coherent body of hard skills, which even many university students lacked but which increasing numbers of jobs required. Today, however, it is making less and less sense to identify skill in the use of computers and other digital technology as an educational goal in its own right. Aside from a few basics, what you need to learn that involves technology is inseparable from what you learn through using it in any up-to-date school course. This is one place where just-in-time knowledge makes sense: Provide instruction in some particular use of technology at the time it is needed for students to get on with their knowledge building. However, today's students will often prove adept at getting how-to-do-it knowledge from their peers or from trial and error.

Another favorite of 21st century skill lists is information search skills. However, information search skills (as well as many other technology-using skills) can become obsolete—perhaps more rapidly than most other knowledge, because of the rate of technological progress. In the early days of web search engines, if you were looking for information to help solve a problem the best you could usually do was define a topic and keep refining it until it retrieved information useful for your purpose. Now all you have to do is ask a question and you are likely to get a flurry of direct answers. As information search engines become increasingly powerful, the challenge for users becomes increasingly that of building trustworthy and coherent knowledge out of the fragmentary information retrieved. This, however, is not a technology skill; it is a knowledge-building skill highly dependent on the quality of one's existing base of world knowledge. This skill is a defining character-istic of *transliteracy* (Liu, 2012). Although it gets no attention from 21st century skills enthusiasts, it is arguably the most "21st century" of 21st century skills—in that the problem of information fragmentation that it addresses can be seen as a product of 21st century technology (Scardamalia & Bereiter, 2014a).

Identification of 21st century educational needs and the emergence of new competencies

The vision of the future that appears in the 21st century literature is a familiar one: rapid change, globalization, need for continual innovation, and so on. This vision, even if it is correct as far as it goes, does not translate into educational objectives, except at a bumper-sticker level.

If we back off just a few steps from the exigencies of international competition and the technological juggernaut, three cultural changes become evident that have major implications for education:

1. **Pressure for knowledge creation.** In the private sector this is experienced as pressure for constant innovation—not only in products but also in manufac-turing and business practices. But the demand for new knowledge extends far beyond the economic sphere. In *The Ingenuity Gap* and subsequent publications, Homer-Dixon (2000, 2006) has documented the shortage of usable knowledge and ideas for addressing the gravest problems facing contemporary societies. Each new crisis generates a demand for new knowledge on the basis of which solutions will be sought. This was not always true and is not true now in soci-eties dominated by tradition or orthodoxy. At the least, education ought to be helping people understand and recognize needs for knowledge creation.
2. **Abstractness.** More and more of the world's work is mediated through in-formation technology that puts the worker at one or more removes from the concrete reality the work is supposed to affect. Whereas at one time diagnosing car engine problems depended on opening the hood and interacting directly with the engine, it is now mostly a matter of interacting with computer read-outs. Work with abstract representations permeates all kinds of occupations and daily life. The dangers of losing hold of concrete reality have long been recognized in education (cf. Judd, 1925) and 21st century students need to be able to move intelligently between dealing with abstractions and dealing with the concrete realities to which those abstractions relate.
3. **Complexity.** Homer-Dixon (2000, 2006) has made the case that complexity itself is becoming a formidable barrier to solving the world's most serious problems. There is both a material increase in the complexity of the interac-tions composing a problem and an increase in the complexity of the knowl-edge that bears on it; in practice they come to the same thing, difficulty in

marshaling sufficient "ingenuity" (Homer-Dixon's term) to solve the problem. This is true of the whole range of problems from global warming and international conflict to deciding what to eat and whether to send one's toddler to day care. We may put it as axiomatic that any educational approach to 21st century needs is inadequate if it fails to deal with the understanding and management of complexity.

Twenty-first century skill lists—the main examples of which are reviewed by Binkley et al. (2012)—fall short on all three of these counts. Teaching creativity is quite likely a futile response to the need for knowledge creation as a personal or societal value. Ability to deal with abstract representations, except perhaps as a media skill, is largely ignored despite the fact that it is central to modern STEM instruction, especially mathematical modeling. As for addressing the increasing complexity of problems, complexity is just beginning to make it into the discourse on 21st century skills.

The movement to test and teach 21st century skills has been mainly driven and funded by big businesses. There is nothing intrinsically wrong with this, but even if we allow that business executives know what their company's needs are, and even if they draw on outside experts for help, it does not follow that they know how the schools should address them. Beyond political objections that may be raised about the heavy involvement of the corporate sector in identifying 21st century education needs, the whole top-down way of identifying objectives and methods warrants criticism. Is any group of stakeholders, no matter how representative of the public interest, qualified to sit around a table and define skill objectives for 21st century education? Shouldn't there be room for discovery, based on what young people are able to accomplish under favorable conditions? In a report prepared for one of the 21st century skills projects, Scardamalia, Bransford, Kozma, & Quellmalz (2012) argued that in a project with such forward-looking aspirations, the traditional working-backward-from-goals approach ought to be augmented by provisions for the discovery of new needed competencies and new opportunities for advancing the state of the art in education, rather than supposing that these can all be identified in advance. In order to discover new competencies, however, there need to be educational environments in which new competencies and new advances have a chance to emerge. The authors proposed a systemic approach containing various feedback loops enabling qualitative and not just quantitative shifts at all levels of the policy-maker to practitioner to learner hierarchy.

The role of project-based learning and knowledge building

The 21st century skills movement has two faces as far as curriculum development is concerned. One is the skills face, with skills tests driving movement toward activities that have skill learning as their main purpose. The other face is development of intellectually live content needing a richer conception of knowledge to provide the needed foundation.

Around the world educators are looking to project-based learning to address both skill and content needs. While there are many instances of old-fashioned projects, which consist of collecting information on a topic and presenting it in a form similar to that of an encyclopedia article, modern project-based learning differs from this in that it is usually collaborative and concerned with a question rather than a topic (Krajcik & Blumenfeld, 2006). Claims that such projects simultaneously build subject knowledge and develop 21st century skills are common; for instance "Projects that have depth, duration, and complexity will challenge students and motivate them towards construction of knowledge. They will acquire problem-solving, communication, collaboration, planning, and self-evaluation skills" (4 Teachers, n.d.).

Where does project-based learning stand with respect to the distinctive 21st century educational needs noted earlier: knowledge creation, abstractness, and complexity? This question can best be answered by looking at examples. Two typical, popular, and widely advocated projects are planning a trip to Mars and evaluating water purity in an actual stream. The first mimics and the second actually engages with a real-world problem. Both have considerably more duration and complexity than conventional classroom units of study, and with suitable teacher guidance they can go into topics in some depth. In carrying out their projects, students may incidentally acquire a lot of worthwhile knowledge, but knowledge creation in the sense of inventing something or producing a theory is not typical. As regards complexity, planning a trip to Mars, when carried out as an elementary or middle school project, can be as simple as planning a vacation trip. A flowing stream is a highly complex ecosystem, but in a structured project investigating water quality students may get no glimpse of this complexity, unless a teacher fills the void. Planning a trip to Mars can engage students with a great variety of knowledge about the solar system, space travel, rocketry, and human biology (similarly, planning a vacation trip can engage students with a variety of geographical and touristic and possibly some health and historical knowledge). Doing an environmental assessment of a stream and its water purity can involve a good deal of biological and some chemical knowledge and perhaps information about industrial processes and government regulations as well. But the "big ideas" in the relevant domains of knowledge, if they are touched on at all, are typically introduced by the teacher using traditional means and do not themselves become objects of inquiry.

Compared to the examples just cited, project-based learning can be upgraded in conceptual content and emphasis on understanding (Krajcik & Shin, 2014). It could be further upgraded to include more knowledge creation, more negotiation between abstract and concrete representations, and more coming to grips with systemic complexity. Instead of relying on "guided discovery" supplemented by conventional instruction, there could be projects in which *big ideas themselves are made the objects of inquiry*. But if project-based learning is upgraded in these ways it ceases to be project-based learning as commonly understood and instead becomes Knowledge Building—an approach in which production of community knowledge and sustained creative work with ideas are paramount (Scardamalia, 2002; Scardamalia & Bereiter, 2006, 2014b).

Acculturating students to a knowledge-creating society

Early in this chapter we contrasted a thinking skills approach with a cultural approach, to which we applied the term "acculturation." In anthropology, "acculturation" refers to initiating people (immigrants, usually) into a culture that is new to them. This is the meaning we intend here. Although the culture of knowledge creation is spreading worldwide, in developing as well as developed nations, for most children (and most teachers) it is a foreign culture. Surveys of epistemological beliefs indicate that students, teachers, and the public in general see the growth of knowledge as the unproblematic accumulation of facts (Carey & Smith, 1993; Windschitl, 2004). At the same time the public believes science will find technical solutions to problems of global warming, supergerms, and internet crime. Education for the 21st century will have failed—arguably is failing—if it can do no better than tool up test-defined skills.

If neither the students or the teacher are already socialized into a knowledge-creating culture, then the only way to get to it is either by guidance from on high, which is generally not available, or by some form of bootstrapping. The best explanation of bootstrapping we have found was retrieved from fusionanomaly.net/bootstrapping.html:

> Bootstrapping is the problem of starting a certain system without the system already functioning. It seems just as impossible as "pulling oneself up by the bootstraps" which Baron Münchhausen, according to stories, could do. However, solutions, accordingly called bootstrapping, exist: they are processes whereby a complex system emerges by starting simply and, bit by bit, developing more complex capabilities on top of the simpler ones.

There is no tested procedure for what amounts to cultural bootstrapping. There is reading good books, which was the way Abraham Lincoln and people like him made their own way into learned society; it also figures prominently in Bertrand Russell's advice on teaching children to think. But modern constructivist thought suggests a more active approach (which is not to deny that one can read a book or listen to a lecture in an intellectually active and creative manner). This has given rise to project-based learning, guided discovery, and other approaches that engage learners in actually *doing* something of an educationally proactive nature—that is, going out after knowledge instead of waiting for knowledge to come to them. Our concern is that while these approaches engage students in doing things that produce learning, the actual work of a knowledge-creating culture remains on the other side of the schoolyard wall. To some a knowledge-creating culture is to be repudiated and avoided. "Populism" is the current name for a backlash against knowledge-based institutions, privilege, and Enlightenment values in general. But probably for most people a knowledge-creating culture is remote and little understood; for those engaged it tends to be a great enhancer of life goals and well-being. Research on Knowledge Building (see, for instance, Scardamalia & Egnatoff, 2010) has shown that authentic knowledge creation and work on idea improvement can be brought into the classroom with considerable benefit for students and teachers. Teachers play a valuable role as fellow bootstrappers who have more knowledge and may have more relevant experience than their students. Their main contribution as far as acculturation is concerned is to engage with students in shaping a community centered on goals, values, and practices of a knowledge-creating culture and having these inform their daily interactions around knowledge and ideas.

References

4Teachers.org. (n.d.) Project based learning: Building motivation. Web document. Retrieved April 1, 2017, from http://pblchecklist.4teachers.org/more.shtml

Anderson, L. W., & Krathwohl, D. R. (Eds.). (2001). *A taxonomy for learning, teaching and assessing: A revision of Bloom's taxonomy of educational objectives: Complete edition*. New York, NY: Longman.

Binkley, M., Erstad, O., Herman, J., Raizen, S., Ripley, M., Miller-Ricci, M., & Rumble, M. (2012). Defining twenty-first century skills. In B. McGaw & E. Care (Eds.), *Assessment and teaching of 21st century skills* (pp. 17–66). New York, NY: Springer.

Bloom, B. S. (Ed.). (1956). *Taxonomy of educational objectives: Handbook 1. Cognitive domain*. New York, NY: David McKay Company.

Bransford, J. D., & Donovan, S. (Eds.). (2005). *How students learn: History, science, and mathematics in the classroom*. Washington, DC: National Academies Press.

Bransford, J. D., & Schwartz, D. (1999). Rethinking transfer: A simple proposal with multiple implications. *Review of Research in Education, 25*, 61–100.

Bransford, J. D., Brown, A. L., & Cocking, R. R. (Eds.). (1999). *How people learn: Brain, mind, experience, and school*. Washington, DC: National Academies Press.

Brookhart, S. (2010). *How to assess higher-order thinking skills in your classroom*. Alexandria, VA: ASCD.

Carey, S., & Smith, C. (1993). On understanding the nature of scientific knowledge. *Educational Psychologist, 28*(3), 235–251.

Chase, W. G., & Ericsson, K. A. (1982). Skill and working memory. In G. H. Bower (Ed.), *The psychology of learning and motivation* (Vol. 16, pp. 1–58). New York, NY: Academic Press.

Cramond, B., Matthews-Morgan, J., Bandalos, D., & Zuo, L. (2005). A report on the 40-year follow-up of the Torrance Tests of Creative Thinking: Alive and well in the new millennium. *Gifted Child Quarterly, 49*(4), 283–291.

Detterman, D. K., & Sternberg, R. J. (Eds.). (1993). *Transfer on trial: Intelligence, cognition, and instruction* (pp. 99–167). Norwood, NJ: Ablex.

Ericsson, K. A., & Chase, W. G. (1982). Exceptional memory. *American Scientist, 70*, 607–615.

Gardner, H. (1999). *The disciplined mind: What all students should understand*. New York, NY: Simon & Schuster.

Homer-Dixon, T. (2000). *The ingenuity gap*. New York, NY: Random House.

Homer-Dixon, T. (2006). *The upside of down: Catastrophe, creativity and the renewal of civilization*. Toronto: Knopf Canada.

Johnmar, F. (2013). The rise of just-in-time information systems. Retrieved April 18, 2017, from www.mediapost.com/publications/article/203009/the-rise-of-just-in-time-information-systems.html

Johnson, P. (2009). The 21st century skills movement. *Educational Leadership, 67*(1), 11–11.

Judd, C. H. (1925). Language as a higher form of reaction. *Elementary School Journal, 25*(5), 335–345.

Kolodner, J. L. (2006). Case-based reasoning. In K. Sawyer (Ed.), *Cambridge handbook of the learning sciences* (pp. 225–242). New York, NY: Cambridge University Press.

Krajcik, J. S., & Blumenfeld, P. C. (2006). Project-based learning. In R. K. Sawyer (Ed.), *The Cambridge handbook of the learning sciences* (pp. 317–334). New York, NY: Cambridge University Press.

Krajcik, J. S., & Shin, N. (2014). Project-based learning. In K. Sawyer (Ed.), *Cambridge handbook of the learning sciences* (2nd ed., pp. 275–297). New York, NY: Cambridge University Press.

Lipman, M. (1988). *Philosophy goes to school*. Philadelphia, PA: Temple University Press.

Liu, A. (2012). *This is not a book: Transliteracies and long forms of digital attention*. Paper presented at the Translittératies Conference, ENS Cachan, Paris, 7 November 2012. Retrieved from www.academia.edu/2774081/This_is_Not_a_Book

McKeough, A., Lupart, J., & Marini, A. (Eds.). (1995). *Teaching for transfer: Fostering generalization in learning* (pp. 21–34). Mahwah, NJ: Lawrence Erlbaum Associates.

Maulik, P. (2010). Ideas are the easy part. StrategyDriven blog. Retrieved from www.strategydriven.com/2010/02/17/ideas-are-the-easy-part/

Mayer, R. E., & Wittrock, M. C. (2006). Problem solving. In P. A. Alexander & P. H. Winne (Eds.), *Handbook of educational psychology* (2nd ed., pp. 287–303). Mahwah, NJ: Lawrence Erlbaum Associates.

Newell, A., & Rosenbloom, P. S. (1981). Mechanisms of skill acquisition and the law of practice. In J. R. Anderson (Ed.), *Cognitive skills and their acquisition* (pp. 1–55). Hillsdale, NJ: Lawrence Erlbaum Associates.

Nietzsche, F. W. (2007). *Twilight of the idols with the antichrist and Ecce Homo*. Hertfordshire: Wordsworth Editions Limited (original work published in 1889).

Piirto, J. (2004). *Understanding creativity*. Scottsdale, AZ: Great Potential Press.

Quammen, D. (1996). *The song of the dodo*. New York, NY: Scribner.

Resnick, L. B., & Klopfer, L. E. (Eds.). (1989). *Toward the thinking curriculum: Current cognitive research*. Alexandria, VA: Association for Supervision and Curriculum Development.

Sawyer, R. K. (Ed.). (2006). *Cambridge handbook of the learning sciences*. Cambridge: Cambridge University Press.

Sawyer, R. K. (Ed.). (2014). *Cambridge handbook of the learning sciences* (2nd ed.). Cambridge: Cambridge University Press.

Scardamalia, M. (2002). Collective cognitive responsibility for the advancement of knowledge. In B. Smith (Ed.), *Liberal education in a knowledge society* (pp. 67–98). Chicago, IL: Open Court.

Scardamalia, M., & Bereiter, C. (2006). Knowledge building: Theory, pedagogy, and technology. In K. Sawyer (Ed.), *Cambridge handbook of the learning sciences* (pp. 97–118). New York, NY: Cambridge University Press.

Scardamalia, M., & Bereiter, C. (2014a). Education in an open informational world. In R. Scott & S. Kosslyn (Eds.), *Emerging trends in the social and behavioral sciences*. Wiley Online Library. doi: 10.1002/9781118900772

Scardamalia, M., & Bereiter, C. (2014b). Knowledge building and knowledge creation: Theory, pedagogy, and technology. In K. Sawyer (Ed.), *Cambridge handbook of the learning sciences* (2nd ed., pp. 397–417). New York, NY: Cambridge University Press.

Scardamalia, M., & Egnatoff, W. (Eds.). (2010). *Canadian Journal of Learning and Technology, Special Issue on Knowledge Building*. *36*(1). Retrieved December 18, 2017 from www.cjlt.ca/index.php/cjlt/issue/current

Scardamalia, M., Bransford, J., Kozma, R., & Quellmalz, E. (2012). New assessments and environments for knowledge building. In P. Griffin, B. McGaw, & E. Care (Eds.), *Assessment and teaching of 21st century skills* (pp. 231–300). New York, NY: Springer Science+Business Media B.V.

Schallert, D. L. (1982). The significance of knowledge: A synthesis of research related to schema theory. In W. Otto & S. White (Eds.), *Reading expository prose* (pp. 13–48). New York, NY: Academic Press.

Swartz, R. J. (1987). Teaching for thinking: A developmental model for the infusion of thinking skills into mainstream instruction. In B. B. Joan & R. J. Sternberg (Eds.), *Teaching thinking skills: Theory and practice* (pp. 106–126). New York, NY: W. H. Freeman and Co.

Swartz, R. J., & Parks, S. (1994). *Infusing the teaching of critical and creative thinking into content instruction*. Pacific Grove, CA: Critical Thinking and Software.

Wegerif, R. (2010). *Mind expanding: Teaching for thinking and creativity in primary education*. Maidenhead: Open University Press.

Weisberg, R. W. (1999). Creativity and knowledge: A challenge to theories. In R. J. Sternberg (Ed.), *Handbook of creativity* (pp. 226–250). New York, NY: Cambridge University Press.

Whitehead, A. N. (1929). *The aims of education*. New York, NY: Macmillan.

Windschitl, M. (2004). Folk theories of "inquiry": How preservice teachers reproduce the discourse and practices of an atheoretical scientific method. *Journal of Research in Science Teaching, 41*(5), 481–512.

6

A DIALOGIC THEORY OF TEACHING THINKING

Rupert Wegerif

Introduction

The growing recent movement for dialogic education overlaps with the project of teaching thinking. Philosophy for Children, for example (see Kerslake, Chapter 4, this volume), is both an excellent example of dialogic education and also, according to evaluations, one of the most effective stand-alone approaches to teaching for general and transferable thinking skills.[1] Dialogic education programmes that integrate thinking through dialogue within the curriculum such as Thinking Together and Alexander's approach of Dialogic Teaching are clearly intended to promote general thinking strategies, skills and dispositions as well as any other goals that they might have such as oracy skills and curriculum learning. Recent surveys of evaluation studies in the area have even suggested that dialogic education might be the most effective way of teaching for general thinking skills and dispositions (Clarke, Howley, Resnick, & Rose, 2016; Resnick, Asterhan, & Clarke, 2015; Resnick & Schantz, 2015). However, if we take the dialogic theory that lies behind dialogic education seriously, then this has important implications for how we understand what thinking is and therefore what teaching thinking means. Thinking, or, more specifically the kind of socially valued thinking that many teachers and researchers want to promote in education, looks rather different through a dialogic theory lens than the kind of general thinking skills and dispositions originally aimed at by the teaching thinking movement. The idea of a discrete cognitive skill, for example, now becomes an aspect of situated dialogues and intellectual dispositions are translated as aspects of relationships within cultures. In this chapter I will explore what dialogic theory has to say about what it means to teach for thinking, looking first at what it has to say about learning and teaching in general, then about what it has to say about thinking and learning to think. Finally, I draw these different strands together into a coherent dialogic theory of how we can teach for thinking by opening, widening, deepening and sustaining dialogic spaces and dialogic space.

What is a dialogue?

Imagine if we were to get two robots – or chatterbots – each programmed to respond to words and categories of words with pre-prepared utterances and we made them interact, the results might look externally like a dialogue but it would not actually be one. Some so-called dialogues in social life can be a bit like that. It is quite possible for people to falsely claim 'we are having a dialogue' when they are just talking at each other or talking past each other. Fortunately we know when social interaction is not real dialogue because we all know the experience of engaging in a real dialogue. Real dialogues happen when people listen to each other and learn from each other. Real dialogues tend to feel exciting and enjoyable. One way to characterise real dialogues, so as to distinguish them from mere external interaction of the robot kind, is to point out that in a real dialogue shared thinking occurs such that it is not always possible to say who is thinking. One could say that in a real dialogue there is no longer just 'I am thinking' and 'you are thinking' but there is also the experience that 'we are thinking together'. But the idea of 'we' thinking might not be quite right; it might not even go far enough. The experience of dialogue, especially dialogue about a shared interest, can also be of a kind of thinking in general that takes hold of us both and carries us along further than we might have thought possible. Describing this experience Merleau-Ponty writes of a successful dialogue that:

> Life becomes ideas and the ideas return to life, each is caught up in the vortex in which he first committed only measured stakes, each is led on by what he said and the response he received, led on by his own thought of which he is no longer the sole thinker.
>
> *(Merleau-Ponty, 1964, p. 159; 1968, p. 119)*

I find the concept of entanglement as this has been developed in quantum theory useful as a way of thinking about what happens to voices in dialogue. Entanglement, perhaps the key defining concept of quantum physics (Schrödinger, 1935), occurs when pairs or groups of particles interact in ways such that the quantum state of each particle cannot be described independently of the others, even when the particles are separated by a large distance but instead, a quantum state must be described for the system as a whole. In dialogues voices become entangled.[2] And not just human voices but also objects and domains of knowledge can become entangled within dialogues.

One way to understand the entanglement involved in dialogues is through the kind of circularity of reference that Rommetveit refers to, quoting Barwise and Perry, as 'attunement to the attunement of the other' (Rommetveit, 1992). In communications theory, Rommetveit points out, messages go one-way from a sender to a receiver, whereas in a dialogue the process is more circular. The 'other' is always already on the inside of every utterance. This is because each utterance responds to what the other has said in a way intended to relate to the other. This model of dialogic inter-subjectivity through mutual attunement needs to be extended to include apparently non-human voices: the voice of mathematics for example. We know in education that an area of discourse like mathematics can appear external and static or can enter inside a learner to become a living voice (Cobb & Hodge, 2010).

Every theorist who can be referred to as dialogic addresses the entanglement aspect of dialogue, but each does so in different ways. Bakhtin explicitly links dialogue to learning through his concept of the 'internally persuasive discourse' (Bakhtin, 1981, p. 376). Authoritative discourse, he writes, remains 'outside' us and remains static in meaning. You either accept it or reject it but you can't engage with it. In contrast the internally persuasive word or discourse is one that enters inside you as if it was one of our own words; it is 'half ours half someone else's' and so it is able to reorganise our words from within and also to engender new words and new ideas.

In a similar way Buber contrasts the objectifying 'I-it' attitude that turns the other into an object with the 'I-thou' attitude that engages responsively with the subjectivity of the other. The 'I-thou' attitude leads to entanglement which Buber characterises with a spatial metaphor, the space between or simply 'the between' ('Zwischen', Buber, 1958). Buber extends the apparent inter-subjectivity of the I-thou relation to include relationships with non-human subjects such as 'God' and also non-human objects such as trees. This extension of dialogic relationships beyond human voices is found in Bakhtin, who remarked 'I hear voices in everything' and is important to educational dialogic theory (Bakhtin, 1986).

What is dialogic space?

Dialogic means seeing things (or feeling things or thinking things) from at least two points of view at once. Monologic means only acknowledging one correct point of view as if everything was visible all at once laid out flat on a table in front of us. It is only through entering into dialogue that ideas change and new perspectives can be taken on board. To enter into dialogue with each other, ideas need to move into a shared space where they can resonate together, merge in some ways, clash in others and stimulate the emergence of new ideas.[3] This shared space of mutual resonance is 'dialogic space' and without it there is no real dialogue and no real learning.

An article I wrote with Neil Mercer introduced the idea of dialogic space into our analysis of classroom talk (Wegerif & Mercer, 1997). The issue at the time was how to understand social cognition in the way in which the upper primary children (aged 8 to 11) were talking together in small groups. There seemed to be at least three significant types of talk: disputational talk when children disagreed with each other without giving reasons; cumulative talk when they agreed without reasons; and 'exploratory talk' when they genuinely engaged with each other's ideas.

We realised that each type of talk reflected an inter-subjective orientation related to a form of individual identification. In disputational talk children identified with their own self-image or ego and each wanted to be the one to win the game and get the answer and in cumulative talk children identified with their image of the group as a harmonious unit and so did not want to criticise. This seemed clear but then we asked ourselves, what is the form of identification involved with 'exploratory talk'? A key feature of exploratory talk is being able to change one's mind. The question then was, from what position is it that individual children are able to look at what they have said, find it wrong and so change their minds? This way of thinking about this practical issue led me to introduce the idea of identification with a 'space of dialogue' or 'dialogic space' as a key part of learning to think (Wegerif, 2007). Many years before this I had read and been inspired by Buber's 'I and Thou' (1958) and, although I was not fully aware of this at the time, I can now see that the idea of dialogic space opening up in classrooms is an applied version of Buber's concept of the 'Between'.

While Buber's 'Between' is always referred to as if it was an abstract notion, the idea of dialogic space has a material aspect. Dialogic spaces can be felt to open up and to close down at specific times that could potentially be recorded. We saw the material side of dialogic space recently in a classroom where a group of three upper primary children were arguing about a puzzle presented in a tablet. Not only did their body language converge on this central focus but so did their fingers. Each put their hand on the tablet to point out what they thought the key aspect of the puzzle was and how it could be solved through moving the pieces. Pretty soon it was clear that much of the shared thinking was being done by their fingers (Wegerif, Fujita, Doney, Linares, Richards, & Van Rhyn, 2017). When thinking becomes embodied in this way it occurs in a shared physical space and creates a shared dialogic space out of that shared physical space. Merleau-Ponty makes a similar point when he says of real dialogue, 'No one thinks any more, everyone speaks, all live and gesticulate within Being' (Merleau-Ponty, 1964, p. 159; 1968, p. 119). His point is that thought moves from the idea we might have that it is something individual occurring silently in separated brains to being something shared because it is audible in a shared space where the words and gestures and intonation and body language carries the shared thinking.

In this sense dialogic space is similar to the notion of a 'blended space'. 'Blended space' is a new term for using augmented reality to link objects in a physical space with digital objects in a digital space (Wu, Lee, Chang, & Liang, 2013). In augmented reality the blend is usually a simple match between physical space and digital space. A park bench in physical space might be blended with a Pokémon GO monster in virtual space such that, with the right glasses or smart phone, the monster can be seen sitting on the bench. In dialogic space the blend is more complex since it is between physical space-time on one side and on the other the open-ended cultural space of ideas where all ideas are embodied and all forms of embodiment can be read as ideas.

Let me explain dialogic space using a café table as an illustration. Before dialogic space opens up things tend to be thought of on the model of the ontology of identity (Wegerif, 2008). Identity ontology says that 'a thing is what it is and not another thing'. The pepper and salt pots plus cutlery on the café table are just pepper and salt pots plus cutlery. When dialogic space opens then material things, bodies, hands, voices, gestures, pixels on the screen, become signs for other things and representative of voices that are not present. Depending on the dialogue the pepper pot could become Lionel Messi scoring a goal for Barcelona, dribbling brilliantly around the salt pot and into a goal marked out by knives and forks, or the two pots could represent the relationship between a proton and a neutron in a deuterium atom surrounded by an electron cloud of scattered pepper on the table, or they could stand in for almost anything at all.

Although all dialogic spaces are unique due to their context they also share something in common which is the opening of the space itself. While in practice any given dialogic space might have a limited range of themes and probable outcomes, these cannot be determined in advance because, in principle, any real dialogue opens up the potential for infinite meaning. This is just another way of saying that the context that could be brought into any dialogue is unbounded. In practice the children might just mention references from the TV that they saw last night but in principle anything could be brought to bear on the problem at hand. I tend to refer to dialogic space rather than dialogic spaces in order to draw attention to this unity of the structure of dialogic space as always opening up unbounded contextual meaning within the diversity of specific contexts. But, of course, dialogic spaces are also all different in their physical location. The neologism of 'dialogic space(s)' would be the most accurate term with the singular 'space' referring to the unbounded ideas side of the blend and the plural 'spaces' to the physical, concrete side.

It is important to have a notion of dialogic space(s) or other cognate term in education (entanglement, dialogic flow, intertextuality, internal relations, etc.) to avoid the reduction of dialogic education to the hegemony of the external. I have read studies that refer to 'dialogic' in education in an entirely external way, coding each utterance and trying to pin everything down to the visible and tangible surface of things. This is a conceptual confusion. Dialogue is interesting because of its dialogic nature; to study it monologically excludes that essential aspect. The only reason dialogue works and is in fact necessary for learning is because it opens up an invisible space of potential in which the logic of the surface – a logic where every identity is fixed and separated, in its proper place – becomes turned inside out such that the surface becomes richly resonant. In real dialogue you are part of me, I am part of you and we together are part of the surrounding world. Each of our words then has the potential to resonate in an unbounded way and so to bring new aspects of reality into visibility for us and perhaps also to bring them into being where they did not exist before as nameable differences.

What is thinking?

Defining thinking is inevitably difficult because thinking is already implied behind the action of defining. The task of understanding thinking is a bit like a short cartoon I recall watching as a child in which the Pink Panther sucks himself up entirely in a vacuum cleaner that he himself is holding – this sucking yourself up in your own vacuum cleaner move is not really possible but we enjoy imagining it as if it was possible.

When people write and talk about 'teaching thinking' they do not just mean teaching any and all types of thinking because some thinking is obviously quite bad. They mean teaching 'good thinking' which they might call 'intelligence' or 'higher order thinking' or some other technical sounding term which always really translates most accurately as 'the kind of thinking that we do not think we see enough of and that we want to see more of'. Since this idea of good thinking is dependent on a social context, one sensible research strategy to find out more about good thinking is simply to ask many people how they understand this concept. In the 1980s Lauren Resnick chaired a US Government inquiry into teaching thinking in the USA and asked many expert teachers what they understood by 'Higher Order Thinking' of the kind that they wanted to teach. The phrases Higher Order Thinking and Higher Order Thinking Skills come from Bloom's taxonomy (Bloom, Engelhart, Furst, Hill, & Krathwohl, 1956) where 'higher' skills such as evaluation and synthesis were separated from 'lower' skills such as 'memory' and 'reading'. There is no good research basis for this distinction but in this study Resnick is not really using Higher Order in any technical sense, she simply uses it in a way that refers to the kind of thinking we value and want to teach. She concluded that Higher Order Thinking was hard to define in advance because it was surprising. In her final report she wrote: Thinking skills resist the precise forms of definition we have come to associate with the setting of specified objectives for schooling. Nevertheless, it is relatively easy to list some key features of higher order thinking. When we do this, we become aware that, although we cannot define it exactly, we can recognize higher order thinking when it occurs. The following are all characteristics of Higher Order Thinking made by Resnick:

- Higher order thinking is non-algorithmic. That is, the path of action is not fully specified in advance. Higher order thinking tends to be complex. The total path is not "visible" (mentally speaking) from any single vantage point.
- Higher order thinking often yields multiple solutions, each with costs and benefits, rather than unique solutions.
- Higher order thinking involves nuanced judgment and interpretation.
- Higher order thinking involves the application of multiple criteria, which sometimes conflict with one another.
- Higher order thinking often involves uncertainty. Not everything that bears on the task at hand is known.
- Higher order thinking involves imposing meaning, finding structure in apparent disorder.

(Resnick, 1987)

Resnick was referring to thinking as something that individuals do when she wrote these criteria, in keeping with the dominant assumptions of the cognitive psychology of that time in the USA, but it is noticeable that these points could equally apply to dialogues as defined by Bakhtin.

In order to try to account for the nature and origin of the complex and surprising thinking that we value and want to teach more of, dialogic theory puts forward the metaphor of thinking as embodied dialogue. This metaphor is offered not in order to replace all the other possible metaphors but in order to add a useful new voice to the ongoing dialogue. Educational research has confirmed that the metaphor of thinking as dialogue is a fruitful one. This metaphor lies behind programmes that have been successful at teaching thinking. Bakhtin's clarification that dialogue occurs when answers give rise to new questions suggests that the dialogue we refer to is not just interaction but those kinds of dynamic relationships in which there is mutual illumination across a gap of difference.

Considering what is wrong with existing and previous metaphors for thinking in cognitive psychology can help us to understand the potential value of the metaphor of thinking as dialogue. I am thinking here of behaviourism's metaphor of thinking as 'nothing but talking to ourselves' producing sub-vocalisations that can be measured as behaviour (Watson, 1958); or the metaphor of thinking as nothing but information processing using a machine code programming language which Pinker referred to as 'mentalese' (Pinker, 1999); and now the new metaphor of thinking as nothing but neural activity in the brain. These various metaphors or lenses have all proved insightful in different ways. The problems with them arise from their tendency to be taken up as 'nothing but' theories. Dialogic theory says that, where we really do not know something, and there are good reasons why we should not pretend to ever completely understand thinking, then the 'truth' is unlikely to be found in any one metaphor; but truth as an aim is more likely to be advanced by having a range of different metaphors in dialogue with each other. This is the polyphonic version of truth put forward by Bakhtin, truth as a direction tended towards by a dialogue of multiple perspectives and not as something that can be found in a single voice (Bakhtin, 1981). This is also the epistemology of transdisciplinarity in science – the idea that the truth is not normally the product of increasing rigour in applying a single model but, on the contrary, truth is often best found in flashes of insight that occur across and between different models, metaphors or, more generally, different points of view (Nowotny, 2004).

Some might challenge applying the metaphor of dialogue to thinking by saying that some individual thinking is done alone and in silence. However, there are good reasons to think that this silent individual thinking takes the form of inner dialogue (Fernyhough, 2008). Sometimes this is obvious and we engage in an explicit dialogue between voices. At other times the inner dialogue is significantly transformed from outer dialogue, more abbreviated and grammatically much simplified but nonetheless with traces that indicate its origin in social interaction (Fernyhough, 2008).

Dialogue as a metaphor for thinking is both specific and general. Specifically it draws attention to and promotes real face-to-face dialogues in classrooms when the thinking is found in the speaking or the gestures and the movements of fingers together on a screen. More generally it offers a new way of thinking about the relationship between social dialogues and silent inner thought that others have previously imagined as non-dialogic or as quasi-mechanical operations in the brain of individuals. The way that small groups work together to solve problems and to pose problems is already thinking (Stahl, 2006; Woolley, Chabris, Pentland, Hashmi, & Malone, 2010). The way in which cultures, societies and communities respond to challenges and design together for a collective future is also thinking (cf. Dewey on the importance of 'social intelligence' 1993, p. 104).

Learning to think

According to Vygotsky, children learn to think as individuals by internalising cultural sign-tools that are first used in social interaction. Vygotsky claimed that children learnt the first sign, pointing, when they found that their reaching for a cup or a toy that they wanted led their mother to complete the gesture by giving them the cup or the toy. As Vygotsky argues, such 'sign-tools' are, at one and the same time, both external tools and internal cognitive tools guiding our cognitive activity (Vygotsky, 1987). More recent empirical research on how children learn to point suggests that Vygotsky was wrong. His account, while broadly on the right lines, misses out the essential dialogic element in learning to think or, as Tomasello puts it (2008), the important caveat that inter-subjective relationships have to precede signs and language.

Baron-Cohen conducted a series of studies on infants' first use of signs and he argues, from the evidence, that to understand the genesis of symbolising we need to distinguish between two kinds of pointing: just pointing to get what you want (proto-imperative) and pointing to draw another's attention to something (proto-declarative). The first kind of pointing, the kind Vygotsky referred to, does not imply inter-subjective awareness and so is not the beginning of language and of thinking. Baron-Cohen provides convincing evidence that autistic children have no trouble mastering 'proto-imperative' use of pointing to show that they want something even when they fail to master more communicative 'proto-declarative' use of pointing as a sign intended to direct another's interest (Baron-Cohen, 1994). The concern that the other understands the sign and has their attention appropriately directed is shown only when the child follows the eyes of the mother. The significance of this is that in order to use pointing as a sign it is necessary first to have a sense of the other person as someone with their own distinct perspective on the world. Thinking then, if we define this as intentional sign use, begins with drawing others to pay attention within a relationship while also being drawn to pay attention within a relationship. In other words thinking as symbolic sign use begins by being drawn out within a dialogic relationship (Bråten & Trevarthen, 2007).

The dialogic relationship behind thinking is characterised as much by difference as by unity. The unity can be found in the coupling of two entities following each other's eye gaze to judge each other's intentions. The difference is why things need to be pointed out by signs in the first place. It is because we do not understand each other and do not know what each other is thinking that we need to communicate and create spaces of partially shared meaning that are also spaces of thought.

One way of thinking about why using shared signs within relationships to direct each other's attention leads on to the kind of complex and nuanced thinking that Resnick described is through the idea of the superaddressee developed by Bakhtin (1981). This is the idea that having two perspectives on the world, one's own and someone else's, implies a third perspective, the perspective of the relationship itself or what Bakhtin referred to as the superaddressee or also as the witness position (1981). The child does not learn to see herself only by seeing herself reflected in the eyes of her mother; she learns to see herself from the perspective of her relationship with her mother. We can see this effect clearly if, when, playing alone with a toy car, the child says to itself 'Sarah can drive'. This is important to understanding how thinking is not just being called out in a specific relationship, for example a child's relationship with her mother, but also in relationship with a world or the outside in general. This outside point of view is really present in thinking in the form of an invisible dialogue partner. This world or outside point of view can sometimes seem to us as if it was a fixed context, as if we knew where and when the child was situated, but it does not strike the child as a fixed context but rather as a series of questions.

Good thinking of the kind we want to teach is creative. The emergence of creative thinking in imaginative play is described well by Hobson (2002) as an inevitable result of seeing things from two points of view in relationship. Once the child discovers that the same thing, perhaps a toy, can be seen in one way by the child and in another way by her mother, then it becomes possible to see the world as a set of perspectives or, as Bakhtin put it, to see voices in everything. A toothpick can become a javelin and a napkin can become a blanket for a doll. The world has a thousand voices and a thousand eyes. Universal metaphoricity is described by Merleau-Ponty as when every part of the world can become a total part from which to see and 'understand' the rest of the world. That advanced thinking also remains rooted in this more primordial experience of metaphoricity is now a widely accepted theory of thinking (Lakoff & Johnson, 2008).

But good thinking of the kind we want to teach also includes criticality which is about using judgement to select the good metaphors and reject the bad. Judgement begins in responsibility to others. First the child needs to explain herself to significant others such as her mother. She learns that she cannot say just anything, she learns which reasons for actions are accepted and which are not. The next key stage in learning to think is marked by the use of the term accountability in the successful educational programme 'Accountable Talk'. This is about accountability to standards of good thinking within a community. In learning to think for ourselves we create a fictitious dialogue partner which could be called 'what everybody thinks' – a personification that George Herbert Mead called 'the Generalised Other'. The Generalised Other is your community. It can tell you whether your thinking is good or bad and whether or not you are following the appropriate rules for thinking.

Creative thinking comes from discovering, out of our engagement in dialogic relationships, that everything and anything can be experienced as a kind of light or metaphor for illuminating the world. Critical thinking comes from internalising the judgements of others and seeing through the eyes of 'what everyone thinks' in order to select down from the infinite metaphoricity of things to the few pathways of meaning that are appropriate and useful to the context. On the whole what most people think of as being reasonable or being rational remains at this level of accountability to a community. But increasingly we find ourselves members of many communities and they do not always agree on what are and what are not the rules of good thinking. This leads to a certain responsibility to think beyond our community or an accountability to what Lingis (1994) calls 'the community of those who have absolutely nothing in common'. Adapting an idea from the French philosopher Levinas (1961), I have referred to this third aspect of learning to think as dialogue with the Infinite Other. The Infinite Other is not a thing or a real person but it manifests as a kind of voice that questions us and disrupts our certainty. For every community it is possible, if you listen closely enough, to hear a voice from outside the community challenging its claims to rationality. For every answer there is always a further question in an infinite regress. The innovation involved in the concept of the Infinite Other is the recognition of the phenomenological reality that this process of apparent infinite regress can manifest as if it was a voice in a dialogue.[4] This voice from the outside has been there from the beginning, from the moment the child learnt to say 'Sarah can drive a car'. It is always the most important voice to learn to listen to in learning how to think.

Teaching thinking

The word 'teach' comes from an old German root 'tæcan' which means to point out. Teaching is about pointing things out. It is only possible to point things out in the context of a relationship where you can follow my gaze and I can follow yours. So teaching involves first building a relationship and then directing the attention of students within the context of that relationship. If we want to teach thinking then the most important thing to point out is ignorance: just how much we do not know. Rather than simply being a model for ignorance, by asking questions a teacher can serve as a model for curiosity.

Teaching questioning

People might say that questions are always asked in a context and are always questions about something. I am not so sure. I think that, independent of any language or any sign system there is somehow always the archetypal question. Not a questioning of this or that but just a general questioning. This is perhaps what Heidegger meant with his 'fundamental question' which he expressed as 'why is there something rather than nothing?' But this fundamental question should not be verbally expressed, it is not a specific question, it is more of an attitude. This attitude is one of curiosity certainly but it is also one of humility. The point is that however much we think we know, we know that only within a context, the larger encompassing context of what we do not know, including the many things that we do not yet even know that we do not know. As we find out more about this context we will find that we have to re-interpret all the things that we think we know meaning that really we do not know anything at all for certain.

Whatever you point out to learners it is possible to point it out in a way that closes down the fundamental question or in a way that opens it up. Knowledge, as this is taught in schools, is only the dialogue so far meaning that it consists only of answers that have been given to questions that have been put. Teaching knowledge as the story of a dialogue leaves a space for the learners to enter into that ongoing dialogue themselves as thinkers able to ask further questions and so to find further answers. In this way anything and everything can be taught as an invitation to join a dialogue and so as an invitation to think (Langer, 2016).

Opening, widening and deepening dialogic space

Constructivist accounts of thinking tend to emphasise the positive ability to build models and systematically apply thinking tools (Holyoak & Morrison, 2015). A dialogic approach lays more stress on what the poet Keats referred to as 'negative capability' or the ability to remain in uncertainty until a creative solution emerges (Keats, 1817). The idea that we can teach teaching indirectly simply by opening a space for reflection can be illustrated by the extensive evidence on the value of introducing pauses into teacher–student interaction. Research has shown clearly that the quality of students' understanding of new concepts can be increased in classrooms simply by extending the length of time that teachers pause after asking a question and before expecting a response (Dillon, 1990). Simply pausing after asking a question is a good illustration of what it might mean in practice to teach thinking by opening a space.

The kind of talk moves promoted in dialogic education usually include asking open questions such as 'why do you think that?' Such moves do not work as positive tools to co-construct meaning but as a negative and indirect way to open a space for reflection and the resonance of multiple voices out of which a creative response might (or might not) emerge.

Opening a dialogic space begins with a relationship within which it is possible to shape the attention of the other. The opening teacher move is drawing attention to unknowing by asking a question or posing a challenge. In some cases this is drawing students into dialogue about immediately present objects or issues but in others it might be helping to graft them onto long-term dialogues of the culture so as to ask questions within a tradition, questions that will take the tradition further. Widening the space is asking everyone what they think and also actively seeking out a range of views perhaps by going to the Internet to find alternatives and to invite in different voices. Deepening the space is questioning the frame that has been assumed up to now, asking 'what are the assumptions that we have taken for granted? Are we sure that they are right? Could the whole area or issue be seen differently?'

Dialogic switch in perspective

In a dialogue we sometimes do not understand the other person's point of view initially and have to work to reconstruct it so that we can practise inhabiting it ourselves. This switch in perspective to facilitate understanding is not a once and for all switch, we do not lose our initial perspective in making the switch, but it is more about being able to hold different perspectives in tension together. The ease with which children can make this switch depends on the quality of their relationships. However nicely children talk together to ask each other questions and give each other reasons this will not automatically translate into insight unless they allow themselves to switch positions with other speakers. Such switches do not only occur with physically present voices and physically present tools but also with virtual cultural voices, for example the virtual voice of a 'generalised other' (Mead, 1934) or a 'superaddressee' (Bakhtin, 1981) position which might be that of, for example, the personified point of view of the community of scientists or the community of mathematicians (Kazak, Wegerif, & Fujita, 2015).

Identification with dialogue

Different ways of talking in classrooms are related to different kinds of identification (Wegerif & Mercer, 1997). Where children identify with themselves only and reject the other they might be prone to what Mercer calls 'disputational' talk (Mercer & Littleton, 2007) and what Habermas refers to as 'strategic' reason, which is reasoning that does not take the other seriously (Habermas, 1984). However when they identify strongly with their group they might be prone to what Mercer calls 'cumulative talk' and what is often referred to in psychology as 'group think' (see Brown, Chapter 7, this volume), which is when the harmony of the group prevents critical questioning and good reasoning. Issues of identification seem important to group thinking and one mechanism of successful dialogic thinking might be shifting that identification away from all static bounded objects, whether an image of the self or an image of the group, onto identification with the open-ended process of dialogue itself (Ligorio, 2010; Rajala & Kumpulainen, 2017; Wegerif, 2011).

Changing the culture

Many of the proposed mechanisms for understanding why dialogic education works are psychological, focussing on changes within individuals. But individuals are shaped within cultures. One way to understand this, informed by Rom Harré's positioning theory (Harré, 1999), is about how different cultural 'discourses' offer different 'speaker positions'. In standard classroom cultures, for example, students are often positioned as not being able to initiate dialogues. An element that is common to all dialogic education approaches is a concern to address behavioural norms directly by explicitly questioning old norms and teaching new norms or what Mercer calls 'ground rules'. These new ground rules or behavioural expectation in turn shape how individuals see themselves and their possibilities (Wegerif, 2002).

Teaching ground rules is a way of teaching thinking through changing the culture such that a different experience of individual agency is produced, an experience that is less egotistical, less tribal and more tolerant of uncertainty and multiplicity because it is open to learning from the others and from otherness.

Design for collective global intelligence

Thinking on the metaphor of dialogue is as real, if not more real, when conducted between people in small groups or in whole cultures than in the internalised form of silent individual thought. Designing the culture of classrooms to support small group dialogue is one way to teach thinking. Designing a global culture that thinks together better is another way.

Designing for social intelligence is a technical issue and a political issue as well as being an educational issue in the broad sense. Even if the dialogues of oral thinkers in oral societies are intelligent they do not tend to reach very far in their influence across space and time simply because they disappear almost as soon as they are spoken (Ong, 2013). We know that the dialogues of oral thinkers like Socrates, Gautama Buddha and Confucius were intelligent because their followers wrote them down. Because of the technology of literacy and because of mass education policies we have something that Oakeshott (1962) referred to as the 'Conversation of Mankind' and the associated ideal of education as joining this ongoing conversation or dialogue. Education in this sense depends upon technology, the technology of literacy, and so it is not surprising that schools focus so much on what has been called the 3 'R's = reading, writing and arithmetic. The advent of the Internet brings this ongoing dialogue of humanity into real-time. Through access to the Internet we can all potentially participate in global dialogues that respond to challenges and design the future together as well as building shared understanding and knowledge in every area. Realising this new potential for real-time global collective intelligence requires teaching thinking as a form of educational design. Literacy is a communications technology that does not work without education. Perhaps the same is true of dialogue mediated by the Internet. The Internet without supporting education into effective dialogue online could lead to increased stupidity and tribalism. The Internet with education might be the beginning of a new age: not so much a 'post truth' age as a 'new truth' age or an 'everyone involved in creating truth together' age.

Summary and conclusions

The metaphor of thinking as dialogue leads to an understanding of teaching thinking as drawing students into dialogue. This has some overlap with other models of teaching thinking and also some differences. It overlaps in seeking to produce thinking dispositions such as curiosity and thinking strategies such as asking questions and reasoning. The main differences stem from the understanding that dialogue between people and dialogues carried by media in society as a whole is already thinking such that silent inner thought is just a modality of this larger dialogue. One aspect of teaching thinking is to be concerned to teach individuals to think through internalising dialogue such that they end up carrying their own inner dialogic space around with them. But more than that a dialogic approach to teaching thinking is concerned to open, widen and deepen shared spaces of dialogue in the school classroom and beyond. A dialogic theory of teaching thinking suggests that it is important to teach cultures to think as well as individuals and ultimately to teach our increasingly global society to think. The project of teaching thinking through engaging students in dialogue therefore connects a focus on dialogues in classrooms to the design of educational technologies, including pedagogies, which will promote and sustain a more global dialogue.

Notes

1   Using skills here in the sense of a socially valued performance (Bailin, 1987).
2   This could just be a useful metaphor borrowed from another strand of science – or it might refer to a hypothesis about the nature of thought and of dialogues on the material level of analysis. Time will tell.
3   Ideas here are not assumed to be non-material but rather parts of the visible, tangible, audible world that turn back upon it to reflect it. Just like words and gestures, signs all have a material aspect.
4   This idea that an infinite regress can return as an active response to our question is also inspired by Hofstadter in his book, *Godel Escher Bach* (1979, p. 121). He refers to this as a strange loop and links it to the nature of consciousness (Hofstadter, 2007).

References

Bailin, S. (1987). Critical and creative thinking. *Informal Logic, 9*(1), 23–30.
Bakhtin, M. M. (1981). Discourse in the novel. In M. M. Bakhtin (Ed.), *The dialogic imagination. Four essays by M. M. Bakhtin* (pp. 259–422). Austin: University of Texas Press.
Bakhtin, M. M. (1986). *Speech genres and other late essays.* Austin: University of Texas.
Baron-Cohen, S. (1994). The mindreading system: New directions for research. *Current Psychology of Cognition, 13*, 724–750.
Bloom, B. S., Engelhart, M. D., Furst, E. J., Hill, W. H., & Krathwohl, D. R. (1956). *Taxonomy of educational objectives: The classification of educational goals. Handbook I: Cognitive domain.* New York: David McKay Company.
Bråten, S., & Trevarthen, C. (2007). Prologue: From infant intersubjectivity and participant movements to simulation and conversation in cultural common sense. In S. Bråten (Eds.), *On being moved: From mirror neurons to empathy* (pp. 21–34). Amsterdam: John Benjamins.
Buber, M. (1958). *I and Thou* (2nd ed., R. Gregory Smith, Trans.). Edinburgh: T. and T. Clark.
Clarke, S. N., Howley, I., Resnick, L., & Rose, C. P. (2016). Student agency to participate in dialogic science discussions. *Learning, Culture and Social Interaction.* http://dx.doi.org/10.1016/j.lcsi.2016.01.002
Cobb, P., & Hodge, L. L. (2010). Culture, identity, and equity in the mathematics classroom. In E. Yackel, K. Gravemeijer, & A. Sfard (Eds.), *A journey in mathematics education research* (pp. 179–195). Springer Netherlands.
Dewey, J. T. (1993). *The political writings.* Indianapolis, IN: Hackett Publishing.
Dillon, J. T. (1990). *The practice of questioning.* London: Taylor & Francis.
Fernyhough, C. (2008). Getting Vygotskian about theory of mind: Mediation, dialogue, and the development of social understanding. *Developmental Review, 28*(2), 225–262.
Habermas, J. (1984). *The theory of communicative action* (Vol. 1.). Cambridge: Polity Press.

Harré, R. (1999). *Positioning theory. The international encyclopedia of language and social interaction.* New York, NY: John Wiley and Sons.

Hobson, R. P. (2002). *The cradle of thought: Exploring the origins of thinking.* London: Macmillan.

Hofstadter, D. R. (1979). *Gödel, Escher, Bach: An Eternal Golden Braid.* New York: Basic Books.

Hofstadter, D. R. (2007). *I am a strange loop.* New York: Basic Books.

Holyoak, K. J., & Morrison, R. G. (2015). Introduction. In K. J. Holyoak & R. G. Morrison (Eds.), *The Cambridge handbook of thinking and reasoning* (pp. 1–13). Cambridge: Cambridge University Press.

Kazak, S., Wegerif, R., & Fujita, T. (2015). The importance of dialogic processes to conceptual development in mathematics. *Educational Studies in Mathematics, 90*(2), 105–120.

Keats, J. (1817). Letter to George and Thomas Keats. December, 28, 1817. Retrieved from https://en.wikisource.org/wiki/Letter_to_George_and_Thomas_Keats,_December_28,_1817

Lakoff, G., & Johnson, M. (2008). *Metaphors we live by.* Chicago: University of Chicago Press.

Langer, E. J. (2016). *The power of mindful learning.* Boston, MA: Da Capo Lifelong Books.

Levinas, E. (1961). *Totalité et Infini: essai sur l'extériorité.* Paris: Le Livre de Poche.

Ligorio, M. B. (2010). Dialogical relationship between identity and learning. *Culture & Psychology, 16*(1), 93–107.

Lingis, A. (1994). *The community of those who have nothing in common.* Bloomington, IN: Indiana University Press.

Mead, G. H. (1934). *Mind, self, and society* (Charles W. Morris, Ed.). Chicago, IL: University of Chicago Press.

Mercer, N., & Littleton, K. (2007). *Dialogue and the development of children's thinking: A sociocultural approach.* London: Routledge.

Merleau-Ponty, M. (1964). *Le Visible et L'Invisible.* Paris: Gallimard.

Merleau-Ponty, M. (1968). *The visible and the invisible.* Evanston, IL: Northwestern University Press.

Nowotny, H. (2004). The potential of transdisciplinarity. In H. Dunin-Woyseth & M. Nielsen (Eds.), *Discussing transdisciplinarity: Making professions and the new mode of knowledge production* (pp. 10–19). Oslo: The Nordic Reader, Oslo School of Architecture.

Oakeshott, M. (1962). The voice of poetry in the conversation of mankind, rationalism in politics and other essays. In M. Oakeshott (Ed.), *Rationalism in Politics and Other Essays* (pp. 197–247). London: Methuen.

Ong, W. J. (2013). *Orality and literacy.* Abingdon, UK and New York: Routledge.

Pinker, S. (1999). How the mind works. *Annals of the New York Academy of Sciences, 882*(1), 119–127.

Rajala, A., & Kumpulainen, K. (2017). Researching teachers' agentic orientations to educational change in Finnish schools. In M. Goller & S. Paloniemi (Eds.), *Agency at work: An agentic perspective on professional learning and development. Professional and practice-based learning* (Vol. 20, pp. 311–329). Cham: Springer. doi:10.1007/978-3-319-60943-0_16

Resnick, L. B. (1987). *Education and learning to think.* Washington, DC: National Academies.

Resnick, L. B., & Schantz, F. (2015). Re-thinking Intelligence: Schools that build the mind. *European Journal of Education, 50*(3), 340–349.

Resnick, L. B., Asterhan, C., & Clarke, S. (2015). *Socializing intelligence through academic talk and dialogue.* Washington, DC: American Educational Research Association.

Rommetveit, R. (1992). Outlines of a dialogically based social–cognitive approach to human cognition and communication. In A. Wold (Ed.), *The dialogical alternative: Towards a theory of language and mind* (pp. 19–45). Oslo: Scandinavian Press.

Schrödinger, E. (1935, October). Discussion of probability relations between separated systems. In *Mathematical proceedings of the Cambridge Philosophical Society* (Vol. 31, No. 4, pp. 555–563). Cambridge, UK: Cambridge University Press.

Stahl, G. (2006). *Group cognition: Computer support for building collaborative knowledge.* Cambridge, MA: MIT Press.

Tomasello, M. (2008). *Origins of human communication.* Cambridge, MA: MIT Press.

Vygotsky, L. S. (1987). Thinking and speech. In R. W. Rieber, & A. S. Carton (Eds.), *The collected works of L. S. Vygotsky (Vol. 1), Problems of general psychology* (pp. 39–285). New York: Plenum Press. (Original work published 1934.)

Watson, J. B. (1958). *Behaviorism*. New Brunswick, NJ: Transaction Publishers.

Wegerif, R. (2002). Walking or dancing? Images of thinking and learning to think in the classroom. *Journal of Interactive Learning Research, 13*(1), 51–70.

Wegerif, R. (2007). *Dialogic education and technology: Expanding the space of learning*. New York: Springer.

Wegerif, R. (2008). Dialogic or dialectic? The significance of ontological assumptions in research on educational dialogue. *British Educational Research Journal, 34*(3), 347–361.

Wegerif, R. (2011). Towards a dialogic theory of how children learn to think. *Thinking Skills and Creativity, 6*(3), 179–195.

Wegerif, R., & Mercer, N. (1997). A dialogical framework for investigating talk. In R. Wegerif & P. Scrimshaw (Eds.), *Computers and talk in the primary classroom* (pp. 49–65). Clevedon: Multilingual Matters.

Wegerif, R., Fujita, T., Doney, J., Linares, J. P., Richards, A., & Van Rhyn, C. (2017). Developing and trialling a measure of group thinking. *Learning and Instruction, 48*, 40–50.

Woolley, A., Chabris, C., Pentland, A., Hashmi, N., & Malone, T. (2010). Evidence for a collective intelligence factor in the performance of human groups. *Science, 330*, 686–688. doi:10.1126/science.1193147

Wu, H. K., Lee, S. W. Y., Chang, H. Y., & Liang, J. C. (2013). Current status, opportunities and challenges of augmented reality in education. *Computers & Education, 62*, 41–49.

7

LEARNING TO THINK COLLECTIVELY

A response to the wicked problems of our times

Valerie A. Brown

Context: collective knowledge

Responses to the current radical environmental and social change require changes in the ways in which we think. Since the risks to human lives are serious and continuing, planning legislation and social services are already taking account of the storm surge and floods of climate change; there is increasing urban violence in crowded cities; and a need for accommodation for countless millions of refugees (Millennial Ecosystem Assessment, 2005). To address these changes, teachers everywhere from primary to adult education, are faced with uncertainty and the need to use all of their minds in order to cover all aspects of accounts of each issue. Such a holistic way of thinking contrasts with that of the scientific era, with its objectivity and reduction of an issue into its parts (Drysek, 1997).

For all educators the changes mean that evidence relied on yesterday needs to be re-examined in the context of today. It also needs to take account of how things will be tomorrow. In embracing this complexity, all members of a society need the capacity to capture both the detail and the essence of the issues involved. They need to look beyond their own personal interests to include the diverse interests concerned with those issues (Bawden, 1998).

At present, in both schools and universities Western thinking is divided into compartments, each with its own way of approaching knowledge. Individuals, a community, relevant specialists, influential organisations and innovative thinkers of Western culture have each shaped their own form of thought, forming sub-cultures of knowledge (Berger & Luckmann, 1971; Brown, 2008). These interest groups are each asking different questions, drawing on different sources of evidence and compiling a different body of content (Brown & Lambert, 2013). Each rejects the other's ways of knowing by referring to individuals as biased, communities as only having anecdotes, specialists as talking in jargon, organisations as self-interested and holistic thinking as airy-fairy.

Traditionally, in this divided thinking, each group tackles only one aspect of complexity, relies on its own observations, works within established frameworks and accepts the primacy of objective thinking (Toulmin, 1972). This reduces the complexity of an issue and makes it easier to find a part-solution. On the other hand, it separates an issue from its changing context, and trains its members in their own mode of compartmentalised thinking (Chalmers, 1994).

Responses to changing events are currently based in the different modes of decision-making in each of the knowledge sub-cultures. In realising that these sub-cultures are socially determined, it becomes clear that decision-making on complex issues will continue with modes of thinking suited to technological solutions of the past. Since many of the social and environmental changes are due to the activities of one species, our era has been labelled the Anthropocene, a human-centred world.

Ways of addressing issues of the Anthropocene will include the need to tackle wicked problems (Brown, Harris, & Russel, 2014). A wicked problem is defined as one that can only be resolved by changes in the society that generated it. It is wicked in that it resists ready-made solutions and requires a different form of hard thinking. The originators of the work on wicked problems, Rittel & Webber (1973), commented that, while problems such as these are not morally wicked, it would be morally wicked to treat them as tame problems with predetermined answers. The characteristics of wicked problems have been comprehensively examined in the development programme of the Australian Public Service Commission (APSC, 2007). For this paper, each item has been linked to initiatives in ways of thinking about the whole, as follows:

- Wicked problems hold multiple interpretations from multiple interests, with no one version completely right or completely wrong (Transdisciplinarity – drawing on the disciplines and beyond) (Funtowicz & Ravetz, 1990).
- Wicked problems are multi-causal with many interdependencies, requiring trade-offs between conflicting goals (Systems thinking – everything is connected to everything else) (Ison, 2008).
- Wicked problems are often unstable; problem-solvers are forced to adjust to a moving target (Resilience thinking – the capacity to respond positively to change) (Walker & Salt, 2006).
- Wicked problems rarely sit conveniently within any one person, discipline or organisation, making it difficult to identify responsibility (Triple Loop Learning – learning from previous learning) (Churchman, 1979).
- Each wicked problem is unique in that it is a product of time, place and people; ways of learning can be transferred from one wicked problem to another, but solutions cannot (Experiential learning – learning from practice) (Kolb, 1984).

The learning experiences of transdisciplinarity, systems thinking, resilience thinking, triple loop learning and experiential learning appear in everyday life as embracing insight while coping with learning to live with change. They each aim to address the whole of a wicked problem. There is considerable overlap between their introductions to the multiple ways of individual thinking. Taken together the learning programmes draw attention to significant relationships among human ways of thinking, linking the biophysical, social, ethical, creative and sympathetic understanding (Brown & Harris, 2014). Together these ways of thinking form a practical foundation for *collective thinking*.

Issue: divided knowledges

Rittel and Webber's work follows the quip attributed to Einstein 'You cannot solve a complex problem through the same thinking that created it'. Nowhere is this more evident than in the usual school curriculum, with its division into geography, history, literature and science. Work on wicked problems has taken on many fresh ways of thinking, not only in educational innovation, also in cutting-edge information systems, engineering designs and systems thinking (Rittel, 1972). Wicked problems typically incorporate multiple ethical positions, multiple world views and multiple ways of constructing knowledge: the three foundations of an open critical inquiry. In responding to simple problems, the approach is usually to hold one form of world view and applying one type of knowledge. While social and environment aspects of an issue are usually addressed, the ethical, creative and sympathetic perspectives of an issue are rarely examined at all (Drysek, 1997).

Previously, the learning task has been to work within the traditional divided and socially bounded knowledge sub-cultures of individual, community, specialised and organisational knowledge (Brown, 2008). The change to multiple ways of individual thinking about change requires a different construction of the task. No longer is an inquiry into a wicked problem the sole responsibility of one specialist discipline or profession.

The learning programmes, described above in relation to wicked problems, and the evidence collected in the Local Sustainability Project, identified the multiple ways of thinking needed to resolve wicked problems. While there is a shared understanding between the interests at the end, the findings of a collective inquiry are not expected to be final, certain or complete, just the best possible for the time (Rittel, 1972).

The contrasts between the bounded knowledge sub-cultures and open-ended multiple ways of thinking are significant. The sub-cultures are socially determined groups, while multiple ways of thinking are at the discretion of an individual. This approach to wicked problems draws on the multiple ways of thinking of which each human mind is capable, in other words, *collective thinking* in an individual, and then in groups (Midgely, 1995).

Reflection on the evidence presents the greatest challenge for would-be collective thinkers. After so many generations of specialised thinking, the challenge is just beginning to make its presence felt. Imagination, creativity, intuition are invaluable uses of the mind to support the final leap. Ever since the dawn of the scientific era more than 300 years ago, access to these abilities have been denied to scientists. Scientists have been told that all valid scientific evidence must be reliable, repeatable and reproducible. That is, they must be able to repeat their investigation with the same methods and get the same results, and other scientists must be able to reproduce the results for themselves (Funtowicz & Ravetz, 1990).

This may work for physical experiments under conditions of control in a laboratory. The minute the inquiry goes into the field, the conditions cannot be held constant. When biological systems are added to the evidence, the living forms initiate mutual feedback systems which need to be taken into account. Once the inquiry involves human beings, issues of choice and learning come into play.

In becoming transdisciplinary and introducing multiple sources of evidence, there is still the challenge of conveying the collective understanding to the wide range of interested parties. Under present conditions, each of the contributing interests is likely to rely on only one of the sources of evidence, and use only the terms associated with that source, often condemned as using jargon. In collective thinking, there will be different languages. Biophysical inquiry speaks in numbers; social inquiry uses narrative; ethical inquiry applies principles; creativity produces artefacts; and sympathy evokes emotions. In collective thinking, while all the ways of thinking are of equal importance, the response to an issue may start with any one.

Social pressures turn the knowledges into a hierarchy. Specialised thinking is treated as superior to community knowledge. Organisational knowledge carries more weight than individual knowledge (Ralston Saul, 1992). However, collective ways of thinking accept that all ways of thinking are equal – each with its own mode of inquiry and type of evidence. Implicitly or explicitly, every human being accesses the multiple ways of individual thinking for every important decision. Interpreting the relationships among multiple ways of thinking is an underlying principle of collective learning.

Collective learning asks a different type of question from any of the specialist disciplines. The philosopher John Passmore (1980) differentiates between questions of ecology and ecological questions. In the first, an inquirer perceives their task as adding to the knowledge base of the discipline of ecology. In the second, the aim of the inquiry is to unravel a complex problem, such as climate change. While the trigger may be ecological, the effect is on all aspects of the socio-environmental system. A tame problem addresses a question to a single discipline, while a wicked problem is approached through multiple ways of thinking.

A key issue for the next generation is to find a way of thinking that can address the environmental and social changes already under way. The hurdles that stand in the way are the compartmentalised forms of knowledge that are the inheritance of the scientific era, and the competitiveness that accompanies them. The barriers to addressing wicked problems holistically are part of that inheritance. On the other hand, the use of multiple ways of thinking has already been established in education, change management, environmental management and the professions in general (World Commission on Dams, 2000), so there is hope.

Resolution: collective thinking

> No man is an island, entire of itself...any man's death diminishes me, because I am involved in all mankind. So never send to ask for whom the bell tolls. It tolls for thee.
>
> (Donne, 1967 [1607])

Collaborative action research was the research method employed by the Local Sustainability Project of the National University 1990–2015. The first phase of the inquiry explored the characteristics of the socially constructed knowledge subcultures which have proved a barrier to collective thinking (Brown, 2008). The second phase of the inquiry developed a framework and a set of questions for collective learning from over 200 councils and community organisations. Since 2010 the Project has conducted training programmes for those wishing to use collective learning methods. The learning framework was an adaptation of David Kolb's work on individual experiential learning, extended to incorporate collective learning (Kolb, 1984). The details of applying this framework and 16 case studies can be found in *Collective learning for transformational change: a guide to collaborative action* (Brown & Lambert, 2014).

The inquiry found that the individuals in the second study tackled their wicked problems from multiple ways of thinking. The ways of thinking were the same set as in the learning programmes responding to wicked problems: biophysical, socio-economic, ethical, creative and sympathetic avenues of response. Since the research was collaborative, each source of evidence was regarded as equally important, not dominated by either the physical or the emotional, but taking account of each.

When an individual collective thinker contributes to a group, the group is likely to expand their approaches to resolving the topic. Such a multi-faceted response could be expected to harness the most resources and political support. It is worth noting that this is a completely different activity from those that lead to group-think. In group-think there is a single set of beliefs and one way of thinking, leading to an unshakable commitment to one answer. Examples of uncompromising group-think are the tragedies of collective suicide in Jonestown and the dictatorships that led to ethnic cleansing. The open processes of collective thinking are so very different from those of group-think, that in practice there is little room for confusion.

The example on collective thinking in individuals and in groups is drawn from a ten-year-long national project reclaiming Australia's degenerating land, Landcare. To best understand that example, there follows details of the multiple ways of thinking in theory and in practice. While the capacity for collective thinking is inherent in all human thinking, it is common for people to only be conscious of using one; the others may only be used unconsciously.

- **Biophysical thinking.** Exploring the material world. This is the world we can see, touch, measure. We have invented highly creative tools, telescopes, computers and mind maps, as extensions of the human mind. Numbers alone, without the other four ways of thinking, make little or no contribution to understanding or decision-making (Chalmers, 1994).

- **Socioeconomic thinking.** Exploring the social world. Every human society develops ways to make a living, talk, cook, count, build shelter, make artefacts, store resources, rear children and govern themselves. Humans are a social species. Socially based thinking covers the wide range of human activities that are taking place in every locality (Mills, 1970).

- **Ethical thinking**. Exploring the ethical world. Ethical thinking takes the form of what should be? How should we live? How should we treat each other? Every human community has a reference point for ethical rules; choosing between religion, agnosticism, humanism and mysticism. Every individual should be free to make that choice for themselves, even if shaped by their own society (Mackie, 1990).

- **Creative thinking.** Individuals differ widely in their choice of artistic expression, in art, music, movement and in their work. Creative thinking heightens the emotions, giving the thinker a 'high'. Outcomes of a project are described as 'a beautiful experiment', 'an elegant solution', 'a fantastic result' (Budd, 1998).

- **Sympathetic thinking.** In any community, there are many avenues for mutual understanding, within long-established relationships and newly made friends. Wenger has described how loyalty to colleagues leads to tightly bonded communities of practice (Wenger, 1998).

Reflection on all these ways of thinking draws on imagination, intuition and past experience to bring them together. In the case of the Landcare study not all members of the group adopted collective thinking. However, the group as a whole was influenced by members who had. Since the situation involves humans, issues of personal choice and learning come into play. Since the multiple ways of thinking are interconnected within each individual mind, when an individual reflects one way of thinking, others may follow.

The need to combine the results of using multiple ways of thinking on wicked problems has emerged into the mainstream. Biophysical inquiries into global warming and the world development goals have issued synthesis papers in addition to the usual inches-thick research report. Social inquiries, with their multiple case studies and diverse study populations, are choosing to issue final reports as narratives that encapsulate the more detailed findings. Ethical responses are the foundation for recommendations to influential agencies, a recent addition to formal reports. Creative thinking now contributes diagrams, illustrations and images to the driest exchange of information. Sympathetic communication has become part of an inquiry, with community consultations and the opportunities to put one's own case (Aslin & Brown, 2004).

In usual practice, the issue of conveying the collective understanding to the wide range of interested parties remains. Each of the contributing interests is likely to mention only one source of evidence, and use only the terms associated with that source. Numbers provide the language of scientists; social inquiry uses narrative;

principles convey the lessons from ethical inquiry, artefacts for aesthetics, emotions for the interpersonal and musings for the individual.

The reflective question, the 'so what' question that brings all this evidence together, remains a considerable challenge for all collective thinkers. Scientists have been trained never to be anthropocentric. For their inquiries to be human-centred is regarded as morally and scientifically wrong. Scientists are taught to recognise logic alone rather than to include their insights from their imagination, creativity and intuition, even though brilliant scientists from Einstein to Oppenheimer have vividly described these contributions to their work. Scientists are expected to think independently and alone. Collective thinkers can become a tightly cohesive group. There is a wide gap between group-think, in which everyone is convinced of one way of thinking and a collective mind.

For the collective thinking, two sets of questions need to be asked. Five are outward looking, asked by investigator(s) who are exploring a chosen topic in its context. The other two are inward, asked by the investigator of themselves. For five of the questions, much evidence will already be available. They can be answered through literature reviews, records, interviews and observations of behaviour and events. For the last two questions, the answers lie in the understanding of the investigator(s).

Inward personal reflections are accessed by introspection, that is, reviewing your existing assumptions about how the five ways of thinking apply to you. Reflective questions are answered by bringing together the answers to the other five. Sharing the findings from the answers from the five questions is a different challenge. Whatever type of question an inquiry starts with, there will already be familiar ways of bringing the findings from the different interests together. Synthesis papers, social narratives, ethical discussion, creative illustrations in a sympathetic avenue of communication all allow a shared understanding.

One way of thinking alone may be adequate under conditions of control in a laboratory. Even this is doubtful, given the creativity of a scientific discovery. The minute the inquiry goes into the field, the conditions cannot be held rigidly constant. Once biological systems are added, the context, living forms that initiate mutual feedback systems need to be taken into account. Once the inquiry involves human beings, complex issues of choice and learning come into play.

Multiple ways of thinking in practice

This example tells of collective thinking acting as an agency for exploring a wicked problem. A major Australian government project had brought together two long-time foes, farmers and environmentalists. The issue was the joint management of a difficult and degrading national environment, an issue which met all the criteria for a wicked problem. The government allocated many millions of dollars to a 'Decade of Landcare' expressly to support a partnership between production and conservation of the land.

Halfway into the decade, there was concern on all sides that no one knew where Landcare was going. It was acknowledged that the initiative was an astounding success. A third of Australia's farming families had active Landcare projects. Landcare councils made up of farmers and conservationists had been established in most regions. Tree planting in shelter belts, regenerative management styles and renewal of river catchments were common projects. Nevertheless, the Landcare programme was scattered all over a big country and seemed to have few long-term goals. There was a general sense of having lost what Landcare was doing as whole.

In response, a year-long contract was let with the aim of 'establishing the communication patterns of Landcare'. The results were published as *Landcare languages: Talking to each other about living with the land* (Brown, 1999). The learning objectives were to increase collaboration among Landcare partners, and to identify their collective thinking about Landcare, as individuals and as groups. The data and conclusions below have been drawn from that report.

The starting point was to determine the core threads which made up the general idea of Landcare. The sampling of Landcare was by the snowball method: personal interviews with ten accepted opinion-leaders in Landcare from the chief interests, followed by a sequence circling out from their recommendations. In the event, 200 active Landcare members were interviewed from two hours to two days. The core questions for the investigation were the multiple ways of thinking already established in previous research.

The first step was for the principal researcher (and this author) to reflect on her own position in relation to Landcare. This allowed for her recognition of her own assumptions and possible prejudices. She had a technical knowledge of the Australian physical environment, experience in social science research, a strong environmental ethic, a feel for the patterns of the landscape, and a sympathy with both the farmers and the environmentalists.

The learning process was based on David Kolb's experiential learning cycle. This carried the participants through the four stages of identifying ideals, describing facts, generating ideas and designing action in relation to the chosen issue. In the final workshop, fifty key decision-makers in Landcare from each of the socially constructed groups (individual, community, experts, organisations and holistic thinkers) were distributed to five round tables. Their responses to each of the Kolb stages were recorded and discussed. The aim throughout was to register the range of positions, not to achieve consensus. Each group was asked to appoint a recorder and a chairperson. The output from the two-day process was presented back to the participants for their confirmation.

The process led the knowledge cultures to share their values, agree on facts, brainstorm ideas and develop collaborative action. Further, and most important, some individuals from each of the groups brought collective thinking to each stage. While widely different in their choice of content, all the individuals addressed the biophysical, social, ethical, artistic and sympathetic aspects of the issue, thus including imagination and emotion in the discussion.

Here are the collated results from the interviews, re-examined as collective learning a decade after the first report:

Biophysical thinking

What are your concerns about working with the environment?

Responses were: nutrient decline, soil erosion, soil salinity, feral animals, water and soil pollution, noxious weeds, loss of biodiversity, risks of fire and flood, drought, urban development, depopulation, overuse and loss of sustainability.

Overall: the range and number of environmental risks justify the setting up of the inquiry. A significant point is that these issues were nominated by both farmers and environmentalists, suggesting that Landcare was indeed forming a neutral ground.

Socioeconomic thinking

What does Landcare mean to you?

Landcare interests were internally divided about Landcare as shown in Table 7.1.

Overall: It was expected that there would be tensions between interest groups. However, there were very strong divisions *within* Landcare interest groups, almost to the point of there being two Landcares, one positive and the other negative. This finding re-oriented social learning programmes to teambuilding within, rather than between groups.

Ethical thinking

What ethical principles guide your decisions in Landcare?

Experiment, problem-solving, stewardship, ownership, partnership, conservation, entitlement, resources, land development, social development, love of place, perseverance, instrumental, personal identity, technocentric, ecocentric, and a brave new world.

Overall: the dizzying number of relationships between Landcare members and their land explains why people were so confused about what was the 'real' Landcare.

TABLE 7.1 Multiple interests in Landcare

Elderly farmers	It's the land looking after you	It's a government plot
Young farmers	Gives us the tools to do the job	It's the last straw that will send us broke
Aboriginal owners	It's about healing the land	It's the land telling me who I am
Administrators	Community collaboration	Just like any grant programme
Politicians	A handout for farmers	A powerful social movement
Economists	Can't see how it will work	Needs a cost/benefit analysis
Scientists	A place to test new ideas	Forces farmers to listen
Media	Human interest stories	A significant national policy
Educators	A radical learning platform	Standard agricultural extension
Urban dwellers	Safeguard for our food	A waste of money

On a positive note, 100% of participants in the study had no problems in specifying their relationship with Landcare, an exceedingly strong response in social science terms. The result could be interpreted either as the wide reach of the Landcare movement, or as fragmentation, or most probably, both.

Creative thinking

What opportunities are there for thinking creatively about Landcare?

One source of creative thinking about Landcare are the information sources available. In rank order, as mentioned in interviews: government agencies, farm suppliers, farming organisations, field days, site visits, television and radio, newspaper, Landcare coordinators, conservation articles, workshops, courses and books.

Overall: Any information source can be creative, although many were not. The most read publication was the newspaper *The Land*. Farmers choose field days; environmentalists seminars and workshops.

Sympathetic thinking

Do you feel close to the members of any of the Landcare groups you belong to?

The responses were again broad. Groups mentioned included practitioners and researchers; concerned with large and small problems; government and community groups; rural and urban interests; social and environmental issues; and land managers and agencies.

Overall: the mix of groups might have been expected to bring conflict. However, Landcare members spoke of the mix as needing bonding if they were to achieve Landcare goals. Many saw their participation in Landcare as building bridges:

Reflection on the whole

Landcare is responding to a wicked problem: the future of the Australian environment, biologically and socially. From the collective thinking study it is possible to say that there is a coherent network, which recognises Landcare and is willing to work with dissimilar groups to achieve it. On the other hand there is a sizable group that considers Landcare a waste of time and effort.

To a specialised thinker Landcare is a jigsaw of many pieces. To a practitioner of collective thinking the project generates a collage, a collective understanding of the issues including all ways of thinking; and definitely not a consensus. There is a need for collective avenues of communication capable of linking all the interests: respecting Aboriginal understanding, establishing collective thinking, coordinating networks, using social media, enabling collective learning and monitoring collective standards and goals.

Conclusions

This chapter has reflected on multiple ways of thinking about wicked problems. The present practice of organising people's thinking within socially determined sub-cultures of knowledge is extremely restrictive. In mainstream practice, wicked problems are often reduced to tame problems, solvable by existing reductionist ways of thinking. The socially derived categories of individual, community, specialised, organisational and holistic knowledges each have their own language, methods of inquiry, body of content and standards for performance. They are also tightly controlled by their membership. This compartmentalisation allows for rigorous scholarship on the part, while preventing an understanding of the whole of an issue. Individuals are thereby prevented from reflecting on their own ways of accessing their multiple ways of thinking.

At all levels of education, tackling a wicked problem requires people to change their ways of thinking. When a learning environment encourages independent thinking, people are free to reflect on the multiple ways they can think for themselves. This begins at the primary level, and continues on through life. These multiple ways have proved to include biophysical, social, ethical, creative and sympathetic multi-dimensional ways of thinking.

These dimensions of thinking were identified in a programme on collaborative agricultural management in Australia. The difficulties in reconciling industrial agriculture and regenerative farming make it a wicked problem. The collaborative approach allowed usually opposition forces to listen to each other. The resulting shared understanding of the multiple interest in the issues overcame previous barriers to change.

The result was a shared understanding of each other's positions without the need for consensus. This in turn allowed for collaborative action on the wide range of issues. This early example of inclusive, multiple ways of thinking about issues was a precursor of initiatives in many fields other than agriculture. The future holds possibilities of expanding the collective thinking to include both the social knowledge sub-cultures and each individual's ways of thinking for themselves.

Acknowledgements

Thanks are due to colleagues who contributed to this chapter, particularly John Harris, David Marsh and the 200 contributors to the Landcare study.

References

Aslin, H., & Brown, V. A. (2004). *Towards Whole-of-Community engagement: A practical toolkit.* Canberra: Murray Darling Basin Commission.

Australian Public Service Commission. (2007). *Tackling wicked problems: A policy perspective* (p. 1). Canberra: Australian Public Service Commission.

Bawden, R. (1998). *Systemic development: A learning approach to change.* Hawkesbury: Department of Systemic Development, University of Western Sydney.

Berger, P., & Luckmann, T. (1971). *The social construction of reality: A treatise in the sociology of knowledge*. Harmondsworth: Penguin.

Brown, V. A. (1999). *Landcare languages: Talking to each other about living with the land*. Canberra: Department of Environment and Heritage.

Brown, V. A. (2008). *Leonardo's vision: A guide to collective thinking and action*. Rotterdam: Sense.

Brown, V. A., & Harris, J. A. (2014). *The human capacity for transformational change: Harnessing the collective mind*. Oxford: Earthscan/Routledge.

Brown, V. A. & Lambert, J. A. (2013). *Collective learning for transformational change: A guide to collaborative action*. London: Routledge.

Brown, V. A., Harris, J. A., & Russel, J. Y. (2014). *Tackling wicked problems through the transdisciplinary imagination*. London: Earthscan.

Budd, M. (1998). Aesthetics. In E. Craig (Ed.), *Routledge encyclopedia of philosophy* (p. 63). London: Routledge.

Chalmers, A. F. (1994). *What is this thing called collective thinking? An assessment of the nature and status of collective thinking and its methods*. St Lucia: University of Queensland Press.

Churchman, C. West (1979). *The systems approach and its enemies*. New York: Basic Books.

Donne, J. (1967 [1607]). *Selected prose*. E. Simpson, H. Gardner & T. S. Healy (Eds.). Oxford: Oxford University Press.

Drysek, J. S. (1997). *The politics of the earth: Environmental discourses*. Oxford: Oxford University Press.

Funtowicz, S. O., & Ravetz, R. J. (1990). *Uncertainty and quality in collective thinking for policy*. Amsterdam: Kluwer Academic Publishers.

Ison, R. L. (2008). Systems thinking and practice for action research. In P. Reason & H. Bradbury (Eds.), *The Sage handbook of action research. Participative inquiry and practice* (2nd ed., pp. 139–158). London: Sage.

Kolb, D. A. (1984). *Experiential learning: Experience as the source of learning and development*. Upper Saddle River, NJ: Prentice-Hall.

Mackie, J. L. (1990). *Ethics: Inventing right and wrong*. Harmondsworth: Penguin.

Midgely, M. (1995). *The myths we live by*. London: Routledge.

Millennial Ecosystem Assessment. (2005). *Ecosystems and human well-being: Synthesis*. New York, NY: Millennial Ecosystem Assessment.

Mills, C. Wright (1970). *The sociological imagination*. Princeton, NJ: Princeton University Press.

Passmore, J. (1980). *Man's responsibility for nature*. Baltimore, MD: Penguin Books.

Ralston Saul, J. (1992). *Voltaire's bastards: The dictatorship of reason in the West*. Toronto: Viking.

Rittel, H. (1972). *Second generation design methods, interview in design methods group*. 5th Anniversary Report, Developments in Design Methodology Occasional Paper 1, pp. 5–10.

Rittel, H., & Webber, M. (1973). Dilemmas in a general theory of planning. *Policy Collective Thinkings, 4*, 155–169.

Toulmin, S. (1972). *Human understanding*. Harmondsworth: Penguin.

Walker, B., & Salt, D. (2006). *Resilience thinking: Sustaining ecosystems and people in a changing world*. Washington, DC: Island Press.

Wenger, E. (1998). *Communities of practice: Learning, meaning, and identity*. Cambridge: Cambridge University Press.

World Commission on Dams. (2000). *Dams and development: A new framework for decision-making*. New York, NY: World Commission on Dams, United Nations.

8

A CONFUCIAN PERSPECTIVE ON DEVELOPING THINKING SKILLS

Li Li

Introduction

Developing higher order thinking skills, such as problem-solving, creativity, criticality and innovative capacity, is an important educational concern in the aim to develop global citizens and future economic growth. Policy reports from around the world stress that education for higher level skills, such as being able to view and solve a problem from multiple perspectives and being resilient, tolerant and collaborative, is essential to personal and collective well-being in an increasingly globalised world (OECD, 2005). Researchers from various philosophical perspectives have studied the meaning of teaching higher thinking skills, their relationship to learning and approaches to develop them (e.g. Wegerif, Li, & Kaufman, 2015). It is important to note that the majority of work and research is predominantly developed from a Western perspective on ways of thinking, learning and knowing, whilst very little is known about Eastern conceptions, understanding and approaches to thinking, specifically from a Confucian perspective.

There are strong reasons for considering a different theoretical position of thinking skills in the Knowledge Age. First, the Knowledge Age is a new, advanced form of social development in which knowledge and ideas are the main source of economic growth. In this era, knowledge is no longer thought of as fixed 'stuff' that is developed in the minds of experts, represented in words and classified into disciplines. It is a new *energy, mind set and network* that make things happen. It is produced not by individual experts, but by collective intelligence – a group of people with complementary expertise who collaborate for specific purposes. In order for people from different social, educational and cultural backgrounds to collaborate to produce relevant knowledge, they need to engage in transdisciplinary work. Second, the world is becoming a globalised one with people living and working in a multicultural and multilingual environment. It is very common to see multilingual families, societies and learning spaces. We also know that thinking is closely related to culture, custom, norms and values; it might therefore be inappropriate to use a Western philosophy of thinking to understand the being, doing and learning of students from other cultures, for example, Confucian cultural heritage (CHC) learners. Against this background, it would therefore be valuable for researchers and educators to take stock and to consider how understanding thinking and knowing from an alternative philosophical position can help us to deal with challenges in society. Furthermore, despite the interest shown by scholars in Chinese learners and the culture of Chinese learning, the dominant discourse in the literature is a negative one and one which depicts CHC learners as valuing surface learning by focusing on memorising, rote learning and reproducing knowledge. This is not an accurate description of CHC learners and recently opposing voices and evidence have shown that they do engage with critical and reflective learning (e.g. Li, 2015; Li & Wegerif, 2013). So, to offer an in-depth understanding of the Chinese culture of learning and the learners, it is important to re-examine the philosophical position of Chinese education.

Although Confucius is widely recognised as one of the greatest proponents of education in human history, his educational philosophy has often been overlooked in the important discussion on this topic and, indeed, is sometimes misrepresented and misinterpreted by researchers. This chapter therefore reconceptualises the importance and meaning of a Confucian perspective of teaching thinking skills through the addition of an understanding of a philosophical stance of a Confucian approach to education. In order to do this, I will first summarise the value and philosophical position of Confucius' theory, and then move on to explore the principles of Confucian educational philosophy. Following this, I present the thinking underlying Confucian philosophy, paying special attention to collaborative learning and reflective thinking. In illustrating Chinese Confucian thinking, I also refer to the literature that discusses the paradox of Chinese learners by discussing the various voices and views offered by different scholars about Chinese learners and the culture of Chinese learning. Finally, I will discuss how Confucian thinking is expressed and valued in contemporary Chinese education.

Confucian (educational) philosophy and principles

We understand that there is a close link between culture and the development of thinking. In order to understand thinking skills from a Confucian perspective, it is essential to understand Chinese philosophy and culture in Confucianism. Kong Qiu (or Kong Fu Zi;[1] Confucius) (551–479 BC) was an educator, philosopher and politician in China during the Spring and Autumn period (approximately 771 BC until 476 BC). It is important to recognise that the origin of Confucius' thought was to reinforce traditional cultural values and was later used by the ruler at that time to solve problems in society. During the Spring and Autumn period, different views emerged to critically challenge the role and status of traditional culture; future social relations and societal development became a central concern for everyone at that time. Many scholars proposed different opinions and positions, among which Confucianism and Legalism were the most influential schools of thought. Later, in the Han Dynasty (300 years after Confucius died), Zhongshu Dong, the philosopher, politician and educationalist, proposed using the principles of Confucianism in governance and lobbied this idea to the ruler. Since that time, the new Confucianism has been widely valued and practised in Chinese and many other Asian contexts.

A number of different works attempt to summarise the key principles of Confucian philosophy, most notably Nguyen-Phuong-Mai, Terlouw, & Pilot (2005). Based on the review of Chinese history and literature, some key ideas of Confucianism can be summarised as follows:

1. The stability of society is based on three cardinal guides and five constant virtues. The three cardinal guides define the unequal relationships between people in society, as Hofstede (2003, cited in Nguyen-Phuong-Mai, Terlouw, & Pilot, 2005) described; the relationships are ruler-subjects, father-son and husband-wife. Such relationships are based on mutual and complementary obligations: subjects, son and wife owe seniors respect and obedience, whereas the ruler, father and husband offer protection and their consideration to the former. The five virtues (benevolence, righteousness, propriety, knowledge and sincerity) are the basic principles of feudal moral conduct. These three cardinal guides and five constant virtues were used to deal with social issues.

2. Confucianism advocates collectivist values rather than individualism, emphasising the responsibility of the individual to the society. For a society, virtues are the most valuable characteristic of moral standards and the quality of having perfect virtue and high moral values is termed Rén (Jen). From Confucius' perspective, everyone in the society should strive for virtue in their life, to achieve Rén. Individuals who exhibit Rén are considered to be Jun Zi, an ideal person or 'Sage', and therefore becoming Jun Zi should be the ultimate goal for individuals. Because the society and culture value collectivism, the individual is viewed first and foremost as a member of a family, and then of an organisation and a community. The family usually plays a critical role in the society because it is the prototype of all social organisations; families make up the community and society in which harmony and consensus are important goals for the life of the individual. Nguyen-Phuong-Mai, Terlouw, & Pilot (2005, p. 405) argue that '[C]hildren grow up and think of themselves as a part of a "we" group, a relationship which is not voluntary but given by nature'.

3. Chinese culture believes in the unity between humans and nature; humans can realise value through interaction with the environment and thereby achieve virtue. This process can also be viewed as the Chinese understanding of personal development. Chinese philosophy emphasises the awareness of the fluid, uncertain and imperfect state of development in human thought.

Confucian philosophy of learning

Confucius set the tone for education in China in a number of important ways and he continues to have a significant influence on modern educational principles. His educational philosophy is very sophisticated and is recorded as Analects: a collection of his conversations with his disciples and between his disciples. Most of his sayings are metaphorical and can be interpreted in different ways.

Confucius' contributions to Chinese society are summarised by Sun (2004, pp. 78–79):

> At least four of his innovations have remained permanent features of Chinese civilization: (1) The creation of the role of the private teacher and the idea and practice of lifelong learning; (2) The creation and establishment of the content of education, its methods, and the ideals; (3) The broad application of liberal arts learning; and (4) the acceptance of students of all social backgrounds, with clearly established principles for doing so. Moreover, he taught social reform by moral persuasion, not by revolution.

Despite their possible hermeneutic complexity, the following Confucius educational beliefs are well-recognised in principle.

- Education should be available for all, regardless of background and ability. Teaching should be based on learners' level and style.
- The purpose of education is to achieve humanity through self-cultivation. Moral training is the most important part of education and such knowledge cannot remain in academic contexts but must be displayed in behaviour.
- Learning is a lifelong course and learning is through thinking and dialogues.

As seen from the above, Confucian philosophy does not suggest that learning is merely the mastery of customs, habits and practice, as is widely represented in the literature, and, in the following section, I will attempt to reveal what Confucius' beliefs about education and learning actually imply.

Education for all

As explained earlier, Rén is the achievement of perfect virtue and high standards of moral values. The value of Rén lies at the heart of Confucius' beliefs about learning, and the formal method for pursuing this personal refinement and self-articulation is Li (礼), the cultivation of moral action. The core value of propriety is the need for self-regulation. Becoming a Jun Zi takes place at a social level and it is not the result of an individual's action but how the person acts within a community. Propriety, which includes every aspect of life, is therefore the underlying syntax of this community. Confucius contended that

> [R]egulated by the edicts and punishments, people will know only how to stay out of trouble but will not have a sense of shame. Guided by virtues and the rites, they will not only have a sense of shame but also know to correct

their mistakes of their own accords (子曰：道之以政，齊之以刑，民免而無恥。道之以德，齊之以禮，有恥且格。).

(Analects 2: 3)

Confucius believed that education should be for all, regardless of social background and cognitive ability, and nobody should be excluded or disadvantaged, as he made explicit in a conversation with one of his disciples: 'In teaching there should be no distinction of classes' (15. 38) (子曰: 有教無類。). He believed that everyone is capable of improving themselves through education in order to reach humanity, except the most intelligent and the most stupid. Taking himself as an example, Confucius demonstrates what education can do to a person: the Master said, 'I am not one who was born in the possession of knowledge; I am one who is fond of antiquity, and earnest in seeking it there' (Analects 7:19) (子曰：我非生而知之者。好古，敏以求之者也). Confucius concedes that his knowledge is not connate and that self-cultivation is the most important aspect of learning. In fact, Confucius advocates treating all people who are willing to learn in the same manner, giving them equal opportunities to learn, because he believed that education can change people and help them to develop good qualities. This is a strong reflection of Confucius' educational beliefs, underpinned by his understanding of achieving humanity through learning.

The purpose of education

The Confucian ideal and ultimate goal is to 'cultivate oneself and bring peace and happiness to the whole populace' (L.Y. XIV 42). For Confucius, 'humanity', a concept with numerous connotations, takes 'benevolence' as its key concept (Hall & Ames, 1998).

As discussed above, the ultimate goal of education and learning is to cultivate oneself to become a person of quality with perfect virtue and high moral values, termed Rén (Jen). The concept of Rén (Jen) or 'perfect virtue' has multiple meanings and interpretations. Rén is not to be understood as an object in the world that can be defined and measured but is perhaps best viewed as a positive orientation towards others and towards otherness, characterised by a sense of unity (love) and constructive participation (reciprocity). Confucius believed that the great principle of reciprocity is the rule of life. Virtuous behaviour towards others includes not treating others as one would not like to be treated; Confucius taught his disciples that 'What you do not want done to yourself, do not do to others' (Analects 15: 23). There are two different ways of interpreting this saying. Some would understand that Confucius is teaching his disciples how to deal with everyday life, in their relationships with others and community; everyone should put themselves in each other's shoes and thus achieve harmony in society. Others believe that Confucius is advocating a process of repositioning, i.e. seeing things from a different perspective. Repositioning here is similar to what is more commonly termed 'creativity' in

Western research: when a person sees a problem from multiple perspectives, he or she can then offer multiple solutions.

Virtue with regard to one's tasks in life consists of trying to acquire skills and education, working hard, not spending more than necessary, being patient and persevering. Such quality is also described as 'sagehood', which is 'a state of oneness with the mind of the universe, evidenced by wisdom and morality' (Starr, 2012, p. 25). For Confucius, a Jun Zi is also someone who 'does not seek to satiate himself in eating, does not seek ease in living, is quick in his dealings and prudent in speech, and keeps to the correctness of those with the way' (Confucius, 2000, 1: p. 14). Only when one does not care about seeking satisfaction from material goods, can one be considered as devoted to learning. Although Confucius preaches the joys of a simple life, he does not condemn the quest for material success. For Confucius, morality is the most important element of humanity and should be placed ahead of material possessions, wealth and honour. Confucius himself demonstrates what a Jun Zi is: he or she must be someone who is honest, respectful and corrects his or her behaviour accordingly. Only by doing so, can one then engage in deep learning and achieve humanity. Sun (2008) elaborates on Confucius' idea of Jun Zi and provides a description of the three characteristics that a Jun Zi should attain: (a) the undivided 'I' with the universe, (b) the unity of 'I' with other human beings, and (c) the wholeness of 'I' with the 'self' (see also Zhao & Biesta, 2011). For both Starr (2012) and Sun (2004), the undivided 'I' with the universe is evidence of attaining sagehood. However, Li & Wegerif (2014) argue that the use of the term 'undivided' is misleading, as Confucius did not wish to claim that he or any other Jun Zi was the universe in any simple sense. His concern was with Rén, which is not about simply acting out of narrow self-interest but is rather about acting in a way that takes into account the interests of the whole society, which implies a dialogic relation with the universe.

Lifelong learning

One contribution of Confucius to education is his idea of lifelong learning, which still influences China today. For Confucius, learning is a lifelong process of self-cultivation and he illustrated this through his own conduct of lifelong learning and cultivation. He said,

> At the age of 15, I determined and devoted myself to learning; at 30, I was established in my profession; at 40, my doubts faded; at 50 I fully committed to my granted mission by heaven; at 60 my ear was attuned; at 70, I followed my heart/desire without overstepping the mark (子曰：吾十有五而志于学，三十而立，四十而不惑，五十而知天命，六十而耳顺，七十而从心所欲不逾矩。).

> *(Analects 2:4)*

Learning was Confucius's lifelong task – a process of developing thinking at different stages of life. He divided the learning process into three critical stages: the first stage is knowledge accumulation when one is 15 to 40 years of age; a second stage, from 40 to 70, is when one realises that one should not be manipulated by the environment; and the third stage, when one is beyond 70, is when a person should be able to integrate subjectivity and be self-regulated, which is not far from being in a state of perfect virtue. The autobiography of Confucius recorded here suggests that learning happens in two distinctive forms: one is the accumulation of knowledge (through transmission) and the other is discovering knowledge (through reflection); the accumulation was necessary and important for Confucius in order to be able to engage in reflection.

A Confucian perspective on thinking

The Confucian perspective on learning, as described above, is not simply acquiring knowledge, but is a way of engaging in self-cultivation to become a Jun Zi or to achieve virtue. Learning to become a Jun Zi does not mean acquiring a set of skills or knowledge but rather developing an attitude which enables one to relate to human society. Learning, therefore, from a Confucian perspective, requires deep thinking. This unity of thinking and learning is highlighted in Confucius' philosophical stance and beliefs: one of his famous sayings is 'Learning without thinking is a vain effort. Thinking without learning is a dangerous effort' (2.15 子曰: 学而不思则罔，思而不学则殆). In the Analects, Confucius emphasises understanding and appropriating knowledge to become a better self, rather than the memorisation of content knowledge. From Confucius' point of view, this deep thinking requires reflection and a sense of being able to relate to the environment: Confucius' thinking, therefore, is reflective and correlative thinking, in which one relates learning to doing and to being in real-life. It does require the learner to take a critical stance, but this form of reflective thinking is different from critical thinking in the West.

Reflective thinking underpinned Confucius' own teaching. Confucian belief is widely acknowledged as honouring and valuing the wisdom of the past, but Confucius did not advocate accepting ancient ideas blindly or unquestioningly. In his own teaching, he demanded challenges and questions from his disciples and rejected obedient, passive learning. He considered students who did not raise questions or think over what he taught them to be dull-witted. The Analects record his reflection on one of his disciples, Yan Hui, who failed to challenge him during their conversation and whom he thought dull-witted; later, when he reflected on Yan Hui's personal conduct, Confucius realised that the student's conversation was sufficiently expressive. As this story illustrates, reflective thinking does not suggest the need to be in debate or disagreement; rather it is about inner reflection and relating others' perspectives to one's own knowledge and interpretations.

Reflective thinking is not a new idea in the literature in the West. Dewey (1897) pointed out the role of reflection in learning and since then numerous articles about reflection have emerged. Nevertheless, it is still quite difficult to find a precise definition for reflection. In many cases it means *thinking about thinking*, which is closely related to metacognition and critical thinking. In fact, some scholars argue that reflective thinking is part of critical thinking and these two terms are occasionally used synonymously. Critical thinking is used to describe:

> ...the use of those cognitive skills or strategies that increase the probability of a desirable outcome...thinking that is purposeful, reasoned and goal directed – the kind of thinking involved in solving problems, formulating inferences, calculating likelihoods, and making decisions when the thinker is using skills that are thoughtful and effective for the particular context and type of thinking task. Critical thinking is sometimes called directed thinking because it focuses on a desired outcome.
>
> *(Halpern, 2014)*

Dewey (1897) suggests that reflective thinking is an active, persistent and careful consideration of a belief or supposed form of knowledge, of the grounds that support that knowledge and the further conclusions to which that knowledge leads. Learners are aware of and regulate their learning by actively engaging in reflective thinking by assessing what they know, what they need to know and how they learn. Reflective thinking in the West therefore recognises how the individual uses thinking to construct their experience, to relate the new to the known, to take different perspectives and to make independent judgements. Reflective thinking is viewed as a systematic, rigorous, disciplined way of thinking, with its roots in scientific inquiry, which happens in a community through dialogue. As Rodgers (2002) pointed out, reflective thinking requires attitudes that value the personal and intellectual growth of oneself and others. Dewey's reflective thinking can be and has been interpreted as focused on individual thinking even though Dewey himself was very interested in what he called social intelligence. In the cognitive psychology approach to teaching thinking skills the focus is on cognitive skills, such as being critical, which are usually seen as properties of individuals (Bailin, Case, Coombs, & Daniels, 1999). In some approaches these individual skills are augmented by habits and dispositions, which also tend to be conceived of as individual (Costa & Kallick, 2000).

Reflective thinking from a Confucian perspective, however, is different from the one that is followed in the Western approach. I will now unpack the idea of reflective thinking skills from a Confucian perspective. For Confucius, reflective thinking is conducted at two levels:

> (a) reflection on the materials of knowledge in order to synthesize and systematize the raw materials into a whole, and to integrate them into oneself as wisdom; (b) reflection on oneself, first in order to ensure that such synthesis, systematization and integration proceed in an open-minded, fair and autonomous way, and, second, in order to integrate knowledge with the self, thus internalizing it until it becomes oneself.
>
> *(Kim, 2003, p. 82)*

Confucius believed in the role of reflection in learning and expected his disciples to engage in active reflection. The Master said, 'If I raise one angel and they do not come back with the other three angels, I will not repeat myself' (Confucius, 2000, 7: p. 8) (子曰：' 不憤不啟，不悱不發。舉一隅不以三隅反，則不復也。'). His disciples were required to reflect on what Confucius taught them in order to come back to him with ideas and questions of their own. What counts for learning from a Confucian perspective is the ability to identify and discover new meanings from the existing knowledge. In other words, the challenging of old traditions and knowledge, or giving them new meanings, is considered to be learning. One of the striking characteristics of Confucian values in education is the role of knowledge: a learner needs to respect and cherish the known in order to develop new meanings and knowledge. In this process, reflection plays a significant role as it is a channel for individuals to acquire and internalise knowledge, as well as to discover new meanings in the known and possibly develop new knowledge. Because of this, revising what one has learnt is an important dimension of the Chinese culture of learning: 'Reviewing the known in order to acquire the new' is a widely shared belief in contemporary Chinese education (see further details in the following section).

One form of reflection sounds similar to contemporary ideas of metacognition: identifying one's own learning attitudes, weaknesses and strengths. For Confucius, knowing one's state of knowledge is fundamental in learning. He says, 'what you know, you know, what you don't know, you don't know. This is knowledge' (Confucius, 2000, 2: p. 17) (子曰：'由，誨女知之乎！知之爲知之，不知爲不知，是知也。'). Therefore, for Confucius, learning is not just about acquiring knowledge and information but also about developing awareness of one's knowledge.

Reflection also involves challenging other people's views and learning from peers. The Confucian perspective on reflective thinking means that one should not be obedient to seniors and authorities; in order to engage in reflection, one should be critical. Teaching students to be critical and not blindly accept ideas lies at the heart of Confucian educational beliefs. It should be acknowledged here that, in ancient China, all the rules were created by and for the ruler. Confucian philosophy was introduced and advocated in order to reinforce the power of the ruler, and the tradition of respecting seniors and authority has been carried forward through the generations. However, this does not mean blind obedience. Despite the principle in Confucius' philosophy of being humble and showing respect for the known, Confucius encouraged his disciples to have the courage to develop new meanings through challenging and questioning each other. The Master said, 'Let every man consider virtue as what devolves on himself. He may not yield the performance of it even to his teacher' (15.35) (子曰：'當仁，不讓於師。'). Confucius demonstrates that one can become perfectly virtuous or knowledgeable by devoting oneself to learning and thinking: using himself as an example, he claims that, by continuously engaging in learning and reflection, one can become knowledgeable like him. Learning and thinking are inseparable and should be ongoing in daily life. The

Master said, 'when I walk along with two others, they may serve me as my teachers. I will select their good qualities and follow them, their bad qualities and avoid them' (Confucius, 1893, 7: p. 21) (子曰：'三人行，必有我師焉。擇其善者而從之，其不善者而改之。').

Reflection also means learning from others and engaging in ongoing improvement. Confucius also made it clear that he practised such reflection himself: the Master said 'When we see men of worth, we should think of equalling them; when we see men of a contrary character, we should turn inwards and examine ourselves' (子曰：'見賢思齊焉，見不賢而內自省也') (Confucius, 1893, 4: p. 17). Through and in reflection, one can foster self-cultivation to develop humanity and become a quality person. Whereas reflection in the West often means the improvement of individuals, reflection from the Confucian perspective means relating oneself to the community and the environment. One of Confucius' disciples, Tsang, engaged in reflection multiple times daily on various aspects: 'whether in transacting business for others, I may have been not faithful; whether, in dealing with friends, I may not have been sincere, whether I may not have mastered and practised the instruction of my teacher?' (曾子曰：'吾日三省吾身：爲人謀而不忠乎？與朋友交而不信乎？傳不習乎?') (Confucius, 1893, 1: p. 4).

Reflective thinking can also be silent. Silence is actually valued as an indication of the importance of reflecting before speaking. Silent reflection can happen at different levels. Confucius proposed a view of thinking as silent 'inner' dialogue with multiple virtual voices, including the voice of the universe. He taught thinking by promoting this kind of reflection indirectly – silence is not seen as individual reflection but as something much more than individual.

> The Master said: 'I would prefer not speaking' (子曰：'予欲無言。')
>
> Tsze-Kung said: 'If you, Master, do not speak, what shall we, your disciples, have to record?' (子貢曰：'子如不言，則小子何述焉?')
>
> The Master said: 'Does Heaven speak? The four seasons pursue their courses and all things are continually being produced but does heaven say anything?' (子曰：'天何言哉？四時行焉，百物生焉。天何言哉?')
>
> (Confucius, 1893, 17: p. 19)

In other words Confucius assumed a relational self or a self that only exists as an emergent property of relationships. He saw education as a means of improving the quality of relationships not only with specific others but also with the horizon of otherness (what Sun refers to as 'the universe') (Li & Wegerif, 2014). Reflective thinking is therefore correlative in nature. In practice, Sun (2008) suggests productive silent reflection consists of three elements: firstly a person should be questioning themselves and their motives from different perspectives; second, they should think about the interests of the community; and finally, they should try to understand the larger point of view of the universe.

In summary, the Confucian perspective of thinking is reflective and has several key features:

- Reflective thinking respects the known, but does not blindly accept the known. Existing knowledge is the foundation for creating new knowledge.
- Reflective thinking includes critical thinking and it encourages the challenging of one's own and others' ideas and being open-minded.
- Reflective thinking is thinking about thinking, and it encourages self-regulation and monitoring.
- Reflective thinking means learning from others.
- Reflective thinking is correlative in nature. Individuals need to put themselves in a larger context, e.g. community and society.
- Reflection can be silent, which can be interpreted as inner reflection.

These thinking skills continue to influence contemporary Chinese education and they can be used to understand the paradox of Chinese learners and the Chinese culture of learning. In the next section, I will describe how Confucius' thinking is practised in modern Chinese schooling.

Confucian thinking in contemporary Chinese education

Confucius's approach to education promotes a number of significant concepts that are still evident in the psyche of Chinese culture (Li & Wegerif, 2014; Zhao & Biesta, 2011), among which the most widely discussed include what constitutes knowledge and learning, teacher and learners' roles in the process of learning, and pedagogy. A significant amount of literature has acknowledged the influence of Confucian values in education, and, having outlined the philosophical underpinning of the Confucian perspective and its thinking, I will now discuss the relevance of these educational values and thinking skills to contemporary Chinese schooling. I will also make reference to the debate and misinterpretation of Confucian education evidenced in the literature.

Moral education and inner satisfaction

In contemporary Chinese education, moral education is still the main educational objective. Although each subject has its focus and curriculum objectives, they all place a significant emphasis on fostering students' moral values in teaching. Specifically, the new curriculum standards for each subject for the first time have a clear statement on the attitudinal goal of developing students' active emotion.

In a school, moral education is required to be implemented and taught in subject instruction activities and through in-class communication. Class time is allocated for moral education through reflection. Students are encouraged to relate what they learn to their everyday practice. In particular, in their reflection children learn how to strive for 'inner satisfaction' by thinking of the self in relation to others and the community they are in. In practice, this concern with inner satisfaction is translated into being honest, keeping one's promises, practising what one preaches and being responsible. This philosophy is advocated throughout education and is known as an educational motto by all primary and secondary school pupils. In schools, students who achieve good academic results but cannot demonstrate 'inner satisfaction' are not considered merit students. When the moral values are implemented in in-class-communication activities, the sense of community is enhanced among the learners. Equally, trust and emotional communication between teachers and students is enhanced (Zhu, 2006).

Collective identity

One important element of developing humanity is to relate oneself to the society and community in which one lives. As I have already discussed, Confucian thinking is correlative and it involves community and society; thus people are expected to behave accordingly and to obey the social rules. Equally, people are expected to place their own interests in relation to the interests of the group, the class, the school, the society and the country. So, when there is a conflict between 'I' and 'we', acts of sacrificing the 'small self' to serve what is referred to as 'the big self' or 'social self' are valued and recognised (Li, 2015). The premise here is that selfishness is the greatest obstacle to the realisation of one's social self as personal fulfilment is structured and shaped by familial, communal, political and even cosmic order. It seems that researchers have reached a consensus that the collectivist mentality and culture which emphasise group characteristics and benefits, in one way or another, guarantee group collaboration and success. When individuals put 'we' ahead of 'I', then there is less conflict and confrontation. Even when disagreement arises, people can resolve the issues in a sensible manner and with a collectivist approach. Perhaps this is the reason why arguing for one's position is less evident in Chinese culture. In school, children are encouraged to think about others when making decisions and put the collective interests first. Chinese education advocates 'self-criticism and peer criticism' to cultivate deep moral values; self-interest is not encouraged.

With these underlying beliefs, team feeling and sense of cooperation are formed among Chinese heritage learners much faster and more easily than in other cultures (Nguyen-Phuong-Mai, Terlouw, & Pilot, 2005). The collectivist culture emphasises the interests of the team itself and the interests of everyone in the team as a whole. In this way a collective goal is identified in a task and a cooperative environment is developed where everyone is obliged to take some shared responsibilities. This philosophy, according to Astorga (2002, cited in Nguyen-Phuong-Mai, Terlouw, & Pilot, 2005), mirrors the modern principles of group building, collaboration and group effort.

Differentiation

Teaching according to ability is a shared education vision among Chinese teachers and it is widely practised throughout education. In practice, it is interpreted as teaching according to students' needs, learning styles and preferences. The depth of learning, coverage of content and curriculum are all guided by this principle.

Respect old knowledge, discover new meanings

In some of the literature on Chinese education, Chinese learners are depicted as obedient, rote and passive learners who rely on repetition, who do not engage in independent learning, who are extrinsically motivated and who merely reproduce knowledge as per examination requirements (see Gu, 2003; Li, 2003). Mok, Kennedy, Moore, Shan, & Leung (2008) claim that the stereotypical Chinese learner is one who wants to save face by not publicly demonstrating inability, engages in rote learning and memorisation, and is performance/achievement motivated. At face value, this might be true in terms of the image of Chinese learners. However, it does not provide a deep understanding of the Chinese culture of learning and thinking, or of its perspective of knowledge. In fact, a Chinese perspective of learning values the role of knowledge in a society, and, in schools, learning means developing the attitudes and ability of relating new to prior knowledge and discovering new meanings from it. As I discussed elsewhere (Li, 2015), this perspective of learning involves two aspects: accumulating and understanding the old knowledge, and critiquing and developing the new knowledge. As outlined above, Confucius' thinking emphasised the role of old knowledge in the process of developing and creating new knowledge and tradition. This, to some extent, involves memorising and accumulating old knowledge; then, based on one's accumulation of knowledge and in-depth understanding of it, one is able to develop new ideas through critical analysis and reflection. In schools, therefore, learners are expected to revise and summarise what they have learnt and to review what they are about to learn in order to understand the relationship between the old and the new. It is recognised as a useful and effective learning strategy, similar to the regulation of cognition, involving planning and evaluation.

The role of memorisation and repetition

Chinese learners are widely recognised as the type of learner who can do well when reproduction of knowledge is required but does less well when discovery is involved (Harris, 1995). However, this view is not a true reflection. The simplistic notion that Confucian philosophy places emphasis on knowledge mastery through rote learning, memorising and repetition is in stark contrast to the reality that Chinese students compete well with other students academically.

As Li (2016) pointed out, the role of memorisation is more complex than the way in which it is understood in the literature. Memorisation has been understood as a technique for knowledge acquisition and enhancement, which prepares students for various levels of tests, but consequently results in lack of creativity. However, the Chinese perspective of learning has a different understanding about the function of memorisation in teaching and learning. Memorisation is critical and fundamental in developing higher order thinking. Memorisation is not and should not be treated as a lower-order thinking skill, but a process that involves analysing, synthesising, applying and making connections. Thus, memorisation is not merely a surface level learning device but involves mechanical memorisation, and memorisation with understanding (Gu, 2003, p. 74). As Watkins (2000, p. 165) explains, 'memorizing and understanding…[are]…interlocking processes'. Jin & Cortazzi (2006, p. 14) acknowledge that in the 'changing practices of Chinese cultures of learning…there is…stress on deep learning which goes beyond memorising or recitation to practical application, through reflective study and high achievement motivation with disciplined effort'. In practice, Chinese learners adopt a methodical series of steps: they initially commit the material to memory; next they seek to understand the intention, style and meaning of the material; they then try to apply their understanding to situations that call for the use of this knowledge; and finally they enter a deeper level of questioning and modification of the original material. Whereas the last step in their approach is verbally interactive by nature, the first three steps may call for more solitary learning and contemplation. In this process, '[R]epetition' plays a role in consolidation and building understanding (Watkins, 2000, pp. 165–166). In this way memorisation provides a space for students to gather information and retrieve and apply their existing knowledge when appropriate. Memorisation is the stepping stone for students to deepen their learning by applying memorised information and, in return, understanding, internalising and appropriating new knowledge.

Reflection and silent engagement

Various scholars have acknowledged that thinking is indeed a key element of Confucian philosophy (see for example, Li & Wegerif, 2014; Starr, 2012; Zhao & Biesta, 2011). In fact, Chinese learners must have good thinking skills to be able to succeed academically and outperform their Western counterparts, as all disciplines require high levels of thinking skills, such as problem-solving collaboratively and thinking 'outside the box'. I would again like to highlight the reflective thinking involved here as a unique characteristic of Confucian learning. Such reflective thinking is relational and deeply rooted in the individual's upbringing as well as in societal values. Chinese children are encouraged to 'digest' knowledge by 'thinking and reflecting internally' from the early years. Reflection takes place in two different forms. First, children engage in reflection through self-appraisal and peer evaluation. The focus is usually put on the rectification of misbehaviour and appropriate conduct of group work. In other words, realising one's own strengths and weaknesses at a particular moment (when doing a specific task) is more important than being able to achieve the perfect outcome. For that reason, Confucian thinking advocates self-reflection and awareness. This sounds very similar to metacognition in the Western literature, yet metacognition refers to one's ability and awareness of level, strategy and regulation, whereas Chinese reflective thinking pays attention to the individual's relationship to their environment. Typical Chinese reflective thinking is the ability to recognise the possible flaws in one's thinking and the need to offer evidence to argue for one's position and course of decision-making. Second, students conduct silent reflection, which is hard to illustrate or observe. Chinese students are depicted as silent and passive learners because they do not actively share their views and opinions. Some scholars attribute this phenomenon to the 'face issue' of Chinese culture or obedience to authorities. In my view, the silence could be a form of inner silent reflection. The practice of not voicing views in class is related to ideas of being responsible and inner reflection. Specifically, children are taught from early years to engage in deeper thinking and reflection before speaking up. The frequently repeated advice to 'think three times before you act (speak)' is advocated by teachers and taken up by students. The idea is that they should engage in silent inner dialogue before engaging in active outer dialogue. Being responsible is linked to the idea of collective interests, as learners are expected to be responsible for their own learning and also for those others who are involved in their learning (e.g. peers and teachers). Chinese learners are thus observed not to raise questions because they are a) engaging in inner reflection and b) relating their own individual needs and voices to the collective interests (relating to otherness – including the universe). However, this does not mean that children are not encouraged to challenge; rather, they are encouraged to challenge only in a responsible manner and only after reflection (see Li & Wegerif, 2013). This educational philosophy of challenging authority underpins Confucian teaching and continues to influence contemporary education in China.

Dialogic teaching

Some Chinese teaching can be considered dialogic teaching, in which multiple voices are valued and inner reflection (dialogue) is encouraged. At face value, Chinese classrooms do not have many opportunities for students to do pair or group work, engaging in discussion and debate. However, the Chinese dialogic teaching rooted in Confucian philosophy values the inner reflection of one's learning and appropriation and internalisation of knowledge. In contrast to the view shared by researchers that CHC learners prefer a didactic and teacher-centred style (e.g. Kirkbride & Tang, cited in Chan, 1999), Li and Wegerif (2013) demonstrate that, in Chinese classrooms, dialogic teaching does exist and is highly valued by learners and the teacher. Dialogic teaching, from this perspective, has three characteristics. First, reflective thinking plays an important role in this process: students are constantly asked to engage in inner and peer reflection; second, multiple voices and views are valued, and the teacher is not the absolute authority, as misinterpreted in the literature; and third, inner dialogue and relating to otherness are necessary. Dialogic teaching can sometimes be observed as having referential questions, extended wait time and using a series of questions in classrooms (e.g. Li, 2011).

Conclusion

This chapter outlines the key aspects of the Confucian perspective on learning and Chinese thinking. Specifically, the Chinese thinking skills referred to here are reflective thinking and collaborative learning. It is important to note that reflective thinking is different from critical thinking, creative thinking or other types of thinking that are emphasised in Western culture, yet it shares some similarities with them. Reflective thinking involves silent inner reflection, self and peer evaluation, knowing the self (metacognition), and multiple voices and perspectives. Collaborative learning refers to developing oneself within a community, being responsible and placing others (and the community) at the centre of doing and thinking. It is correlative and a vital instrument in the achievement of inner satisfaction and high moral values.

Note

1   The words 'Fu Zi' following a last name signify an honorific equivalent to 'Master'.

References

Bailin, S., Case, R., Coombs, J. R., & Daniels, L. B. (1999). Conceptualizing critical thinking. *Journal of Curriculum Studies, 31*(3), 285–302.

Chan, S. (1999). The Chinese learner: A question of style. *Education + Training, 41*(6/7), 294–305.

Confucius. (1893). *Confucian analects* (J. Legge, Trans.). Retrieved from www.cnculture.net/ebook/jing/sishu/lunyu_en/

Confucius. (2000). *The analects* (R. Dawson, Trans.). Oxford: Oxford University Press.

Costa, A., & Kallick, B. (2000). *Habits of mind: A developmental series.* Alexandria, VA: Association for Supervision and Curriculum Development.

Dewey, J. (1897). My pedagogic creed. *The School Journal, LIV*(3), 77–80.

Gu, Y.-Q. (2003). Fine brush and freehand: The vocabulary-learning art of two successful Chinese EFL learners. *TESOL Quarterly, 37*(1), 73–104.

Hall, D. L., & Ames, R. T. (1998). Chinese philosophy: Bibliography. In E. Craig (Ed.), *Routledge encyclopedia of philosophy*. London: Taylor & Francis. Retrieved December 21, 2017, from www.rep.routledge.com/articles/overview/chinese-philosophy/v-1/bibliography/chinese-philosophy-bib

Halpern, D. (2014). *Thought and knowledge: An introduction to critical thinking* (5th edition). New York & Hove, UK: Psychology Press.

Harris, R. (1995). Overseas students in the United Kingdom university system. *Higher Education, 29*, 77–92.

Jin, L., & Cortazzi, M. (2006). Changing practices in Chinese cultures of learning. *Language, Culture and Curriculum, 19*(1), 5–20.

Kim, H. (2003). Critical thinking, learning and Confucius: A positive assessment. *Journal of Philosophy of Education, 37*(1), 71–87.

Li, J. (2003). US and Chinese cultural beliefs about learning. *Journal of Educational Psychology, 95*(2), 258–267.

Li, L. (2011). Obstacles and opportunities for developing thinking through interaction in language classrooms. *Thinking Skills and Creativity, 6*(3), 146–158.

Li, L. (2015). A Confucian perspective on teaching thinking in China. In R. Wegerif, L. Li, & J. Kaufman (Eds.), *The Routledge international handbook of research on teaching thinking* (pp. 45–57). London: Routledge.

Li, L. (2016). Integrating thinking skills in foreign language learning: What can we learn from teachers' perspectives? *Thinking Skills and Creativity, 22*, 273–288.

Li, L., & Wegerif, R. (2013). What does it mean to teach thinking in China? Challenging and developing notions of 'Confucian education'. *Thinking Skills and Creativity, 11*, 22–32. doi: 10.1016/j.tsc.2013.09.003

Li, L., & Wegerif, R. (2014). What does it mean to teach thinking in China? Challenging and developing notions of 'Confucian education'. *Thinking Skills and Creativity, 11*, 22–32.

Mok, M. M. C., Kennedy, K. J., Moore, P. J., Shan, P. W. J., & Leung S. O. (2008). The use of help-seeking by Chinese secondary school students: Challenging the myth of 'the Chinese learner'. *Evaluation & Research in Education, 21*(3), 188–213.

Nguyen-Phuong-Mai, M., Terlouw, C. & Pilot, A. (2005). Cooperative learning vs Confucian heritage culture's collectivism: confrontation to reveal some cultural conflicts and mismatch. *Asia-Europe Journal, 3*(3), 403–419.

OECD. (2005). *The definition and selection of key competencies.* Retrieved from www.oecd.org/pisa/35070367.pdf

Rodgers, C. (2002). Defining reflection: Another look at John Dewey and reflective thinking. *Teacher College Record, 104*(4), 842–866.

Starr, D. (2012). China and the Confucian education model. *Universitas, 21*, 1–27.

Sun, Q. (2004). To be Rén and Jun Zi: A Confucian perspective on the practice of contemporary education. *The Journal of Thought, 39*(2), 77–91.

Sun, Q. (2008). Confucian educational philosophy and its implication for lifelong learning and lifelong education. *International Journal of Lifelong Education, 27*(5), 559–578.

Watkins, D. (2000). Learning and teaching: A cross-cultural perspective. *School Leadership and Management, 20*(2), 161–173.

Wegerif, R., Li, L. & Kaufman, J. (2015). *The Routledge international handbook of research on teaching thinking.* London: Routledge.

Zhao, K., & Biesta, G. (2011). Lifelong learning between 'east' and 'west': Confucianism and the reflexive project of the self. *Interchange, 42*(1), 1–20.

Zhu, X. (2006). Moral education and values education in curriculum reform in China. *Frontiers in Education China, 2*, 191–192.

9

AN OUTLINE OF ASSESSMENT IN HUMANISTIC CONVERSATIONS

Definitions, aims, and design

Benzion Slakmon and Baruch B. Schwarz

Formative assessment of collaboration

Three dimensions are intertwined in the design of assessment of learning, referred to as the assessment triangle (Pellegrino, DiBello, & Goldman, 2016): observation, interpretation, and cognition. If individual cognition is replaced by group cognition, the two other vertices have to be replaced accordingly. That is, observation and interpretation must refer to the group as an entity. Remembering these well-known facts about assessment is necessary when tackling the assessment of dialogic learning, or learning to participate in dialogues. We will see that although the reference to educational dialogues has become ubiquitous, the evaluation of the quality of the dialogue as a form of talk is a challenge. We start by outlining our account of the notion of humanistic conversation, pointing out similarities and differences between its various forms and other kinds of talk. We then explain that this evaluation must encompass talk as well as the design (by the teacher or by other stakeholders).

The purpose of assessment practices in education – the improvement of student learning – depends on the theoretical framework of the practitioners and researchers, their assumptions and beliefs about the nature of the human mind, the origin of knowledge, and the process of learning (Pellegrino, 2014). The kind of assessment we refer to is formative, which provides feedback to students on performance and informs the teacher about design and curricular needs. Usually such assessment is done through quizzes or the inspection of portfolios that include various artifacts, achievements, and student actions while creating projects: usually games, models, inquiries, and essays. All of the above can also serve summative assessment. The current literature on formative assessment does not include oral assessment.

Let us show (or recall) first what humanism is. Humanism is a philosophical and ethical stance that emphasizes the value and agency of human beings, individually and collectively. Seeing "man as the measure of all things", as suggested by Protagoras, means accepting the complex sovereignty of the passions as well as the logic of freedom and its inhibitions. The humanistic project acknowledges the tension within our lives, yet thrives for coherence. The subject becomes then a condensed, reflective site of tension. Amid these tensions, human powers are creative (Sennett, 2011). The humanistic stance, therefore, had to develop critical thinking based on evidence as a measure for overbalancing views and transcending dogma or superstition.

The term "humanism" was coined by theologians, and is based on reflection of the history of Western philosophy and theology. In its budding years, religious humanism (e.g., with Pico della Mirandola's work in the 15th century [1998/1486]) dealt heavily with the question of the presence of the divine in humanity. Progressively, however, humanism has typically aligned itself with secularism, or with at least a minimal level of autonomy for individuals to become their own makers, to paraphrase della Mirandola. Being versed in the humanities relies on learning to participate in a certain ideal of a civilized conversation, which can be understood as an attempt to weave different voices (forces) into a coherent meaning.

The humanistic conversation

The humanistic conversation brings together different commitments. These include a commitment to the full expression of one's voice and to critical inquiry, through hermeneutical practices (Gadamer, 2006) applied to texts and discussants alike. It also involves commitment to the norms of the disciplines in which the conversation steps, but without the commitment to its boundaries. Indeed, the humanistic conversation celebrates the freedom to cross these boundaries for the joy of following the inquiry where it leads. The commitment to the other, which was so central during the Middle Ages and the Renaissance, and which had characterized more than any other commitment the essence of the humanist as participating in dialogues, disappeared for two centuries (Bergman, 1974). The rise of the Philosophy of Intersubjectivity with Hegel and Husserl, followed by the philosophy of dialogue (e.g., with Buber, 1971/1923; Rosenzweig, 2005/1921) brought back the commitment to the other at the foreground of humanism, and brought forward in a forceful way the centrality of certain forms of talk to humanist essence. To a large extent, the idea of humanism, which was seriously shaken in the 20th century, now owes its persistence to the return to the centrality of the dialogue to human experience and ethics.[1]

Quite naturally, these sharp fluctuations in the idea of humanism, and the re-identification of the importance of dialogue impinged on education. A new Zeitgeist emerged, according to which the educated person is now the one who can participate in forms of talk that are committed to these triadic relations – to the other and/ or the community, to rigorous reasoning, and to disciplinary knowledge (Bingham & Sidorkin, 2004; Michaels, O'Connor, & Resnick, 2008). However, progressive pedagogies that bring talk to the forefront have encountered enormous obstacles (see also Lefstein, 2010). The first obstacle is ideational: Alexander (2006) pointed out that it is difficult for teachers to lead *cumulative* talk, in the sense that participants fail to contribute to each other's ideas towards the elaboration of new insights. Second, a major challenge of implementation is intrinsic to the curricular organization of school learning in an inexorable progression of concepts "to be acquired". Such an organization makes it difficult to develop a dialogic approach, which is based on negotiation of meanings, and has, by definition, an open, unexpected dimension (Biesta, 1994, 2012). The third challenge is derived from the evasive nature of relationality (Todd, 2012). Although the dialogic dimension of talk precedes learning and knowing, realizing it in school can only take place within a setting in which the latter precedes the former. As a result, dialogic learning is always only a hinted option of the learning environment. Our question is how to pedagogically design and work towards such a realization. It is argued that although the dialogic dimension is present in every educational, and more generally, interactional setting, it is the mission of the humanities to uncover and invite students to reside within it. We suggest that in order to be visible rather than simply being hinted at, we must incorporate the evaluation of dialogic talk into educational practice.

Although resembling other intellectual talk genres, especially in vocabulary, the humanistic conversation has its own codes and rituals. It resembles ordinary, mundane talk, but unlike disciplinary discourse, changing, diverting directions are legitimized; the emotions and the character of the discussants are welcomed, as discourse does not confine itself to critical reasoning of arguments (Noddings, 2011; Tannen, 2013). The discussants are expected to fully engage in the conversation so that the logos, pathos, and the ethos are all present. All are celebrated as part of the manifestation and fulfillment of the humane. From this perspective, dialogue is perceived as a mode of existence, with a distinct epistemology, and as an educational end in itself (Bingham & Sidorkin, 2004; Shor & Freire, 1987; Wegerif, 2007). In this view, the humanizing mission of schools is achieved through relationships because schools are the cultural institutions for practicing practical intersubjectivity (Biesta, 1994). Proponents of this approach hope that the methodology of educational research will move closer to dialogism, believed to be more appropriate to human science (Jenkins & Lyle, 2010).

The humanistic conversation comprises aesthetic values of performing wisdom and enjoying its beauty. Despite the learning attributes associated with it, it is not perceived of as work, but as a creative making (poiesis) made by investing it with personal residues. In this process, the conversation itself, which is the process and outcome of becoming, and the subjectivity of the participants, are being developed (Arendt, 1958/1998). The conversation embodies ethical living in its rich set of codes, among those meeting the other, arguing, reconciling, caring, 'living together', and hospitality in the presence of otherness, both as an ethical imperative (Biesta, 2016; Kristeva, 1991) and as a semiotic foundation of the dialogic (Bakhtin, 1981; Nystrand, 1997).

This conversation brings together past achievements, wider contexts, and present concern. It is based on the quartet of the (two at least) participants, the past, and the openness of the future. New meanings are reached when discussants go beyond rote and repetition of past traditions through the investment of personal resources. Yet the process of generating new knowledge is based on the practice of reference, as without dialogue with the historical, new achievements will be meaningless. In other words, a humanistic conversation always engages the tradition as its *third addressee* (Bakhtin, 1981) and is stamped by the dialogic tension between the old and the new. Whereas the emergence of the new or the realization of one's idiosyncrasy is achieved in the dialogue, it must be weaved through tradition in a way that transforms it, and turns it from a muting, paralyzing burden, to a correspondence and creative impetus. In some sense, there is a similarity between the micro practice of using the conversation's past resources to make it a coherent whole, and the larger cultural pattern of weaving the past into one's actions and words.

The problem with living culturally outside the aura, or the presence of the past, can be better understood when thought of in a temporal manner. It is then that the rupture is best realized as displaced existence. This rupture is a central theme in contemporary philosophical writings in the philosophical discourse on modernity (Habermas, 1987). In his book, *The Man without Content* (1999), Agamben discusses this rupture as a crisis in terms of the transmissibility of cultural dialogue across generations, or of past experience as its destruction, labeled intransmissibility. Agamben points to the symphysis attributes of the aesthetic forms, but the space opened by the aesthetic for new transmissibility can only be filled by the meta-content of the discussion about the impossibility of transmission. Contemporary conversation in the humanities must bring together, according to Agamben, both the historical and aesthetic in a way that entails the reflection over the relations with the past and the dialectic of subjectification through socialization to past traditions. The questions of meeting the other and the possibility of obligation towards a tradition lie at the heart of the conversation.

Evaluating dialogue as an enacted humanistic act

The tradition that sees dialogue as a learning device dates back to Plato. Presently, some see in the study of dialogue a sophisticated, fundamental mechanism that plays a crucial developmental role in children's upbringing, a primary resource in children's development as thinkers, knowledge builders, problem-solvers, and efficient peers (Mercer & Littleton, 2007; Reznitskaya et al., 2009; Schwarz & Baker, 2016; Vygotsky, 1980). For many decades now, dialogue has entered the educational realm under the name of 'learning together' for different purposes (Baker, Andriessen, & Järvelä, 2013; Howe & Abedin, 2013; Mercer & Dawes, 2014). Therefore, at first glance, after four decades of research on classroom talk, it seems that researchers have already covered this domain. Building on Barnes (1979), Mercer, Wegerif, & Dawes (1999) have proposed a categorization of school talk ranging from *cumulative talk* (in a very different sense from the sense given by Alexander), to *disputational talk* and *exploratory talk*. To these, Wegerif (2007, 2013) added what he called *playful talk*, referring to the more dialogically fundamental aspects of talk, namely, its creativeness, infinity, and a refusal to see the mediation of the teacher as a domestication of novices' interpretations of the world. Most assessments of dialogic interventions are based on the recognition of the above categories that develop during these interventions. Wegerif and colleagues' (2017) approach is based on an external (to the activity) assessment. They use Raven tests. The approach was recently updated and now offers two different Raven-like tests, validated for the same level of difficulty to be used at the beginning and the end of the group activity (Wegerif, Fujita, Doney, Linares, Richards, & Van Rhyn, 2017). Another progression in the field was made by the interactional focus of the *collaborative reasoning* research group (Reznitskaya et al., 2009) and more recently by Rojas-Drummond and colleagues' notion of 'dialogic literacy' (2017). A highly operationalized and useful approach to achieve this is the coding scheme for analyzing classroom dialogue across educational contexts (Hennessy et al., 2016). The utterance-based approach is useful for correlating talk with cognitive development. Asterhan & Schwarz (2016) adopted an intermediary approach between an utterance-based approach and an approach based on the recognition of a category of talk and identified the importance of a form of talk recognizable by distinctive patterns they call *deliberative argumentation* for many aspects of cognitive and social development. However, here also, the recognition of talk characteristics or patterns such as explorative talk or deliberative argumentation is quite restrictive, taking into account the humanistic mission because it leaves aside important dimensions. Although Schwarz & Baker (2016) elaborate on the link between the practice of deliberative argumentation and the constitution of a deliberative democracy (first alluded to by Michaels, O'Connor & Resnick, 2008), this general suggestion is quite vague.

There are no clear boundaries delineating the beginning of dialogue and the diminishing of talk. This fuzzy situation makes it difficult to advance the educational dialogue as a humanistic enterprise. There are, however, some principles on which any educational dialogue should be comprehended. First, if we are to educate students to become more dialogic, the educational setting needs to rearrange itself around talk activities. This principle makes the evaluation of the educational dialogue a challenging task since talk leaves no easily referable and measurable objects. The similarity of dialogue to other forms of talk might lead the students to confuse it with other talk forms, such as exploratory talk. However, evaluating educational talk as a humanistic enterprise is something else. As a phenomenological occurrence, the dialogue can neither be pointed out externally nor be grasped and discussed as an object. It should be an experience, a wonder. And this wonder should be articulated to learners as a joint achievement emerging in culturally supportive environments. In the next section, we summarize well-known developments on collaborative learning, presented in two ways, first as research findings, then articulated as an indispensable component of pedagogy for humanistic conversations.

The current emphasis on small groups

Progressively, although the small group was first considered to be an instrumental arrangement for collaboration and cooperation (Sharan, 1980), researchers began to understand that this setting is the scene of a wonder – a context that enables much more than the sum of the cognitions of its members (Aronson, 1984; Schwarz, 1995; Schwarz, Neuman, & Biezuner, 2000 who exemplified the two-wrongs-make-one-right effect). Currently, there is an increasing emphasis on group work, cooperation, and collaborative learning (Bellanca & Brandt, 2010; Trilling & Fadel, 2009). With over a decade of research, starting with Barron's seminal studies (2000, 2003), evidence has accumulated not only about the value of small group learning for achievement, but also on the practical knowledge about the conditions in which productive collaboration occurs. There is also a considerable body of knowledge on teachers' practices supporting classroom collaboration (Cohen, 1994; Jolliffe, 2007; Kutnick, Blatchford, Baines, & Tolmie, 2013; Webb et al., 2009).

Researchers who developed the Computer-Supported Collaborative Learning (CSCL) Research Community (Cole & Distributive Literacy Consortium, 2006; Scardamalia, 2002; Scardamalia & Bereiter, 1991) realized that the small group (with 3–4 students) is a natural context for meaning making:

> Group practices mediate between individual cognition and community culture. They can be observed and analyzed in small-group interactions. Thereby, the theory of group practice provides a solution to the obstinate issues of meaning-making, inter-subjectivity, structuration and connecting levels of learning while focusing analysis on the small-group unit, which is central to collaborative learning.
>
> (Stahl, 2017, p. 16)

The wonder provided by the small group grew in the presence of tools especially designed to afford certain behaviors: Stahl's idea of *group cognition* indicates that the affordances of the tools help in collective meaning making (2006, 2017). However, for Stahl, the community and its tools form a complex system that cannot be modeled through simple causal relationships, because the whole is both over-determined and open-ended; the community is made possible by its infrastructure, but also interprets the meaning of its tools and adapts to their affordances. Group work is no longer perceived only as instrumental to the individual learners. The small group of three to four students allows for cooperation and collaboration, for full common engagement, for group practices, and most fundamentally, for what Stahl defines as "co-experiencing a shared world". Expanding Stahl's ideas beyond his initial STEM focus, the small group is the natural context for the deployment of educational dialogue (see also Wegerif and colleagues' (2017) similar idea of "group thinking").

Developed mostly in CSCL settings, Stahl's group cognition theory emerged out of the materiality and the visualization of the interactive practices between learners and artifacts. By now, as it addresses the larger field of the Learning Sciences (Stahl, 2016), time has come to incorporate its main ideas into various contexts that may lack computer-supported mediation, yet integrate textual and physical technologies for learning together, namely the culturally rich genre of the humanistic conversation, with its practices, language, rules, and tradition. In other words, the notion of the "practice turn" (Stahl, 2017, p. 28) is central to Stahl's linking between group practices and group cognition. As a learning theory it is not confined to its CSCL settings, but can be applied to more abstract activities such as humanistic conversations and other non-CS mediated discussions. The theory helps us see the existing parts of the conversation as group practices, of which the cognitive dimension is already embedded. The metaphors that the CSCL community elaborated – co-construction of knowledge as meaning making, or the identification of artifacts as physical objects created by people that embody human meaning, thereby overcoming the distinction between what is in the mind vs. in the world – are forceful ideas that should be part not only of the scientific discourse but also of classroom talk. Moreover, the small group is the site for practicing living together across differences. It is enacted learning, in the face of the other. It is in this encounter that the humanistic values have to be fulfilled, simultaneously with the work on the tasks.

Holistic design for the evaluation of the dialogue as a deliberate humanistic act

Beyond the explicit design decision to give precedence to the group as a natural context for experiencing dialogue as a humanistic act, other design principles are necessary. Realizing dialogue from the general classroom dialogue involves practicing several discursive actions, one on top of the other, with the hope that higher levels of engagement will emerge. We argue that the ideas about the importance of weaving the past into the present and the philosophy of group cognition, with its revolutionary consequences for the way the subject and learning are understood, should not be confined to the academic realm of studying learning. The new knowledge on group cognition has ramifications that go beyond its analytical attributes and are of crucial and timely pedagogical importance. Beside their theoretical significance, they should serve as design principles. Realizing the dialogic nature of subjectivity and of knowing, to introduce oneself to the latent dimensions of the humanistic conversation ought to be seen as fundamental educational aims of the humanities. The design for learning to participate in the humanistic conversation is then aimed at how to integrate this new dialogic paradigm into the curriculum. The opening of the reflective dimension about talk has intersubjective significance, and a role to play in bringing back the past to the present as part of the subjectification. It puts strong emphasis on recursive discursive activities and on reflection on them. It is not done for the sake of idolizing the 'Homo academicus' but for the sake of apprenticing young students to the humanistic conversation as a cultural system. The new academic knowledge on group cognition is turned into an ethical and practical learning challenge for the students. Questions are asked in a certain way, for example, not only because this enhances group learning, but also because the better one is at asking, the greater one's participation in the humanistic conversation and the greater one's realization.

Curriculum design for such realization demands inflexibility in three dimensions: The learning activities are meant to be recursive so that students will be able to practice them and teachers will be able to draw clear trajectories of collaboration across time. The inflexibility also means the attempt to maintain fixed groups. Finally, learning cycles include inspirational texts and deliberation on the ethical, epistemological and pedagogical underpinnings of collaboration. The centrality of collaboration, time, and of inspirational texts brings to the fore dialogue located among participants between the past and the future. The knowledge on classroom dialogue is discussed not as rules, but as values. In terms of content radical openness to new, unexpected ideas is expected. Expecting the new in dialogue is something that is welcomed and learned. The social and the cognitive are intertwined and presented as such. The principle of strong structural design that enables radical openness in terms of content was a leading theme in the writings of Ann Sharp, founder of Philosophy for Children.

The design presented here is based on a year-long interdisciplinary humanities course taught to 28 Jewish, 8th grade, junior high school students comprising 15 boys and 13 girls, ages 13–14. The specific pedagogical design of the classroom from which the data was taken, which is termed the 'reflexive paradigm' (Lipman, 2003), is an educational environment rich in discursive resources. The course was inspired by *Philosophy for Children* (P4C, Lipman, Sharp, & Oscanyan, 2010; Lipman, 2010) – a program aimed at fostering students' thinking skills: critical, creative, and caring, through apprenticeship in a community of philosophical inquiry. P4C is regarded as a manifestation of *dialogic pedagogy* (Hardman & Delafield, 2010; Slakmon, 2015), known for its demonstrated achievements in promoting sustainable cognitive learning gains and socio-emotional effects, such as students' self-perception as learners and as problem-solvers (Topping & Trickey, 2007; many chapters in the book *Socializing intelligence through academic talk and dialogue* (Resnick, Asterhan, & Clarke, 2015)).

The year-long six hour per week course was organized in a circular fashion to include three major iterations, organized around three general themes. The first theme was justice and its manifestations or neglect in issues of equity and inequality. The second was truth, especially as manifested in the notions of "understanding" and "interpretation". The third was the idea of "the good" and its manifestation in the "good conversation" (the dialogue). Each iteration lasted for approximately eight weeks, consisting of 50–60 hours each. The iterations themselves were structurally recursive, so that every week resembled the others and had reciprocal activities with constant transversal engagement in dialogue. As Barnes (1979) noted, communication is the main mode of curriculum design so courses might be best understood in terms of activities and modes of communication. The teacher contributed less than 40% of the talk in whole class discussions, and was not present during small group discussions. This structure was maintained throughout the year, with changes being made in the resources presented to the students to work with (for the detailed activity plan see Slakmon, 2015). The activity week comprised the following activities:

1. Reading:
    a. Weekly hour of free voluntary reading (Krashen, 2011).
    b. Guided (in several degrees) reading in adapted philosophical texts from *Discourse on Inequality*, Jean Jacques Rousseau; *Discourse on the Sciences and Arts*, Jean Jacques Rousseau; Different entries from Diderot's *Encyclopedia*; *Nicomachean Ethics*, Aristotle; *I-Thou*, Martin Buber; *Allegory of the Cave*, Plato; Epigrams concerning the notion of enlightenment and the freedom of reason from *What is Enlightenment?*, Immanuel Kant, and *The Wanderer*, Friedrich Nietzsche (from *Human, all too human*).
    c. Guided reading of short stories, poetry, editorial column, and stories from the bible, including: *Good Day*, Tuvia Rivner; *Urgent Warning,* Tahel Porush; *The Crucifixion of the Jews*, Philip Roth; *No Title Required*, Wisława Szymborska; *Nick Adams Stories,* Ernest Hemingway; and Biblical stories including Cain and Abel and the Tower of Babel.

    Moderation of the discussion is of great importance. As a site of decision making, it is the nexus of intellectual and public power. To learn to moderate is to learn to navigate oneself and others in the ambiguity of the yet to be learned. It is easy to understand the educational importance of such traits to citizenship. There is a great difference between collaboration among students when the moderation is carried out by the teacher and collaboration regulated and moderated by the students themselves by their own faculties. The same is true with regard to setting the agenda for the discussions. Citizens are expected to be free to pursue their own interests and not only to perform in the confines established by an external authority. As a consequence, small group discussion did not include teacher moderation. The teacher's moderation was limited to the plenary reflective session. The large group modeled the small groups in all aspects except the authoritative; as the students went back to collaborating in small groups, they had to assume responsibility over the power management of the talk and space, without external authority to lean on for approval. In other words, cultural norms of classroom talk, which can also be seen as the learning subject, are usually produced and maintained by the teacher. Our pedagogical design required that the students will maintain the cultural talk norms *without* the teacher's presence. The teacher's physical absence contributed to the liberation of conversational space.

    Here we see an example of how the official curriculum can be used for the introduction of higher forms of dialogue. Reading about the higher forms of dialogue and discussing it, as with Buber's introduction, is an important and necessary supplement to the interactional activities, that is, the discussions themselves. Learning about something cannot replace experiencing it, and whole class discussions about dialogue might lead some students to mark it as unwanted disciplinary knowledge. On the other hand, it is a way to point out that talk has other dimensions worth exploring, without coercion.

2. Writing: Weekly hour of writing from:
   a. Free voluntarily writing (of stories, poetry, diary entries, epigrams), or
   b. Personal or collaborative essay writing (as concluding assignment of 4c).

3. Contemplation of works of art, training in looking, depiction and suspension of judgment, using the following works: Brueghel, P. (The Elder) (1563), *The Tower of Babel;* (1564), *The Procession to Calvary;* (1590–1595), *Landscape with the Fall of Icarus;* Doré, G. (1866), *Cain and Abel Offering Their Sacrifices;* Doré, G. (1866), *The Murder of Abel;* Dürer, A. (1498), *Self Portrait at 26;* Dürer, A. (1503), *The Large Turf;* Rembrandt (1631), *The Anatomy Lesson of Dr. Nicolaes Tulp.*

4. Settings for talk:
   a. Text-based whole class discussions (accompanies 1b)
   b. Whole-class community of inquiry circle, based on 1b (above), followed by:
   c. Small group discussions on the questions arising in 4b (in face-to-face setting in the first two iterations and in computer-supported collaborative learning discussions throughout the third (Slakmon & Schwarz, 2014, 2017).
   d. Teacher-led whole class discussions.

5. Weekly hour of reflective sessions, in which certain talk modality that was performed during the final week of the school year, was analyzed either by the teacher or by the students themselves by using their own audio recordings or CSCL protocols and comparing them to their previously created ground rules for talk.

The first cycle serves as an illustration of the learning structure of the program. As mentioned, the theme of the first cycle was justice. The starting point was a joint reading of the Cain and Abel story, followed by a discussion in the Community of Philosophical Inquiry structure (CoPI). The meaning making is carried out collaboratively from the outset, relating to Stahl's phases of joint experiencing the shared world. The first level of interpreting the text was to clarify unclear words and terms. The next level was questioning and building a wide, general list of questions that arise from the text, according to the students' understanding. Next, the students were asked to evaluate the list of class questions in order to categorize them. Minor or "small" questions were the terms used for factual, closed, informative questions; "Big" questions was the term used for interpretive and evaluative questions that reveal the shared *point of doubt* the group reached (Splitter & Sharp, 1995; Haroutunian-Gordon, 2014). This was followed by adding external viewpoints on the story readings of legends, on the story from the Mishna and the Talmud and analyzing works of art, all referring to the opening story. The students proceeded to write essays on the questions they found interesting from the general list. Then continuing the first CoPI, the students practiced ways to deepen their original questions by regression. Subsequently, they continued their discussions in small groups. They wrote essays about the origins of inequality, and then read Rousseau's essay on the subject.

In the weekly "reflective sessions", the audio/video recordings of the lessons were used as representations and learning materials of the oral dimensions. Students' attention was drawn to the way they replied to others' comments; cases of problematic participation structures were introduced; students were encouraged to include all participants in the conversation and to build on each other's ideas as a way of realizing collaboration.

Evaluating classroom dialogue

The evaluation of classroom dialogue as a humanistic act in the course we described is a complex endeavor. The first natural step in this evaluation is that the course took place. This is not an empty statement when one takes into consideration the multiple constraints of school learning. The second step is to scrutinize the *responsibility* groups took during the course. The groups were responsible for discussions, documentation, and reflection over their activities. The audio documented conversation of the small groups is an accomplishment, the thing that needs to be learned, practiced, and improved through reflective analysis. Other aspects of this distributed responsibility could be detected in numerous moments of *collective reflection, mutual engagement*, and *peer assessment* (see Schwarz, de Groot, Mavrikis, & Dragon, 2015 about the detection of such moments as manifestations of *learning to learn together*).

Assessment of group learning – participation in activities, norms, or cognition – does not exclude individual assessment. On the contrary, the levels complete each other. The problem of inadequate assessment of collaboration begins when one level of activity is being assessed by measures of another level. In most cases, the collaborative parts will be ignored in favor of individual learning.

The curriculum of the course was designed to include three learning cycles. While the texts and questions for inquiry changed, the activities remained so that students will gradually master the practices and develop strong norms with regards to them. The students practiced the same abovementioned practices every week. Each learning cycle ended with an evaluation day that lasted for five or six consecutive lessons in which the groups participated in an encapsulated learning cycle. Like with the grand three months cycle, throughout these assessment days, the students went through the entire set of learning activities and talk modalities. They had to participate to the best of their abilities while dealing with new, unfamiliar texts, both the initial one and the supplementary.

The assessment day included five major activities: a joint reading of the text, a joint plenary CoPI, and the small group activities of discussing, joint writing, and presenting the process to the plenum at the end of the day. Dialogue about the assessment of each activity was held continuously throughout the year between the teacher and the students. The resulting criteria were then served as a learning device.

An example for this assessment as reflection process can be found in refinements made in the classroom regarding discussions: raising questions, differentiating the factual questions from the interpretive and the evaluative ones, regressing towards questions of definition.

Such criteria were used by small groups to reflect and assess their discussions. The teacher capitalized on this activity to deepen the classroom understanding of the criteria, refine it, and negotiate it in the weekly plenary sessions. The assessment process was then negotiated and built in an accumulated, bottom-up manner, with constant reference to it as part of the learning process. It is not new that evaluation measures in education are turning into educational aims and have strong, crucial impact on pedagogy. However, turning the assessment explicitly into a negotiated, normative process that is done recursively with the students is important for creating the conditions for group reflection (see also: Slakmon & Schwarz, 2017). The actors must develop their own assessment over the activity using their own conceptions of what high quality activity means. This constraint demands ongoing reflection. The group needs to develop ways to observe its actions as they happen, by documenting, remembering, and raising them again in later parts of the discussion, in order to decide how the actions reconcile with the criteria and whether the actions or the criteria need refinements. The sensitive reader will by now realize that this small-scale, small group process of assessment resonates with the grand ideal of the humanistic conversation, in terms of its dialectic relation to the past. On a small scale, the sedimentation of the group reflection – the assessment – as part of the learning discussions embodies the desired humanistic move. Working at this micro scale does more than moving from an idealistic stance regarding humanism towards realizing, or fulfilling it in action. First, it moves from advocating it to opening a dialogue about the ideal and its meaning and the possibilities for exercising it. Second, it hints at its realization through dialogue. Third, this design provides countless opportunities for improvements with its recursive cycles of actions, observations, reflection, and reformulations.

Finally, the entire process bears epistemic, moral, and aesthetic significance that is important to the students' education. On the epistemic level, the groups experience the realization of their consideration, ideals, criteria, and values of assessment as they accepted as external reality, as the "objective" assessment. The external process of assessment fits and reflects their in-group thinking on assessment. The moral significance comes from the process of setting the shared, pragmatic (in the sense of small group made), normative criteria for how we ought to discuss, as a social imperative. A strong congruence occurs between the small group normative ideals and the "worldly" social assessment process. The normative does become a norm, for a change. Aesthetically, the small group adaption of the scientific knowledge about assessment in group-cognition involves translating it into applicable and accepted measures and, as we argued, it also involves its transformation into a normative matter. Turning an action that has external utility ("assessment") into a purposeful act of inner interest, whose importance is not drawn from its external importance, is an aesthetic move.

Conclusions

Talk in schools has been subdued to the regime of the written word. It has seldom been perceived as an educational aim in itself. The primacy of the written is sometimes maintained even in learning environments that work under the new paradigm of dialogic teaching and well after the recognition of the importance of talk to thinking processes (or as thinking processes). In other words, even when talk is not regarded as opposite to learning, but as part and parcel of it, there is the habit of seeing the completion of the learning process in the written word, in forms of written answers, essay writing, and so forth. Talk is instrumentalized by being conceived as a vehicle rather than as simultaneously the process and the pinnacle of learning.

The instrumentalization of the conversation and its reduction to knowledge building mechanism has severe ramifications across the curriculum but the greatest damage is done to the humanities and civic education. Certain forms of humanistic discussion – critical reasoning, dialogic inquiry, and symposium – are perhaps the ultimate end and the highest achievement of the culture of the humanities.

Discussion is a knowledge-informed and value-based event. It brings together in one multidimensional activity the core civil skills: learning, voicing, persuading, and deciding. In discussions, these skills are interrelated. Learning is a process that is also a precondition for the discussion, but also an ability one must have to excel throughout. Voicing is the ultimate form of expression and a precondition for the dialogue, but it gets its value from the ability to perform it in a pluralistic environment, in the natural demanding conditions of the public sphere. Persuading involves high quality of arguing, listening, and critical thinking skills, moral imagination as well as, once more, voice. Unlike dull learning environments, the act of discussing is naturally followed by deciding and reaching resolutions. It is a merging point of the humanistic conversation, which carries in it aesthetic values of performing wisdom and enjoying its beauty; it embodies ethical leaving in its rich set of codes for "living together" in the conversation. It brings together past achievements, wider contexts, and present concern.

We have been arguing that both on the pedagogical and the research level, a consistency must be maintained between the level of the activity that is developed and the level of activity that is evaluated and assessed at the completion of the iteration/curricular unit. If certain cultured forms of discussion are at the focus of learning, then the assessment should focus on such discussions as the ultimate educational goal. The discussion and the practice that construct it should be assessed by themselves, without reducing them to individualistic level of learning in forms of for example, essay writing, test for content, etc. The sociogenetic level of the activity is irreducible. In spite of that, there is no tension between the levels, especially in an educational setting. Teachers are interested in developing all levels; hence the efforts to evaluate learning outcomes should be put on all levels, without reduction. There is compliance between the two (Schwarz & Baker, 2016).

The *practice turn* in learning means that assessment also should focus on practices, and treat them as the locus of the learning activity, at the expense of more traditional educational end products. This idea signifies that the assessment of the activity should be recursive and that, in some cases, performances of the learned practice are declared as "definitive", but, at the same time, they are similar to the learned practice.

Note

1   The reader is invited to read the chapter "Separation and Discourse" in Levinas' *Totality and infinity* (1991) on this endeavor.

References

Agamben, G. (1999). *The man without content*. Palo Alto, CA: Stanford University Press.

Alexander, R. J. (2006). *Towards dialogic teaching: Rethinking classroom talk*. Cambridge: Dialogos.

Arendt, H. (1958/1998). *The human condition*. Chicago: University of Chicago Press.

Aronson, E. (1984). *The social animal* (6th ed.). New York, NY: NH Freeman and Co.

Asterhan, C. S. C., & Schwarz, B. B. (2016). Argumentation for learning: Well-trodden paths and unexplored territories. *Educational Psychologist, 51*(2), 164–187.

Baker, M., Andriessen, J., & Jarvela, S. (Eds.) (2013). *Affective learning together*. London: Routledge.

Bakhtin, M. M. (1981). *The dialogic imagination: Four essays by MM Bakhtin* (M. Holquist, Ed.; C. Emerson & M. Holquist, Trans.). Austin, TX: University of Texas Press.

Barnes, D. R. (1979). *From communication to curriculum*. Harmondsworth, UK: Penguin Books.

Barron, B. (2000). Achieving coordination in collaborative problem-solving groups. *Journal of the Learning Sciences, 9*, 403–436.

Barron, B. (2003). When smart groups fail. *Journal of the Learning Sciences, 12*, 307–359.

Bellanca, J. A. (Ed.). (2010). *21st century skills: Rethinking how students learn*. Bloomington, IN: Solution Tree Press.

Bergman, S. H. (1974). *Dialogical philosophy from Kierkegaard to Buber*. Jerusalem: The Bialik Institute.

Biesta, G. J. (1994). Education as practical intersubjectivity: Towards a critical-pragmatic understanding of education. *Educational Theory, 44*(3), 299–317.

Biesta, G. J. (2012). No education without hesitation. Thinking differently about educational relations. In C. W. Ruitenberg (Ed.), *Philosophy of education yearbook* (pp. 1–13). Urbana, IL.

Biesta, G. J. (2016). *Beyond learning: Democratic education for a human future*. New York: Routledge.

Bingham, C. W., & Sidorkin, A. M. (Eds.). (2004). *No education without relation* (Vol. 259). New York: Peter Lang.

Buber, M. (1971). *I and Thou*. New York, NY: Charles Scribner's Sons.

Cohen, E. G. (1994). Restructuring the classroom: Conditions for productive small groups. *Review of Educational Research, 64*(1), 1–35.

Cole, M., & Distributive Literacy Consortium. (2006). *The fifth dimension: An after-school program built on diversity*. New York: Russell Sage Foundation.

Della Mirandola, P. (1998/1486). *On the dignity of man*. Indianapolis & Cambridge: Hackett Publishing.

Gadamer, H. G. (2006/1975). *Truth and method* (2nd ed.). London & New York, NY: Continuum.

Habermas, J. (1987). *The philosophical discourse on modernity.* Cambridge, MA: The MIT Press.

Hardman, M., & Delafield, B. (2010). Philosophy for children as dialogic teaching. In K. Littleton & C. Howe (Eds.), *Educational dialogues: Understanding and promoting productive interaction* (pp. 149–164). London: Routledge.

Haroutunian-Gordon, S. (2014). *Learning to teach through discussion: The art of turning the soul.* New Haven, CT & London: Yale University Press.

Hennessy, S., Rojas-Drummond, S., Higham, R., Márquez, A. M., Maine, F., Ríos, R. M., … & Barrera, M. J. (2016). Developing a coding scheme for analysing classroom dialogue across educational contexts. *Learning, Culture and Social Interaction, 9,* 16–44.

Howe, C., & Abedin, M. (2013). Classroom dialogue: A systematic review across four decades of research. *Cambridge Journal of Education, 43*(3), 325–356. doi:10.1080/030576 4X.2013.786024

Jenkins, P., & Lyle, S. (2010). Enacting dialogue: The impact of promoting philosophy for children on the literate thinking of identified poor readers, aged 10. *Language and Education, 24*(6), 459–472.

Jolliffe, W. (2007). *Cooperative learning in the classroom: Putting it into practice.* London: Paul Chapman.

Krashen, S. D. (2011). *Free voluntary reading.* Santa Barbara, CA: ABC-CLIO.

Kristeva, J. (1991). *Strangers to ourselves.* New York: Columbia University Press.

Kutnick, P., Blatchford, P., Baines, E., & Tolmie, A. (2013). *Effective group-work in primary school classrooms: The SPRinG approach.* London: Springer.

Lefstein, A. (2010). More helpful as problem than solution: Some implications of situating dialogue in classrooms. In K. Littleton & C. Howe (Eds.), *Educational dialogues: Understanding and promoting productive interaction* (pp. 170–191). London: Routledge.

Levinas, E. (1991). *Totality and infinity: An essay on exteriority.* Dordrecht, The Netherlands: Kluwer Academic Publishers.

Lipman, M. (2003). *Thinking in education.* Cambridge: Cambridge University Press.

Lipman, M. (2010). *Philosophy goes to school.* Philadelphia, PA: Temple University Press.

Lipman, M., Sharp, A. M., & Oscanyan, F. S. (2010). *Philosophy in the classroom.* Philadelphia, PA: Temple University Press.

Mercer, N., & Dawes, L. (2014). The study of talk between teachers and students, from the 1970s until the 2010s, *Oxford Review of Education, 40*(4), 430–445. doi:10.1080/030549 85.2014.934087

Mercer, N., & Littleton, K. (2007). *Dialogue and the development of children's thinking: A sociocultural approach.* New York: Routledge.

Mercer, N., Wegerif, R., & Dawes, L. (1999). Children's talk and the development of reasoning in the classroom. *British Educational Research Journal, 25*(1), 95–111.

Michaels, S., O'Connor, C., & Resnick, L. B. (2008). Deliberative discourse idealized and realized: Accountable talk in the classroom and in civic life. *Studies in Philosophy and Education, 27*(4), 283–297.

Noddings, N. (2011). *Peace education: How we come to love and hate war.* New York: Cambridge University Press.

Nystrand, M. (1997). *Opening dialogue: Understanding the dynamics of language and learning in the English classroom. Language and literacy series.* New York & London: Teachers College Press.

Pellegrino, J. W. (2014). A learning science perspective on the design and use of assessment in education. In K. Sawyer (Ed.), *The Cambridge handbook of the learning sciences* (2nd ed., pp. 233–252). Cambridge University Press.

Pellegrino, J. W., DiBello, L. V., & Goldman, S. R. (2016). A framework for conceptualizing and evaluating the validity of instructionally relevant assessments. *Educational Psychologist, 51*(1), 59–81.

Resnick, L. B., Asterhan, C. S. C., & Clarke, S. N. (Eds.). (2015). *Socializing intelligence through academic talk and dialogue.* AREA Books Publications.

Reznitskaya, A., Kuo, L. J., Clark, A. M., Miller, B., Jadallah, M., Anderson, R. C., & Nguyen-Jahiel, K. (2009). Collaborative reasoning: A dialogic approach to group discussions. *Cambridge Journal of Education, 39*(1), 29–48.

Rojas-Drummond, S., Maine, F., Alarcón, M., Trigo, A. L., Barrera, M. J., Mazón, N., & Hofmann, R. (2017). Dialogic literacy: Talking, reading and writing among primary school children. *Learning, Culture and Social Interaction, 12*, 45–62.

Rosenzweig, F. (2005/1921). *The star of redemption*. Madison, WI: University of Wisconsin Press.

Scardamalia, M. (2002). Collective cognitive responsibility for the advancement of knowledge. *Liberal Education in a Knowledge Society, 97*, 67–98.

Scardamalia, M., & Bereiter, C. (1991). Higher levels of agency for children in knowledge building: A challenge for the design of new knowledge media. *Journal of the Learning Sciences, 1*, 37–68.

Schwarz, B. B., & Baker, M. J. (2016). *Dialogue, argumentation and education: History, theory and practice*. New York: Cambridge University Press.

Schwarz, B. B., Neuman, Y., & Biezuner, S. (2000). Two "wrongs" may make a right…If they argue together! *Cognition & Instruction, 18*(4), 461–494.

Schwarz, B. B., de Groot, R., Mavrikis, M., & Dragon, T. (2015). Learning to learn together with CSCL tools. *International Journal of Computer-Supported Collaborative Learning, 10*(3), 239–271.

Schwarz, D. L. (1995). The emergence of abstract representations in dyad problem solving. *The Journal of the Learning Sciences, 4*(3), 321–354.

Sennett, R. (2011). Humanism. *The Hedgehog Review, 13*(2), 21–30.

Sharan, S. (1980). Cooperative learning in small groups: Recent methods and effects on achievement, attitudes, and ethnic relations. *Review of Educational Research, 50*(2), 241–271.

Shor, I., & Freire, P. (1987). *A pedagogy for liberation: Dialogues on transforming education*. London: Bergin & Garvey.

Slakmon, B. (2015). *The emergence of dialogic dimension in philosophy classroom* (Unpublished Doctoral Thesis). The Hebrew University of Jerusalem, Israel.

Slakmon, B., & Schwarz, B. B. (2014). Disengaged students and dialogic learning: The role of CSCL affordances. *International Journal of Computer-Supported Collaborative Learning, 9*(2), 157–183.

Slakmon, B., & Schwarz, B. B. (2017). "Wherever you go, you will be a polis": Spatial practices and political education in computer-supported collaborative learning discussions. *Journal of the Learning Sciences, 26*(2), 184–225.

Splitter, L. J., & Sharp, A. M. (1995). *Teaching for better thinking: The classroom community of inquiry*. Melbourne: Australian Council for Educational Research.

Stahl, G. (2006). *Group cognition: Computer support for building collaborative knowledge*. Cambridge, MA: MIT Press.

Stahl, G. (2016). From intersubjectivity to group cognition. *Computer Supported Cooperative Work (CSCW), 25*(4–5), 355–384.

Stahl, G. (2017). *Essays in philosophy of group cognition*. Lulu.com.

Tannen, D. (2013). The argument culture: Agonism & the common good. *Argument, 142*(2), 177–184.

Todd, S. (2012). *Learning from the other: Levinas, psychoanalysis, and ethical possibilities in education*. Albany, NY: SUNY Press.

Topping, K. J., & Trickey, S. (2007). Collaborative philosophical inquiry for schoolchildren: Cognitive gains at 2-year follow-up. *British Journal of Educational Psychology, 77*(4), 787–796.

Trilling, B., & Fadel, C. (2009). *21st century skills: Learning for life in our times*. San Francisco, CA: John Wiley & Sons.

Vygotsky, L. S. (1980). *Mind in society: The development of higher psychological processes*. Cambridge, MA: Harvard University Press.

Webb, N. M., Franke, M. L., De, T., Chan, A. G., Freund, D., Shein, P., & Melkonian, D. K. (2009). 'Explain to your partner': Teachers' instructional practices and students' dialogue in small groups. *Cambridge Journal of Education, 39*(1), 49–70.

Wegerif, R. (2007). *Dialogic education and technology: Expanding the space of learning* (Vol. 7). Springer Science & Business Media.

Wegerif, R. (2013). *Dialogic: Education for the internet age.* London: Routledge.

Wegerif, R., Fujita, T., Doney, J., Linares, J. P., Richards, A., & Van Rhyn, C. (2017). Developing and trialing a measure of group thinking. *Learning and Instruction, 48,* 40–50.

10

THEORY AND THE EVALUATION OF TEACHING THINKING

Evidence about the impact of thinking skills approaches: what is it important to evaluate?

Robert Burden and Steve Higgins

Introduction

Claims about the value of teaching thinking date back to at least the early Greeks, with similar importance evidence in other educational traditions, such as Confucianism (Li & Wegerif, 2014) and Arabic culture (Allamnakhrah, 2013). At one level the underlying message is indisputable as in generation after generation the disastrous consequences of the lack of critical, careful, caring and creative thought within society are all too evident. However, the issue of what can be counted as acceptable and convincing evidence for the successful outcomes of cognitive education is rather more challenging. There are those such as Smith (1992), who dispute the very value of the word 'thinking', because of how the use of the term varies according to time, place and circumstance. There is also a longstanding debate as to whether thinking can best be taught as a stand-alone activity, as advocated by Feuerstein and his followers, or should be taught by infusion into various aspects of curriculum studies, as concluded by McGuinness in an influential report to the UK Government (McGuinness, 1999). This chapter explores the role of theory in developing our understanding of what we should be looking for in terms of understanding the efficacy of teaching thinking.

If we are to be able to answer the fundamental question to which this chapter is aimed, we must first seek to define our terms.

- What exactly are we implying when we refer to teaching for thinking and cognitive education?
- What, if any, are the most fundamental ways in which thinking is made evident?
- Is there some form of developmental sequence by which we can tell if our level of thinking is improving?
- What is the exact nature of the relationship between thinking and learning?

- The very nature of cognitive education implies a theory of education with very specific outcomes. How specific or broad should these outcomes be? Over what timescale should they be evaluated?
- What precise inputs are likely to lead to specific outputs and under what circumstances?

These and other related questions underlie the need for some form of conceptual framework within which the ideas can be linked and analysed. The approach to be taken here is that of social interactionism (Shalin, 1986; Williams & Burden, 1997), whereby the contributions made to any form of learning are made by the dynamic interactions between teachers, learners, tasks and context. Such an approach relates to a Pragmatist perspective of the importance of relational understanding, both in terms of Dewey's transactionalism (Vanderstraeten, 2002) and Peirce's 'laboratory philosophy' (Hookway, 2002). As Peirce would argue, once we are clear about what difference an understanding makes to our future experience, we can then investigate and find out.

This enables us to focus our earlier questions further, as follows:

- From an educational perspective, what exactly is it that we require our students to learn?
- What specific approaches are likely to produce the desired outcomes?
- How can we measure success?
- How long is this likely to last?
- Do these approaches work with everyone?
- What are the attributes of a successful teacher of thinking?
- What are the key aspects of a supportive environment?

Many of these questions have been addressed on numerous occasions, some of which have been summarised by Burden (1998) and by Fisher (2012). In particular, Burden refers to seven important aspects of the thinking process identified by Nickerson (1999). These are:

i. the basic operations or processes involved when we think, such as observing, using space/time relationships, measuring, classifying, predicting, inferring and problem-solving;
ii. domain-specific (declarative) knowledge;
iii. knowledge of the normative principles of reassuring, such as logic and probabilistic thinking;
iv. the use of thinking tools or routines, such as heuristics or strategies;
v. metacognitive knowledge and skilfulness in relation to one's own thinking processes;
vi. attitudinal and dispositional variables, such as those in 'learning to learn' or identified by Costa as 'habits of mind';

vii. the effects of belief, such as ontological beliefs about the nature of intelligence or epistemological beliefs about the nature of knowledge.

We believe that answers to these questions are most likely to be found from a consideration of the evidence arising from different studies applying a range of methodologies and approaches to evaluation.

First, of course, it is necessary to think about what the term 'thinking' means; how it can be defined and described. Here an invaluable text is Moseley and colleagues' (2005) *Frameworks for thinking*. It reviews philosophical, sociological and psychological perspectives on thinking, then presents an analysis of 43 distinct taxonomies and frameworks which describe and classify thinking. These are organised in three families: frameworks for instructional design; for productive thinking (reasoning and creative thinking); and those describing cognitive structure and/or cognitive development. It includes well-known approaches, such as Bloom's taxonomy of the cognitive domain (with its more recent revision by Anderson and Krathwohl), Guildford's Structure of the Intellect model, Piaget's stage model, and Biggs and Collis' SOLO taxonomy (Structure of the Observed Learning Outcome). It also includes less well-known descriptions and classifications such as Belenky's 'Women's Ways of Knowing' and Romiszowski's analysis of knowledge and skills (Moseley, Baumfield, Elliott, Higgins, Miller, & Newton, 2005). The book provides a comprehensive account of the different ways in which thinking has been conceptualised so as to identify how it might be taught and evaluated. Without clarity about definitions and concepts, both theoretical and empirical studies will flounder.

A number of meta-analytic studies then stand out as indicators of the efficacy of thinking skills approaches in enhancing learning outcomes (Dignath, Buettner, & Langfeldt, 2008; Donker, De Boer, Kostons, Dignath van Ewijk, & Van der Werf, 2014; Higgins, Hall, Baumfield, & Moseley, 2005; Klauer & Phye, 2008; Marzano, 1998). All of these reviews identify medium to strong effect sizes of thinking skills programmes on learning outcomes (Dignath et al. +0.62; Donker et al. +0.66; Klauer & Phye, +0.69; Higgins et al. +0.62; Marzano +0.65). The application of metacognitive or self-regulatory strategies was found in each case to provide a particularly valuable impact.

A detailed consideration of the report by Higgins and colleagues (2005) helps to highlight both strengths and weaknesses of the meta-analytic approach in educational research. Only studies involving comparison groups were considered eligible. This was to control for the effect of maturation or other aspects of teaching with an appropriate counterfactual condition (Higgins, 2017). This meant that only 29 of the original 191 studies identified following a wide literature sweep could be included. These studies were carried out across primary, secondary and special schools in 12 different countries, so were drawn from a wide range of educational settings. Each had a sample size of more than ten pupils. Three forms of outcomes were considered (a) cognitive effects as measured by some form of intelligence or reasoning test (e.g. Raven's Progressive Matrices (Raven & Court,

1998)); (b) curriculum-based assessment in three main areas – science, mathematics and literacy; (c) attitudinal and dispositional change.

The overall effect sizes for both cognitive and curriculum outcomes were established at 0.62, but there was considerable variation across programmes and curriculum subjects. The most widely evaluated programme, Feuerstein's Instrumental Enrichment, employed mainly with those experiencing different forms of disability, produced an overall effect size of 0.52, mainly on the Raven's Matrices test. Programmes geared towards improvement in curriculum subject areas, such as CASE (Cognitive Acceleration in Science Education) and CAME (Cognitive Acceleration in Mathematics Education: Adey & Shayer, 1994), appeared to have considerable impact on examination success, but this tended to vary across subject, age and gender (Chang & Barufaldi, 1991; Cunningham, Brandon, & Frydenberg, 2002; Strang & Shayer, 1993).

Higgins and colleagues point out that only 'fuzzy generalisations' can be drawn from this data, particularly since studies reported little about the programmes or aspects of implementation and use within classrooms, thereby making it difficult to identify common features between programmes. Main points to arise from their conclusions are that use needs to be matched to the particular teaching context and monitored closely to ensure potential benefits. Moreover, further research was needed to clarify specific causes of any benefits and to identify where most impact was likely to occur, in terms of age groups and curriculum aspects. There did not seem to be any particular theoretical position which was superior, though programmes and approaches explicitly using the idea of metacognition did appear to be those which had a greater effect (an effect size of +0.96).

This kind of review can tell us whether learners, on average, make greater progress on tested outcomes, compared with those who have not experienced thinking approaches at the end of the period of research. So, we can therefore be reasonably confident that such approaches *can* be effective. However, there are also important things that we still do not know. We do not know *how* they work, in terms of any particular approaches or techniques. We certainly do not know *why* they work, in terms of validating any underpinning theory or theories. In addition, we just know that they work *on average*; we don't know if there are some groups of learners they are more effective for, or whether there are some teachers who are more successful than others, or how much the context affects the outcomes. Regression analysis of the patterns of findings in a meta-analysis can give us some indicators (such as whether younger or older learners tend to benefit more), but these can only be tentative until further research is undertaken.

Some of these issues have been taken up in subsequent studies. The impressive work of Topping and Trickey, for example, focusing explicitly on the effects of introducing Philosophy for Children (P4C) into the curriculum of mainstream schools, took a longitudinal, multilevel approach. In a review of the literature (Trickey & Topping, 2004) they describe in detail the fundamental aspects of Philosophy for Children and summarise previous investigations into this approach. A subsequent paper (Trickey & Topping, 2006) describes in detail the introduction of P4C into

Scottish primary schools and how the results of this intervention were evaluated. A third paper (Topping & Trickey, 2007) describes the continuing improvement of the students involved after 18 months and also focuses on the changes in the pupils' perceptions of themselves as learners. The Trickey and Topping studies demonstrate a thorough but rare attempt in work on thinking training outcomes. They also show how to overcome some of the weaknesses of previous studies and how studies of this kind can be implemented in schools. They selected what they considered to be relevant outcome measures in both curriculum and affective areas and they followed through the effects for some time after the intervention had finished.

Further studies and analysis

It is not the intention of this chapter to provide a comprehensive list of positive and negative evaluation studies, but to focus rather on a small sample of studies which highlight specific aspects of evaluation that need to be taken into account in developing an understanding of the relationship between theory and practice.

There are several readily identifiable features of Feuerstein's Instrumental Enrichment (FIE) that lend themselves to the evaluation process. It is a highly structured programme, built upon a sound theoretical rationale, involving an intensive period of specialist training, requiring at least two hours input per day over two to three years. This means that FIE interventions have tended to be focused on specific groups of young people and adults rather than general school populations. Several early positive reviews of the effectiveness of FIE (Savell, Twohig, & Rachford, 1986; Shayer & Beasley, 1987) have identified these features while others have identified special groups where positive changes have been found in both intelligence and behaviour.

One group of disabled learners for whom FIE appears to have been particularly effective is those with hearing impairment (Hayward, Towery-Woolsey, Arbitman-Smith, & Aldridge, 1988; Thickpenny & Howie, 1990). A South African study by Skuy and his colleagues (1995) introducing this programme into a disadvantaged mining community produced impressive anecdotal results, while a further study by Kaufman & Burden (2004) revealed a remarkable increase in self-esteem of a group of severely disabled adolescents over 18 months of intensive training. At the other end of the scale, Kaniel & Reichenberg (1992) report the effects of generalisability when the programme was used with a group of talented adolescents in Israel. Kozulin (2000) summarises many similar studies in highlighting the diversity of instrumental enrichment application. Shiell's (2002) doctoral study presents a meta-analysis of 36 separate studies with an analysis of the impact on cognitive, academic and affective domains. Each of these studies helps us to identify important variables contributing to successful outcomes.

One of the most intensive approaches to cognitive acceleration in the UK has been that of the Kings College London team under the leadership of Philip Adey and Michael Shayer (Shayer & Adey, 2002). From the early 1990s onwards their impressive evaluations of their CASE (Cognitive Acceleration through Science

Education) and CAME (Cognitive Acceleration through Mathematics Education) programmes, designed specifically to promote higher level thinking in young adolescents, have provided coherent evidence for positive effects on grades achieved at later stages in formal public examinations (Adey & Shayer, 1994). A further investigation by Shayer (1999) revealed that schools taking this approach produced significant academic added value over a five-year period compared with matched comparisons schools in the same area. Their work was firmly rooted constructivist psychology initially based on Piagetian theory, though later modified to include a Vygotskian perspective. As researchers in this field, they were keen to develop a testable approach which might demonstrate effects in relation to the underpinning theoretical ideas.

Adey, Robertson, & Venville (2002) investigated the evidence of applying the Kings College cognitive acceleration method to 5 and 6 year olds in a disadvantaged inner city area. Approximately 300 children in 14 Year 1 classes in 10 schools for the experimental group and 170 children in eight classes in five schools constituted the control. Children in experimental classes experienced a set of 29 activities designed to promote cognitive conflict and encourage social construction and metacognition over one school year. The experimental group overall made significantly greater gains in cognitive development over the period of the experiment than the controls in both direct (effect size 0.47) and transfer (effect size 0.43) tests, although the difference was significantly more pronounced for the girls than the boys. Of particular interest in this study are the specific tests of cognitive ability constructed by the researchers, the nature of the intervention programme and the findings with regard to gender difference. International replication has shown some consistency on Piagetian measures (e.g. Oliver, Venville, & Adey, 2012, in Australia), though independent validation with curriculum outcomes has been less successful (e.g. Aunio, Hautamäki, & Van Luit, 2005; Hanley, Bohnke, Slavin, Elliott, & Croudace, 2016).

Burke & Williams (2008) devised a programme for explicitly teaching thinking skills to 11/12-year-olds over an intensive period of eight weeks. An infusion approach was taken whereby the language of thinking, the development of metacognition and the promotion of thinking dispositions were introduced across the curriculum. A sample of 178 students were taught across three conditions: individual learning, collaborative learning and a control group. Of particular interest to the present chapter is the approach that was used by the researchers to identify possible changes in the students' thinking skills and their perceptions of their ability as learners. These included an individualised test based on Beyer's (1997) six-task format, qualitative tests of learners' conceptions of good thinking (Burke & Williams, 2008), the Myself-As-a-Learner Scale (MALS) (Burden, 2012) and the Assessment of Learner Centred Principles (McCombs, 1999). The results appear to show a significant improvement in the thinking ability of both the individual and collaborative groups and in the use of metacognitive reflection questions. These findings applied also to the results of the qualitative tests of learners' conceptions of good thinking. However, the main difference between scores on the MALS was in favour of the collaborative learning group, most specifically with regard to enjoyment in problem-solving.

Further light on the importance of collaborative thinking is thrown by the 'teaching thinking through talking' project of Wegerif, Mercer, & Dawes (1999), both through its positive results on improving individual and collective reasoning scores on Raven's Progressive Matrices, but, more significantly by the kind of dialogic reasoning that the primary school children were able to show. While some of the ways of talking taught in the programme were found to promote critical thinking by challenging claims with explicit verbal reasons in the form of 'I disagree with x because of y', creative reasoning was also promoted by means of listening to others carefully, asking open questions and seeking alternatives.

While these results appear to be very encouraging, there was no follow-up data on the possible continuation of the intervention or its long-term impact. Moreover, no information is provided on the potential transfer of thinking skills into different curriculum areas. Finally, as the study was conducted using an experimental-control group methodology, information on the specific and broader context of the study, the reactions of the teachers involved and the effects upon which school community were gathered. The tests themselves nevertheless provide an interestingly creative approach to obtaining outcome measures beyond cognitive measures.

A paper by Hu et al. (2010) describes how a theory-based learn to think (LTT) curriculum for primary school students sought to draw upon the strengths of both out-of-context and infusion approaches. One hundred and sixty-six students in three classes of Grade 1 (6+ years old), Grade 2 (7+ years old) and Grade 3 (8+ years old) in a primary school in Shanxi province, China were randomly ascribed to experimental and control groups. All students were pre-tested for non-verbal intelligence and academic achievement. Experimental students followed the LTT curriculum (one activity every two weeks) for four school years. This was based on a thinking method, thinking quality and thinking context model, which drew on Chongde Lin's theory of intelligence, Piaget's theory of cognitive development, and Vygotsky's social construction theory. All were post-tested on three occasions for thinking ability and four times for academic achievement. Grade 1 and Grade 2 students showed positive effects of LTT from one year after their start, increasing in thinking ability, Chinese and mathematics, with the main effects showing with students in the middle band of initial ability. Of particular value in this study is its longitudinal nature and its randomised control design, together with the specific measure of thinking skills that the researchers constructed.

Taking a broader perspective

A paper by Dewey & Bento (2009) serves to exemplify the complexities of unravelling the outcomes of even sophisticated, well-designed cognitive education projects. A reasonably large-scale sample of 384 primary school pupils were divided into experimental and control groups and taught by the infusion method of activating children's thinking skills (ACTS), as advocated by McGuinness (1999). Pre and post measures of change were implemented over a two-year period involving both quantitative and qualitative instruments. Results showed a slight improvement on cognitive testing with a small effect size and clear signs of more sophisticated use of language and questioning. However, no improvement was found in the pupils' perception of themselves as learners or in their behaviour in problem situations. The teachers nevertheless commented positively on their own satisfaction with the infusion method. One major problem throughout was the issue of programme fidelity. That is, the question of how to monitor whether ACTS was actually being implemented, by which teachers, at what level, and to which (groups of) pupils. This serves to highlight opportunities that can be missed in apparently negative studies in helping our understanding of why an intervention appears not to work and brings us back to the need for even more fine-grained mixed method studies in which quantitative and qualitative data work together in identifying exactly what kind of input leads to what specific output.

Drawing upon an alternative research design utilising an action research framework, Burden & Nichols (2000) were able to investigate in close detail exactly why a promising thinking skills intervention also met with failure. In this instance, an illuminative approach to evaluation based upon earlier work of Stufflebeam (1971) and Parlett & Hamilton (1972) examined the key elements of setting, plans, action and participant reactions in contributing to evaluation as an aid to decision-making. The model, referred to hitherto as SPARE, directed the evaluators to describe in detail the setting of the project in a large urban secondary school, to record the plans or intentions of the instigator of the project (in this instance the school principal), the actions taken by the school faculty to introduce thinking skills across all aspects of the curriculum, followed by the reactions of all stakeholders (staff and students). The main focus of the evaluators in this instance was the very process by which decisions were made at one level of the management hierarchy and carried through by those at the workface, particularly with regard to the attitudes of the participants to the nature of the proposed and implemented changes. It became clear, as a result, that not enough consultation and preparation was carried out before instigating curriculum changes in a directive manner, that the majority of the teaching staff were not only resistant but openly hostile to the proposed changes, and that this reluctance was passed on to the students who were thus unable to comprehend how learning to think was of any value to their own perceived educational objectives.

A further cautionary study

One of the most salutary studies of the effects of introducing Feuerstein's Instrumental Enrichment programme into British Schools was carried out by Blagg (1991). The study has a number of exemplary aspects. It received substantial government funding as part of a Low Achieving Pupil project which enabled researchers to follow through the effects of introducing FIE into four secondary schools in the south-west of England over a three-year period. A comprehensive research design enabled Blagg and his colleagues to obtain wide-ranging data of both a quantitative and qualitative nature relating to the effects on both students and teachers. While the results were somewhat equivocal, the nature of the design made it possible to identify exactly what went wrong and why. It had the benefit of being a well-funded government initiative to explore ways of providing a more effective education for those pupils in their final two years in school who were not benefiting from the traditional system of public examinations. Thus, it was geared at a relatively small, specific group and not aimed at wider generalisations. In many ways, the care and attention given to the evaluation was greater than that given to the implementation of this project. Both quantitative and qualitative assessment procedures were employed within an illuminative design, again based on Stufflebeam's (1971) Context, Input, Process and Product (CIPP) model.

As a 'top down' initiative, all project funding was controlled by administrative officers and advisors without any 'grass roots' commitment from teachers, who were generally ill-prepared and given little choice as to their involvement. This was largely overcome as the project progressed, but, despite the high level of funding, the attrition rate among the four secondary schools involved was high. The assessment procedures included pre and post measures of the pupils' intellectual ability, their reading, mathematics and study skills and their attitude towards themselves as learners and schoolwork in general, largely by means of a critical incident observation schedule. Changes in the teachers, meanwhile, were assessed by means of a critical self-reflection schedule and applications of Cattell's 16PF questionnaire. In terms of outcome, no significant improvements overall were found in any of the pupil basic subjects attainments, although the observation schedules revealed them as being more actively involved in class discussions, more self-disciplined, becoming better listeners and more likely to defend their opinions on the basis of logical evidence. Many gained in confidence and showed improved self-esteem over the intervention period. No improvements were found in intelligence test scores.

Teacher-focused outcomes were considerably more promising. Scores on the 16PF demonstrated that, in general, by the end of the project teachers had become more assertive, confident and self-reliant. Compared with those teaching the control groups, the FIE teachers became more positive about their roles, feeling more satisfied with their job, more confident in their teaching abilities, more committed to their profession and more valued in their work. Their attitudes towards the capabilities of low achieving pupils also became much more positive. One of the most important lessons to be learnt from Blagg's study was the powerful part played by the context into which any thinking skills programme is introduced. While Blagg clearly identifies weaknesses within the rigid structure and transfer difficulties inherent within the FIE programme, the obstacles provided by the historical and social setting of this particular intervention make plain the need for a much broader perspective to be taken than that of a simple input-output design.

Key variables to be taken into account in evaluation studies

Identifying the variables involved in each of the research studies described above makes it possible to draw up the following list:

- Design factors
  ◦ pre/post implementation data to be collected
  ◦ involvement of control/comparison groups

- ◦ randomised sampling
- ◦ quantitative/qualitative methods
- ◦ positivist/illuminative paradigm
- Input
  - ◦ the nature of the programme to be implemented
  - ◦ stand-alone versus infusion methodology
  - ◦ length of input
  - ◦ training and commitment of teachers
- Recipients
  - ◦ general population
  - ◦ age, gender, disability, cultural background
- Nature of assessment producers
  - ◦ structured tasks/standardised tests vs. home-grown
  - ◦ application of a reliable thinking taxonomy
  - ◦ questionnaires
  - ◦ interviews
  - ◦ 'real world observations'
  - ◦ criterion-referenced portfolios
- Time to impact
  - ◦ Concurrent (e.g. process data describing learner interaction/thinking)
  - ◦ Post-test (cognitive/affective/conative impact)
  - ◦ Follow-up (cognitive/affective/conative effects, or wider dispositional outcomes)
  - ◦ Long term (cognitive/affective/conative effects, or wider dispositional outcomes)

A theory-guided evaluation would enable a logic model for the *why* and *how* of effects to be linked to an assessment of *what* effects on *which* pupils and explored as part of the evaluation. As an example, a measure of the quality of learners' collaboration could be correlated with outcomes to identify specific features of interaction related to successful learning. Linking process and outcome evaluation data would allow aspects of a specific theory to be tested.

The importance of context

One further area in need of consideration is that of context. A somewhat independent body of research has investigated the nature of the contexts within which thinking and learning can thrive and argued for the importance of authenticity. Hadjioannon (2007), for example, posed the fundamental question of what classroom environments that support authentic discussion look like. After defining authentic discussions as dialogically oriented interactions where participants present and consider multiple perspectives and often use others' input in constructing their contributions, this author carried out a qualitative analysis of a fifth-grade classroom community where such discussions were frequent. Seven aspects of a supportive classroom environment were identified: the nature of the physical environment, curriculum demands and enacted curriculum, teacher beliefs, student beliefs about discussions, relationships among members, classroom procedures and norms of classroom participation.

A longstanding tradition of research into effective learning environments has emanated largely from Australia, particularly with regard to the teaching of science and mathematics. Although terminology has tended to differ slightly across studies, a paper by Dorman (2001) summarises succinctly nine dimensions of a positive classroom climate contributing to academic efficacy: student cohesiveness, teacher support, investigation task orientation, co-operation, equity, involvement, personal relevance, shared control, student negotiation. Allodi (2010), by contrast, while recognising that social climate is an essential factor in the educational process, identified several reasons why this had been neglected in the Swedish context: dualistic and hierarchical views, bureaucratic systems, reductionist interpretation, difficulties in handling and evaluating social values and goals, and post-modern criticism of scientific knowledge and psychology.

De Corte, Verschaffel, & Masui (2004) have provided a framework for designing powerful learning environments for thinking and problem-solving. Referred to as the CLIA model, the focus here is on competence, learning, intervention and assessment. Building upon the earlier work of Brown & Campione (1996) and their 'Fostering of Learning Communities' (FLC) project, these authors posit that effective learning communities are learner-centred, knowledge-centred, assessment-centred and community-centred which need to be aligned in ways that mutually support each other. In examining more explicitly the four components of the CLIA model, De Corte, Verschaffel, & Masui (2004) identify the importance of developing competence in both cognitive and conative components involving motivation and volition; a definition of learning as active/constructive, cumulative, self-regulated, goal-directed, situated and both collaboratively and individually constructed. Intervention should initiate and support the active, construction acquisition process in all students, the development of self-regulation strategies, preferably in real-life situations and across different subjects, and a culture of self-reflection. Assessment should be aligned with these components; developing competence in specific areas, diagnostic feedback about deep understanding of content and their mastery and productive use of thinking skills, together with alternative forms of assessment geared to both individual and group self-assessment. The De Corte et al. model (2004) is probably the most comprehensive and fine-tuned approach to understanding the contribution of context to learning outcomes that has yet been devised.

Ercikan & Seixas (2011) identify three main areas for outcome-based measures of higher order thinking skills, which they refer to as the *Cognitive and Learning model*, the *Task model* and the *Evidence model*. In applying the Cognitive and Learning model assessment practice will focus on elements of knowledge, competencies and thinking at which the intervention is aimed. The Task model will describe evidence of learning progression in specified areas of the curriculum, while the Evidence model describes criteria for what should be measured as well as how they can be scored. This approach can be very helpful in unravelling the different kinds of evidence on offer in various research studies to support claims of the effectiveness of one or another intervention. Thus, the application of various IQ type measures in a before and after design (e.g. Topping & Trickey, 2007) can be seen as an example of the Cognitive and Learning model. The success of students in public examinations following the application of Adey and Shayer's CASE and CAME programmes, on the other hand, can be seen as an example of the Task model. It can be argued that a combination of assessment techniques reflecting all three models would substantially increase the power of any evaluation study and establish greater validity in terms of outcomes.

Conclusion

Despite the plethora of interventions in recent years aimed at enhancing thinking in classrooms and beyond, this review has shown that critical evaluation of their effectiveness has been limited by different conceptualisations of what it means to be an effective thinker and different theoretical models of how thinking can be taught. In addition to this, it has been argued that our overall understanding of the experience of thinking *in situ* and the importance of context is under-researched and poorly understood. We know it is possible to teach for better thinking, but we know little about whether students then routinely do. This has had a knock-on effect on what researchers are looking for, what it is they are trying to find out, the terms they use to describe what they are looking at and for, how they choose to design their interventions, the population at which they are aiming, and how they choose to design their approach to evaluation including the selection of measuring instruments to determine change. For example, Trickey & Topping (2004, 2006) and Topping & Trickey (2007) focused on Philosophy for Children while Yang & Chung (2009) investigated the cultivation of critical thinking within civic education. Dewey & Bento (2009), on the other hand, took an 'infusion methodology' approach whereby teachers were trained to identify specific types of thinking and map these on to existing areas of the curriculum. Others still such as De Corte, Verschaffel, & Van De Ven (2001) have examined cognitive and metacognitive strategies that facilitate understanding including text comprehension.

Although this chapter has explored the complexity of the situation and the difficulty in drawing out common threads and lessons learnt which, to an extent, has limited the development of knowledge and understanding, it has also demonstrated that much has been achieved. The weight of evidence from a multitude of research studies taking a range of different perspectives is strongly supportive of the value of teaching people of all ages and impairments how to think critically, creatively and ethically, at least in the short and medium term. However, we need to be absolutely clear as to what we want to achieve and what the conditions are under which this can best be accomplished. To do this we need to begin with a theory of education which goes beyond the passing of examinations or even increasing population IQ levels. We therefore need to develop more sophisticated methods to investigate both internal and external change, mentally and behaviourally, particularly with regard to decision-making within real world situations. The issues are too multilevel and complex to encompass within any one research study. However, a finer grained analysis of the contribution played by the variables identified in this chapter, involving both quantitative and qualitative methods within an interpretative paradigm can go a long way in helping to answer many of the questions set at the beginning.

References

Adey, P., & Shayer, M. (1994). *Really raising standards: Cognitive intervention and academic achievement.* London: Routledge.

Adey, P., Robertson, A., & Venville, G. (2002). Effects of a cognitive acceleration programme year I pupils. *British Journal of Educational Psychology, 72*, 1–25.

Allamnakhrah, A. (2013). Learning critical thinking in Saudi Arabia: Student perceptions of secondary pre-service teacher education programs. *Journal of Education and Learning, 2*(1), 197.

Allodi, M. W. (2010). The meaning of social climate of learning environments: Some reasons why we do not care enough about it. *Learning Environments Research, 13*, 89–104.

Aunio, P., Hautamäki, J., & Van Luit, J. E. (2005). Mathematical thinking intervention programmes for preschool children with normal and low number sense. *European Journal of Special Needs Education, 20*(2), 131–146.

Beyer, B. K. (1997). *Improving student thinking: A comprehensive approach.* Boston, MA: Allyn and Bacon.

Blagg, N. (1991). *Can we teach intelligence?* Hillsdale, NJ: Lawrence Erlbaum.

Brown, A. L., & Campione, J. C. (1996). Psychological theory and the design of innovative learning environments: On procedures, principles and systems. In L. Schauble & R. Glaser (Eds.), *Innovations in learning: New environments for education* (pp. 289–325). Mahwah, NJ: Lawrence Erlbaum.

Burden, R. L. (1998). Assessing children's perceptions of themselves as learners and problem solvers. *School Psychology International, 19*(4), 291–306.

Burden, R. L. (2012). *Myself-As-a-Learner scale.* (2nd ed.). Birmingham: Imaginative Minds.

Burden, R., & Nichols, L. (2000). Evaluating the process of introducing a thinking skills programme into the secondary school curriculum. *Research Papers in Education, 15*(3), 203–305.

Burke, L. A., & Williams, J. M. (2008). Developing young thinkers: An intervention aimed to enhance children's thinking skills. *Thinking Skills and Creativity, 3*, 104–124.

Chang, C.-Y., & Barufaldi, J. P. (1991). The use of a problem solving based instructional model in initiating change in students' achievement and alternative frameworks. *International Journal of Science Education, 21*, 373–388.

Cunningham, E. G., Brandon, C. M., & Frydenberg, E. (2002). Enhancing coping resources in early adolescence through a school-based program teaching optimistic thinking skills. *Anxiety Coping and Stress, 15*, 369–381.

De Corte, E., Verschaffel, L., & Masui, C. (2004). The CLIA-model: A framework for designing powerful learning environments for thinking and problem solving. *European Journal of Psychology of Education, 19*(4), 365–384.

De Corte, E., Verschaffel, L., & Van De Ven, A. (2001). Improving text comprehension strategies in upper primary school children: A design experiment. *British Journal of Educational Psychology, 71*, 531–559.

Dewey, J., & Bento, J. (2009). Activating children's thinking skills (ACTS): The effects of an infusion approach to teaching thinking in primary schools. *British Journal of Educational Psychology, 79*, 329–351.

Dignath, C., Buettner, G., & Langfeldt, H. (2008). How can primary school students learn self-regulated learning strategies most effectively? A meta-analysis on self-regulation training programmes. *Educational Research Review, 3*(2), 101–129. www.dx.doi.org/10.1016/j.edurev.2008.02.003

Donker, A. S., De Boer, H., Kostons, D., Dignath van Ewijk, C. C., & Van der Werf, M. P. C. (2014). Effectiveness of learning strategy instruction on academic performance: A meta-analysis. *Educational Research Review, 11*, 1–26. www.dx.doi.org/10.1016/j.edurev.2013.11.002

Dorman, J. (2001). Associations between classroom environments and academic efficacy. *Learning Environments Research, 4*, 243–257.

Ercikan, K., & Seixas, P. (2011). Assessment of higher order thinking. In G. Schraw & D. R. Robinson (Eds.), *Assessment of higher order thinking skills* (pp. 245–261). Charlotte, NC: Information Age Publishing.

Fisher, R. (2012). Teaching writing: A situated dynamic. *British Educational Research Journal, 38*(2), 299–317.

Hadjioannon, X. (2007). Bringing the background to the foreground: What do classroom environments that support arithmetic discussions look like? *American Educational Research Journal, 44*(2), 370–399.

Hanley, P., Bohnke, J. R., Slavin, B., Elliott, L., & Croudace, T. (2016). *Let's think secondary science: Evaluation report and executive summary*. Education Endowment Foundation. Retrieved from https://educationendowmentfoundation.org.uk/our-work/projects/lets-think-secondary-science/

Hayward, H. C., Towery-Woolsey, J., Arbitman-Smith, R., & Aldridge, A. H. (1988). Cognitive education with deaf adolescents: Effects of instrumental enrichment. *Topics in Language Disorders, 8*, 23–40.

Higgins, S. (2017). Impact evaluation: A case study of the introduction of interactive whiteboards in schools in the UK. In R. Coe, M. Waring, L. V. Hedges, & J. Arthur (Eds.), *Education research: Methods and methodologies* (2nd ed.) (pp. 145–152). London: Sage Publications.

Higgins, S., Hall, E., Baumfield, V., & Moseley, D. (2005). *A meta-analysis of the impact of the implementation of thinking skills approaches on pupils*. Project Report. London: EPPI-Centre, Social Science Research Unit, Institute of Education, University of London.

Hookway, C. (2002). *Truth, rationality, and pragmatism: Themes from Peirce*. Oxford: Oxford University Press.

Hu, W., Adey, P., Jia, X., Liu., J., Zang, L., Li, J., & Ding, X. (2010). Effects of a 'learn to think' intervention programme on primary school students. *British Journal of Educational Psychology, 81*, 531–557.

Kaniel, S., & Reichenberg, R. (1992). Instrumental enrichment: Effects of generalization and drivability with talented adolescents. *Gifted Education International, 8*, 128–135.

Kaufman, R., & Burden, R. L. (2004). Peer tutoring between young adults with severe and complex learning difficulties: The effects of mediation training with Feuerstein's instrumental enrichment programme. *European Journal of Psychology of Education, 19*(1), 107–117.

Klauer, K. J., & Phye, G. D. (2008). Inductive reasoning: A training approach. *Review of Educational Research, 78*(1), 85–123. www.dx.doi.org/10.3102/0034654307313402

Kozulin, A. (2000). The diversity of instrumental enrichment applications. In I. A. K. Kozulin & Y. Rand (Eds.), *Experience of mediated learning: An impact of Feuerstein's theory on education and practice* (pp. 257–273). London: Pergamum.

Li, L., & Wegerif, R. (2014). What does it mean to teach thinking in China? Challenging and developing notions of 'Confucian education'. *Thinking Skills and Creativity, 11*, 22–32.

McCombs, B. L. (1999). *The assessment of learner-centered practices (ALCP): Tools for teacher reflection, learning, and change*. Denver, CO: University of Denver Research Institute.

McGuinness, C. (1999). *From thinking skills to thinking classrooms: A review and evaluation of approaches for developing pupils' thinking* (Research Report RR115). London: Department for Education and Employment.

Marzano, R. J. (1998). *A theory-based meta-analysis of research in instruction*. Anvova, CO: Mid-continent Regional Educational Laboratory.

Moseley, D., Baumfield,V., Elliott, J., Higgins, S., Miller, J., & Newton D. P. (2005). *Frameworks for thinking: A handbook for teaching and learning.* Cambridge: Cambridge University Press.

Nickerson, R. (1999). How we know and sometimes misjudge what others know: Imputing one's own knowledge to others. *Psychological Bulletin, 125*, 737–759.

Oliver, M., Venville, G., & Adey, P. (2012). Effects of a cognitive acceleration programme in a low socioeconomic high school in regional Australia. *International Journal of Science Education, 34*(9), 1393–1410.

Parlett, M., & Hamilton, D. (1972). *Evaluation as illumination: A new approach to the study of innovatory programmes.* Occasional Paper. Centre for Research in Educational Sciences, Edinburgh University.

Raven, J., & Court, J. H. (1998). *Manual for Raven's progressive matrices and vocabulary scales.* Oxford: Oxford Psychologists.

Savell, J. M., Twohig, P. T., & Rachford, D. (1986). Empirical status of Feuerstein's 'Instrumental Enrichment' (FIE) techniques as a method of teaching thinking skills. *Review of Educational Research, 56*, 381–409.

Shalin, D. N. (1986). Pragmatism and social interactionism. *American Sociological Review, 51*, 9–29.

Shayer, M. (1999). Cognitive acceleration through science education II: Its effects and scope. *International Journal of Science Education, 21*(8), 883–902.

Shayer, M., & Adey, P. (2002). *Learning intelligence: Cognitive acceleration across the curriculum from 5 to 15 years.* Maidenhead: Open University Press.

Shayer, M., & Beasley, F. (1987). Does instrumental enrichment work? *British Educational Research Journal, 13*, 101–119.

Shiell, J. L. (2002). *A meta-analysis of Feuerstein's instrumental enrichment* (PhD Thesis). The University of British Columbia UBC, Vancouver. http://dx.doi.org/10.14288/1.0055041

Skuy, M., Mentis, M., Durback, R., Cockcroft, K., & Fridjhon, P. (1995). Cross-cultural comparisons of effects of IE on children in a South African mining town. *School Psychology International, 16*, 265–282.

Smith, F. (1992). *To think.* London: Routledge.

Strang, J., & Shayer, M. (1993). Enhancing high school students' achievements in chemistry through a thinking skills approach. *International Journal of Science Education, 15*, 319–337.

Stufflebeam, D. L. (1971). *Educational evaluation and decision making.* Itasca, IL: F.E. Peacock.

Thickpenny, J. P., & Howie, D. R. (1990). Teaching thinking skills to deaf adolescents: The implementation and evaluation of instrumental enrichment. *International Journal of Cognitive Education and Mediated Learning, 16*, 265–282.

Topping, K. J., & Trickey, S. (2007). Collaborative philosophical enquiry for school children: Cognitive effects at 10–12 years. *British Journal of Educational Psychology, 77*, 271–288.

Trickey, S., & Topping, K. J. (2004). 'Philosophy for children': A systematic review. *Research Papers in Education, 19*(3), 365–380.

Trickey, S., & Topping, K. J. (2006). Collaborative philosophical enquiry for school children: Socio-emotional effects at 11 and 12 years. *School Psychology International, 27*(5), 599–614.

Vanderstraeten, R. (2002). Dewey's transactional constructivism. *Journal of Philosophy of Education, 36*(2), 233–246.

Wegerif, R., Mercer, N., & Dawes, L. (1999). From social interaction to individual reasoning: An empirical investigation of a possible socio-cultural model of cognitive development. *Learning and Instruction, 9*(6), 493–516.

Williams, M. D., & Burden, R. L. (1997). *Psychology for language teachers: A social constructivist approach.* Cambridge: Cambridge University Press.

Yang, S. C., & Chung, T.Y. (2009). Experimental study of teaching critical thinking in civic education in Taiwanese junior high school. *British Journal of Educational Psychology, 79*(1), 29–55.

INDEX